The B The MAILBOX BOOK 4

Grades 1-3

Table of Contents

Since the first book published in 1988, **The Best of The Mailbox**® books have become the most popular titles available to teachers of grades 1–3 today. Now we're proud to present the newest **The Best of The Mailbox**® book for primary teachers, **The Best of The Mailbox**®**—Book 4.** Inside these covers, you'll find many of the best teacher-tested ideas published in the 1996–2000 issues of *The* Primary *Mailbox*® magazine. Our editors selected these practical ideas from those sent to us by teachers across the United States. We've included many of our regularly featured sections of the magazine plus special teaching units and reproducibles.

www.themailbox.com

Project Manager: Susan Walker
Copy Editors: Sylvan Allen, Gina Farago, Karen Brewer Grossman, Karen L. Huffman, Amy Kirtley-Hill, Debbie Shoffner
Cover Artist: Clevell Harris
Art Coordinator: Theresa Lewis Goode
Typesetters: Lynette Dickerson, Mark Rainey

President, The Mailbox Book Company™: Joseph C. Bucci
Director of Book Planning and Development: Chris Poindexter
Book Development Managers: Stephen Levy, Elizabeth H. Lindsay, Thad McLaurin, Susan Walker
Curriculum Director: Karen P. Shelton
Traffic Manager: Lisa K. Pitts
Librarian: Dorothy C. McKinney
Editorial and Freelance Management: Karen A. Brudnak
Editorial Training: Irving P. Crump
Editorial Assistants: Terrie Head, Hope Rodgers, Jan E. Witcher

Manufactured in the United States
10 9 8 7 6 5 4 3 2

CLASSROOM DISPLAYS

READING
IS
COOL!

James
and the
Giant Peach

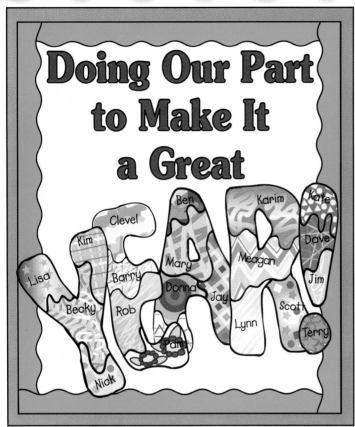

Great things are created with teamwork, and this display is a perfect example! Mount a border and the phrase "Doing Our Part to Make It a Great." From poster board cut large letters to spell "YEAR." Visually divide the letter cutouts into a class supply of puzzle pieces; then label each piece for a different student. Code the back of each letter cutout (for easy reassembly) before cutting it apart. Have each child decorate his puzzle piece. Then, with your youngsters' help, assemble and mount the puzzle pieces as shown. It's going to be a great year!

Mary Jo Kampschnieder—Gr. 2
Howells Community Catholic School
Howells, NE

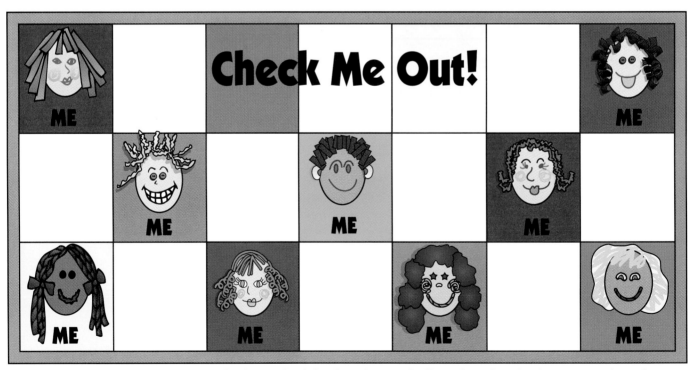

Create miles of smiles with this back-to-school display. Cover a bulletin board with white paper. A student uses assorted arts-and-crafts supplies to create her self-likeness on a construction-paper oval. Then she mounts her self-likeness and precut letters spelling "ME" on a colorful rectangle. Display the projects in a checkerboard pattern, leaving room for the title near the top. You can count on plenty of students, parents, and staff members checking out this display!

Linda Macke—Gr. 3, John F. Kennedy Elementary, Kettering, OH

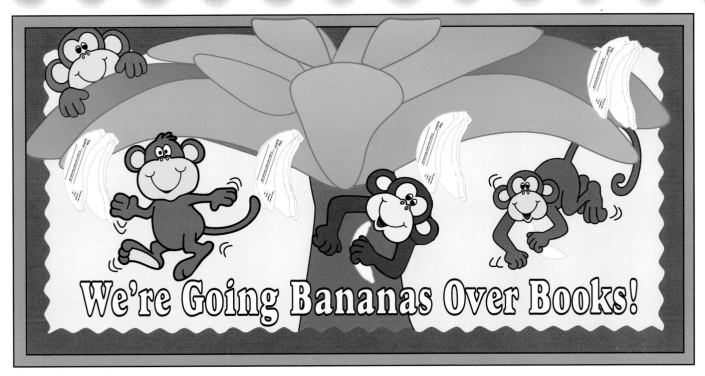

This motivational reading display will have students going bananas over books! Mount a large three-dimensional treetop, a monkey or two, and the title. Using the pattern on page 23, duplicate a supply of banana-shaped book reports. Each time a child reads a book, he completes and cuts out a banana report. Mount the bananas in bunches. Encourage students to check out their classmates' "a-peeling" reading recommendations!

Katherine V. Gartner—Grs. 1–2 Special Education, Oxhead Road Elementary School, Centereach, NY

Keep your happy hive humming with this easy-to-manage helper display. Mount a beehive like the one shown and several sets of bee wings that you have labeled with desired job descriptions. Have each student personalize and cut out a bee pattern (page 23). Pin a bee cutout to each pair of wings; then store the remaining bees in the hive. Each week assign new jobs using an established method of rotation.

Tara Livingston—Special Education, Valley Park School, Overland Park, KS

"WEL-GUM" TO OUR ROOM!

Dispense a colorful classroom welcome with this hallway display. A student uses assorted arts-and-crafts supplies to create her self-likeness on a colorful paper circle. Fashion the base of a gum dispenser from colorful paper. Mount the resulting cutout, the student projects, and the title. For the dome, tape a large circle of clear plastic over the projects. By gum, that's a cute display!

Jo Fryer—Gr. 1
Kildeer Countryside School
Long Grove, IL

If you're planning to invite your students' grandparents and/or older adult friends into the classroom, this display is a must! On a 3 1/2-inch white circle, have each child illustrate one or more grandparents or older adult friends. Then have each child glue her project on a blue construction-paper ribbon (pattern on page 24). Mount the completed projects on a display like the one shown.

Beth Vander Kolk—Gr. 1, The Potter's House, Grand Rapids, MI

Look Who's Hiding in the Pumpkin Patch!

Here's an open house display that's a guaranteed crowd-pleaser! Each student cuts a pumpkin shape from orange paper. On her resulting cutout, she writes three or four self-describing clues followed by the question "Who am I?" Tape a snapshot of the student near the bottom of her pumpkin; then cover the snapshot with a flap of orange paper. Display the projects as shown. During open house challenge parents to find their children in the pumpkin patch!

adapted from an idea by Leigh-Ann Hensal, Lockport, NY

The Cream of the Crop!

Harvest a bumper crop of self-esteem at this manipulative display. Using the patterns on page 25, duplicate for each child a yellow ear of corn and two green corn husks. A child writes his name and why he feels special on his ear of corn. Next he cuts out his patterns, stacks the husks atop the ear of corn, and pokes a brad through the black dots, joining the three cutouts. Display the projects as shown. Let the harvest begin!

Scare up some great student work and a whole lot of fun at this seasonal display. Mount the title, a character, the caption "Bump Board," and samples of exceptional student work. When the display is full, the bumping begins. Each student whose work is chosen for the display gets to bump another paper off the board. You can count on plenty of "boooo-tiful" work during October!

Judy Knight—Gr. 3, Day Elementary, San Angelo, TX

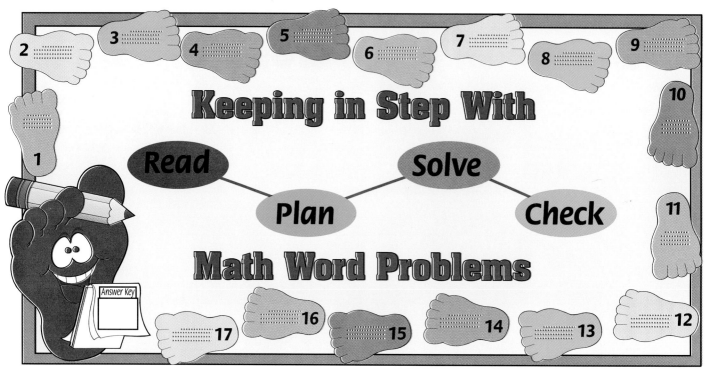

Take the fancy footwork out of solving word problems! Mount the title, a character, and the four steps to solving a word problem. To create the border, have each child write a math word problem on a numbered footprint cutout; then mount the cutouts as shown. Challenge students to use the four-step method to solve the word problems their classmates created. Provide an answer key at the display if desired.

Gina Parisi—Basic Skills Grs. 1–6, Brookdale School, Bloomfield, NJ

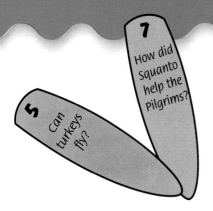

This grinning gobbler has a tail full of questions for students to answer! Number and program feather cutouts with seasonal questions like "What is a female turkey called?" and "What ocean did the Pilgrims cross?" Mount the feathers, a featherless turkey cutout, and the title as shown. Near the display provide books that contain the answers to the posted questions. Great gobbler! Research has never been more fun!

Julie Plowman—Gr. 3, Adair-Casey Elementary, Adair, IA

Fall is a perfect time to snuggle up with a quilt-making project. Each student creates a fall scene on a white paper plate using paper scraps, glue, and other desired supplies. Mount the projects on colorful squares and display as shown. Use a marker to draw stitches. When winter (spring, summer) rolls around, have each student design a new scene for the quilt. Now that's a year-round display that's easy to get comfortable with!

Linda Parris—Gr. 1, West Hills Elementary, Knoxville, TN

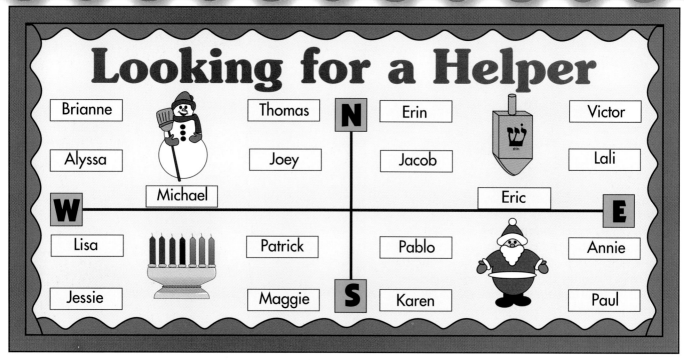

Looking for a Helper

Brianne			Thomas	**N**	Erin			Victor
Alyssa			Joey		Jacob			Lali
W	Michael					Eric		**E**
Lisa			Patrick		Pablo			Annie
Jessie			Maggie	**S**	Karen			Paul

Reinforce cardinal directions with this clever helper display. Visually divide a bulletin board into fourths, label the cardinal directions, and mount a seasonal picture in each quadrant. For each student post a name card that is above, below, or beside a picture or another card. Each day identify a helper by citing a clue like "The name of today's helper is east of the dreidel." Each season or month, replace the pictures and rearrange the cards. To up the challenge, add intermediate directions too!

Vicki Neilon—Gr. 2, Antietam Elementary School, Lake Ridge, VA

WARM WINTER WRITING

Warm students up to wintry writing and create this toasty display! Post a student-generated list of adjectives that describe mittens or wintry weather. Give each student two large mitten cutouts—one lined and one blank. A student decorates the blank cutout; then she writes a descriptive poem or paragraph about her decorated mitten on the lined cutout. Mount the mitten projects and title as shown. Invite students to take the chill off winter by reading their classmates' mitten-related writing!

Jennifer Balogh-Joiner—Gr. 2, Franklin Elementary, Franklin, NJ

In remembrance of Martin Luther King, Jr.'s dream of peace and compassion for all, ask students to ponder their dreams for their community. Have each child write his thoughts on white paper and then trim the paper to create one large thought bubble and several small connecting bubbles. Provide the supplies that students need to create self-portraits like the ones shown; then mount each child's project for all to see.

adapted from an idea by Debbie Dalton—Gr. 2, C. M. Bradley Elementary School, Warrenton, VA

Use this year-round display to promote altruism and foster positive behaviors. Each month showcase a poster or cutout of a person who has contributed to the betterment of others. Add the person's name and a sign that lists his or her most outstanding traits. Then have every student create a personalized cutout for the display. Each time you observe a student or the class exhibiting one of the listed traits, attach a foil star beside that trait. Wow! Look who's making a difference now!

Hope Bertrand—Grs. 2–3, Fremont Elementary School, Bakersfield, CA

Plant a seed of encouragement to create this valentine display that's filled with heartfelt messages. Personalize a large heart-shaped card for each student by writing his name and attaching his photo to the card's front. Distribute the cards, making sure that no one receives his own. Inside the card, a student writes a sentence that describes something he especially likes about the person who is pictured. Display the cards as shown.

adapted from an idea by Jeri Daugherity—Gr. 1
Mother Seton School
Emmitsburg, MD

Your youngsters will be eager to lend a hand in creating this seasonal display! Mount the title; then engage your students in tracing and cutting out their hand shapes from black, white, and red paper. Use the resulting cutouts to form a large heart and arrow. Now that's a "hand-y" heart!

Mary Sue Chatfield—Gr. 1
Central Lee Elementary
Donnellson, IA

Spotlight your readers *and* future leaders at this patriotic display. Have each student illustrate herself on drawing paper as a future leader, glue her artwork on red or blue paper, and add foil stars. Display the personalized projects; then staple a laminated poster-board strip below each one. A student uses a wipe-off marker to keep her strip programmed with the book title she is currently reading. Read on!

Cynthia Adams—Gr. 3, Jefferson Elementary, Hobbs, NM

Greet the arrival of spring with this picture-perfect vocabulary display! Write a student-generated list of words or phrases that contain the word *spring*. Have each child copy a different word or phrase from the list onto a paper strip; then on desired paper have him write and illustrate a sentence that features this word or phrase. Display the students' work as shown. Spring is everywhere!

Sue Lorey, Arlington Heights, IL

Keeping track of March weather is a breeze at this display. Have each child make a lion or a lamb as described in "Lions and Lambs" on page 41. Also duplicate and cut out 33 cards from page 26. Program one lion and one lamb card as shown; then mount these two cards, the student projects, and the title. For each day in March, enlist your students' help in categorizing the weather; then date and display the appropriate card.

Peter Tabor—Gr. 1, Weston Elementary, Schofield, WI

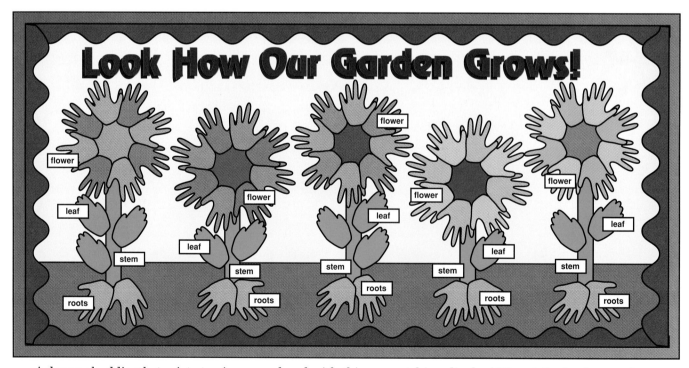

Ask your budding botanists to give you a hand with this eye-catching display! Mount the background paper and title. Give each small group of students glue, scissors, pencils, a paper stem and flower center, and colorful paper. Demonstrate how to trace a hand on paper to create a leaf, a root, and a petal. Mount each group's completed flower in the class garden and label it as shown.

Patti Ghormley—Gr. 1, Liberty Elementary School, Libertytown, MD

April Showers Bring...

Are you experiencing April showers, when you'd rather be enjoying May flowers? No problem! This student-created display can be in full bloom in no time! Ask each student to draw and color a picture of springtime flowers. Trim and mount the students' artwork as shown; then add paper windowpanes, a paper window shade, and a crepe-paper valance. There you have it—a garden of May flowers in April!

adapted from an idea by Linda B. Vaughn—Gr. 2, Franklin Elementary School, Mt. Airy, NC

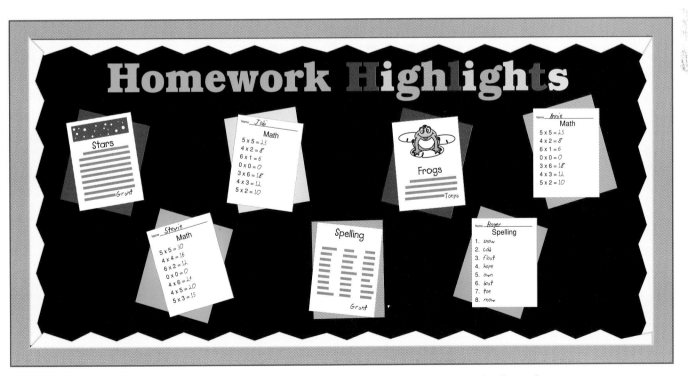

This colorful display is sure to create enthusiasm for homework. Use assorted colors of neon paper to create the title and the individual backdrops for students' homework. When a student's homework merits extra recognition, attach his paper to the display. Keep the display fresh by frequently replacing the posted homework papers with more current samples.

Judy Chunn—Grs. 2–3, Westminster School, Nashville, TN

15

Spill the beans—the jelly beans, that is—about the science process. Mount the title and a large jar cutout that contains a paper jelly bean labeled for each step of the science process. As students experience the different steps, ask volunteers to post their findings. For added appeal, have each volunteer color-code her work with a jelly bean cutout to show the step on which she is reporting.

Lisa Kelly—Gr. 1, Wood Creek Elementary, Farmington, MI

Rub-a-dub-dub! This interactive display may cause student interest in math to bubble over! Program one side of several bubble cutouts with math-related problems. Use pushpins to display the bubbles facedown. When time allows, choose a bubble and challenge students to solve its corresponding problem. When the problem is solved, reattach the bubble to the display faceup. Be sure to plan a bubble-related celebration when all the problems are solved!

Amy Barsanti—Gr. 2, Pines Elementary School, Plymouth, NC

Look who's hard at work! Mount the title and a border of yellow caution tape. Then have each student personalize and cut out a construction paper copy of the hard-hat pattern on page 26. Laminate the cutouts and slit the dotted lines. Ask each student to choose a sample of her best work; then display the papers with their matching cutouts. Invite students to replace their work samples as frequently as desired.

adapted from an idea by VaReane Gray Heese, Omaha, NE

Spotlight your youngsters' weekend experiences at this eye-catching display. Each Monday, every child who has a weekend experience that she'd like to share with the class creates an illustration and a caption about it. Showcase these projects and set aside time for each child to explain her work and provide added details about the pictured event.

Donna L. Hall—Grs. 1–2, Fairview Elementary, St. Louis, MO

Student smiles really add up at this math-related display! Working in pairs, each child uses a different piece of red yarn to measure the width of his partner's smile; then he trims the yarn to smile width and presents it to his partner. Next each child uses a ruler to measure his yarn. Total these measurements; then have each child make a self-portrait sporting his red-yarn smile! Display as shown. Cheese!

Cathy T. Howlett—Gr. 3, Franklin Elementary, Mt. Airy, NC

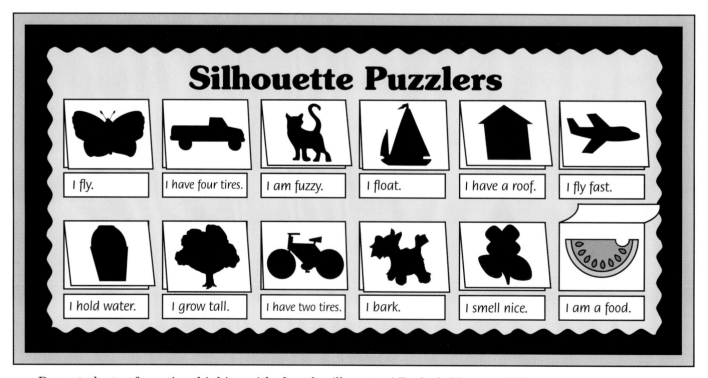

Prompt plenty of creative thinking with shapely silhouettes! Each child cuts a different object from a discarded magazine, traces the cutout on black paper, cuts along the resulting outline, and glues her cutout on folded construction paper as shown. Then she writes a silhouette-related clue on provided paper. The resulting interactive display will be buzzing with creative thoughts!

Jill Hamilton—Gr. 1, Schoeneck Elementary, Stevens, PA

Alphabetizing practice is a breeze at this hands-on display! Securely attach three lengths of heavy string or plastic clothesline to a bulletin board; then clip 26 clothespins to the lines. Have each student decorate a T-shirt with magazine cutouts to match the beginning sound of a prelabeled letter. Laminate these projects for durability; then store them in a laundry basket. Each morning ask a different student to clip the T-shirt cutouts to the line in alphabetical order. Remove the cutouts at the end of each day.

Julie Erthal—Gr. 1, Thomas Jefferson School, Alton, IL

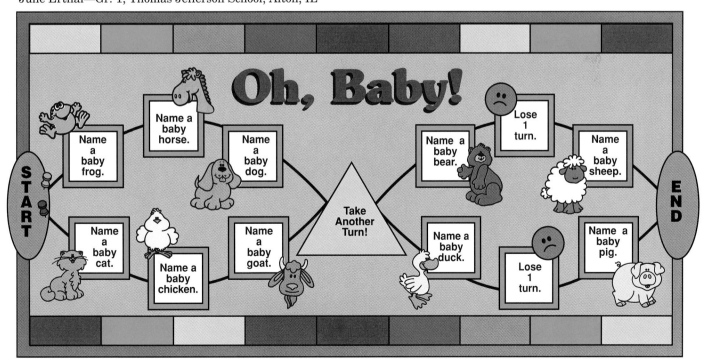

Review any topic with this interactive display! Create a gameboard; then insert two pushpins at START. Make a die that has values of "1" and "2." To play, one of two students (teams) picks a pathway, rolls the die, and moves his pushpin. If he correctly follows the direction, he stays there. An incorrect response at any point along the gameboard returns the player to START. The first player to reach the END wins. Frequently change the programming to keep student interest high.

Terrie Guest Yang—Grs. K–1, Hsin-chu International School, Hsin-chu, Taiwan

Give your end-of-the-year display a space-age spin! Cover a bulletin board with black paper, accent it with foil stars, and add the title. Have each child describe a highlight from the past school year on a colorful comet pattern (page 28), then cut it out. Next he uses a toilet-tissue roll and assorted other supplies to design a rocket. Mount the projects and you have an out-of-this-world finale to the school year!

Mary Mahaffey—Gr. 3, Harrisburg Academy, Wormsleyburg, PA

We're BIG on Memories!

Make a big impression with this colossal collection of memories. A student traces a shape template (oval, square, etc.) onto writing paper and art paper. He cuts out each shape; then, on the lined cutout, he describes a favorite memory from the school year. Assist students in arranging the cutouts on colorful paper to resemble a dinosaur; then have them glue the cutouts in place. Cut out the dinosaur shape and embellish it as desired. Mount the one-of-a-kind lizard for all to enjoy!

adapted from an idea by Sharma Houston—Gr. 2, Pearsontown Elementary, Durham, NC

There's no catch limit at this fishy display! Mount the title and a fishnet; then use the patterns on page 28 to create a supply of colorful fish. Store the fish patterns, pencils, crayons, and scissors near the display. When a child observes or experiences an act of kindness, he describes the event on a fish pattern. Next he customizes, cuts out, and displays the fish for all to see. Wow! What a catch!

Debbie Sietsema—Gr. 2, Allendale Public School, Allendale, MI

Keep the entire class on course by putting each student in the driver's seat! A child adds his name and self-likeness to a car pattern (page 27); then he colors the pattern and cuts it out. Next, he writes (on a precut construction paper shape) one thing he expects to learn in school the following year. Display the projects as shown. Vroom!

Trina Taylor—Gr. 2, High Point Elementary, Cedar Hill, TX

Splish, splash, summer's almost here! For this display a child describes on paper an activity she hopes to enjoy this summer. She trims her paper into a speech bubble. Then she colors a copy of the inner tube pattern on page 27 and cuts it out. Next, she uses art supplies to fashion a self-likeness from her waist up and glues it to the inner tube as shown. Showcase each child's projects together.

Catherine Broome—Gr. 1, Melbourne, FL

Create a stir with this cool 3-D reading display! For every child, cover an empty tissue box with white paper. On each of three sides of his resulting ice cube, a student writes the title of a favorite book and illustrates a scene from it. Mount the projects as shown. Now that's a refreshing way for youngsters to share their favorite literature!

Julia Brown—Gr. 3
Forest City Elementary
Forest City, NC

Use with "We're Going Bananas Over Books!" on page 5.

Title: _____

Author: _____

To learn more about this book, ask _____

(student)

This book was...
(check one)
○ Excellent
○ Good
○ O.K.

Patterns
Use with "Sealed With a Kiss" on page 95.

Use the ribbon pattern with "Our
Grand Prizes!" on page 6.

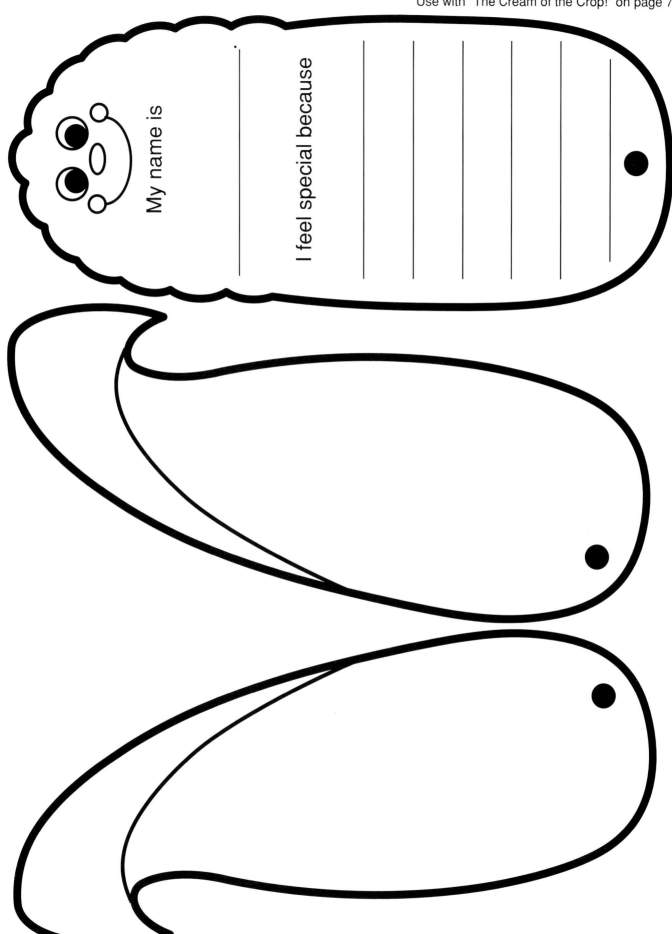

My name is

I feel special because

Cards
Use with "Watching the Weather" on page 14.

Pattern
Use with "Ideas Under Construction" on page 17.

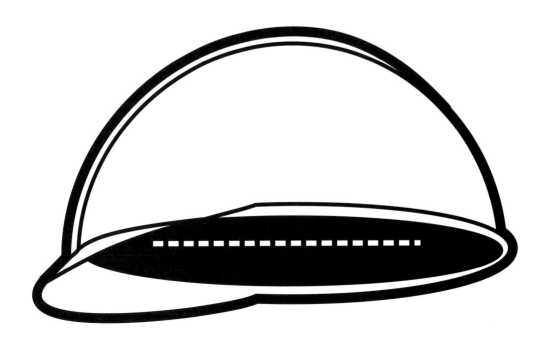

Use the inner tube pattern with " 'Water' We Doing This Summer?" on page 22.

Use the car pattern with "On the Road to Third Grade!" on page 21.

Patterns

Use the fish patterns with "Look Who Has Been Caught Being Kind!" on page 21.

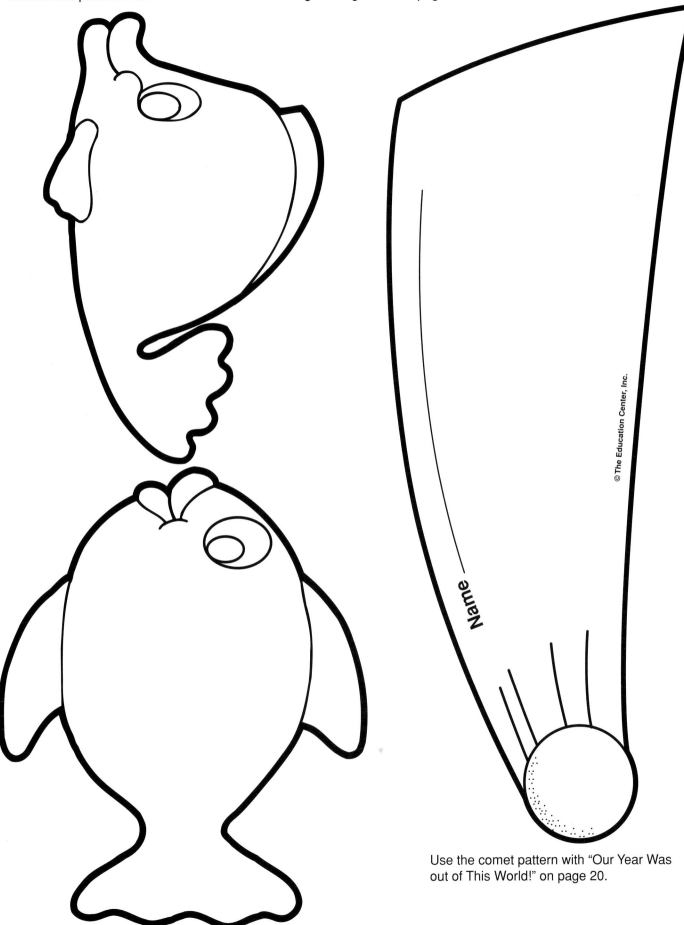

Name

Use the comet pattern with "Our Year Was out of This World!" on page 20.

Arts & Crafts

Arts & Crafts

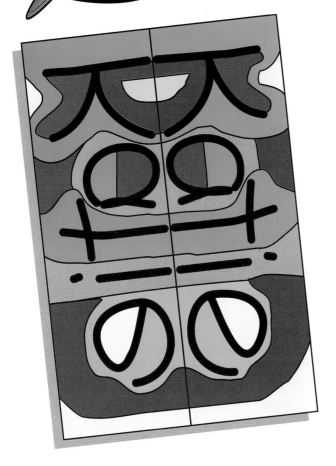

Hidden Names

What's in a name? A very interesting design! To begin this project, fold a 12" x 18" sheet of white construction paper in half lengthwise. Unfold the paper. Then, pressing heavily, use a black crayon to write your first name on the fold line. Re-fold the paper, keeping your name to the inside. Repeatedly rub your hand firmly across the paper to create a second crayon image of your name. Unfold the paper and use a black crayon to trace over the transferred letters. (See the illustration.) Next use crayons or tempera paint to create a colorful design around the writing. Display these one-of-a-kind name posters for all to enjoy and decode!

Colorful Crayons

Create a rainbow of color and promote class unity with these jumbo crayons! As a prelude to the project, discuss the meaning of the phrase "It takes every color to make the rainbow." Help students understand how this phrase applies to their classroom, their community, and their world. Then begin the project with a 6" x 18" piece of white construction paper and a supply of colorful tissue-paper squares. Using diluted glue and a paintbrush, "paint" the tissue-paper squares onto the paper, overlapping the squares as you cover the rectangle. When the rectangle is completely covered, set it aside to dry. The following day trim a 4" x 6" piece of construction paper to resemble the point of a crayon and glue it to one end of the tissue paper–covered rectangle. To the opposite end glue a 2½" x 6" piece of construction paper. Then personalize a construction-paper oval (or other desired shape) and glue it to the side of the crayon. Mount the completed projects on a bulletin board titled "It Takes Every Color to Make the Rainbow."

Jennifer Balogh-Joiner—Gr. 2
Franklin Elementary School
Franklin, NJ

Sunny Delight

If there's a patch of sunflowers your students can visit, make a beeline for it; then march from the patch into this bloomin' art project. In advance, cut several potatoes in half and trim some of the halves to make petal-shaped prints and some to make one-inch-square prints. To create a sunflower, dip a square printer into brown paint; then repeatedly press it onto a large sheet of art paper, creating a circular design. Outside this, use a petal-shaped printer and yellow paint to encircle the brown area. When the paint has dried, cut out the flower. To turn a bulletin board into a patch of sunny sunflowers, staple each student's blossom atop a green-paper strip embellished with some green-paper leaves. That's sunny all right! Now where did I leave my shades?

Teresa Williams—Gr. 1
Coquihalla Elementary
Hope, British Columbia, Canada

Personality Plus

Personality! These projects are packed with it. But not only that; each student's likeness will also reveal something about his family members and pets!

1. Give each child a large T-shirt shape cut from a 9" x 12" sheet of construction paper. Ask that he take the shirt cutout home, decorate it with drawings or pictures of family members and pets, and return the cutout to school.
2. When all the cutouts are returned, have each student paint a 12" x 18" sheet of art paper with a skin-toned paint that approximates his own coloring.
3. When the painted paper has dried, have the student draw two arm outlines and a head-and-neck outline on his paper, then cut them out.
4. Have each student glue the arm and head cutouts onto his T-shirt cutout that was decorated at home.
5. Encourage each student to cut out and decorate a construction-paper hat of his own design, then glue it on the head cutout.
6. Have each student use colorful markers to draw facial features.
7. To complete the effect, have students glue on paper and yarn to represent hair and accessories.

Ellen M. Stern—Gr. 1
Alberta Smith Elementary
Midlothian, VA

Pretty Patchwork Apples

Johnny Appleseed would have to agree—these pretty patchwork apples are definitely the pick of the crop! Start with a large, tagboard apple cutout (pattern on page 48) and a supply of two-inch fabric squares. Using a paintbrush, brush a thin coating of glue on the back of a fabric square; then press the square of fabric onto the apple cutout. Continue in this manner, slightly overlapping the fabric squares, until the entire apple cutout is covered. Let the project dry overnight; then trim away any fabric that extends beyond the tagboard cutout. Attach a brown stem and a green leaf (patterns on page 48) to complete the project.

Donna Oldfield—Gr. 1
Portsmouth Catholic School
Portsmouth, VA

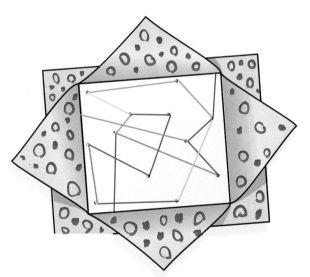

Abstract Artwork

Encourage oodles of creativity with this impressive project. Use a pencil to make several dots on an 8" x 10" sheet of white paper; then use a ruler and colorful markers or crayons to connect the dots. To make a frame for the design, center a 7" x 8" template atop a 9" x 12" sheet of colorful construction paper. Trace around the template; then draw two intersecting diagonal lines in the resulting rectangle. Carefully cut along the diagonal lines and fold back the flaps along the remaining lines. Tape the design to the back of the frame so the artwork is viewed through the opening and then decorate the frame as desired. Each piece of abstract artwork will be unique!

Rita Arnold—Grs. 2–5
Alden Hebron School
Hebron, IL

Schoolwork Frame-Ups

Students and parents will agree that these fabulous frame-ups are perfect for displaying schoolwork. Glue the ends of four poster board strips (two 2" x 12" strips and two 2" x 14" strips) together to create a rectangle. When the resulting frame is dry, decorate it with stickers, construction paper scraps and glue, and/or markers. Next turn the frame over and center a gallon-size resealable plastic bag over the project. Securely tape the bottom and sides of the bag to the frame. Then open the bag, carefully insert the end of a stapler, and staple the bag (just below the zipper) to the frame. Lastly, press lengths of half-inch self adhesive magnetic tape around the perimeter of the back of the project. A student slips a work sample into his frame and then proudly displays his project on his family's refrigerator. Encourage students to replace their works samples one or more times a week!

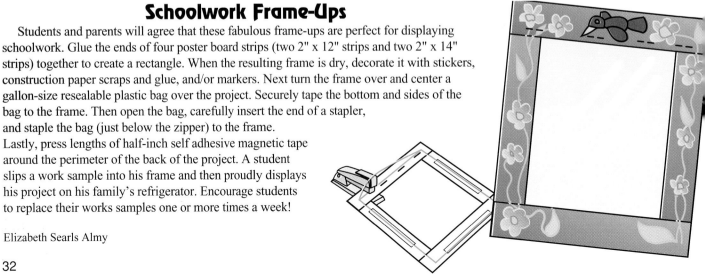

Elizabeth Searls Almy

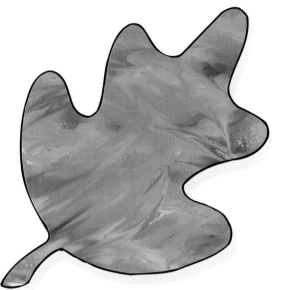

Fall Foliage

Create a dramatic fall-foliage display with these colorful construction-paper leaves. Partially fill each of several shallow containers with fall-colored powdered tempera paint (orange, red, yellow, green, brown). Then, working atop a newspaper-covered surface, cover a 9" x 12" sheet of fall-colored construction paper with irregular paint splotches. To do this, dip a wet paintbrush into a container of powdered paint and splotch the paint onto the construction paper. Clean the brush; then repeat the painting step—using a variety of paint colors—until a desired effect is achieved. When the paint has dried, trim the painted paper into the shape of a large leaf. Laminate the leaves if desired; then display them as embellishments or borders on classroom bulletin boards.

Camilla Law—Gr. 3, St. Timothy's School
Raleigh, NC

Sail On!

Look what's on the horizon—a seaworthy project just in time for Columbus Day! Cut an eight-inch circle from white construction paper. Using watercolors, paint ocean waters on the bottom half of the circle and a colorful sky on the top half. While this dries, cut out a ship's hull, sails, and masts from construction-paper scraps. Add details to the cutouts with crayons or markers. To assemble the project, glue the painted circle atop a slightly larger, black construction-paper circle; then glue the construction-paper cutouts to the painted surface. Land ahoy!

"Hand-some" Leaves

When it comes to making these lovely leaves, students will be more than happy to lend a hand! To make a handprint leaf, paint the palm side of a hand using fall-colored tempera paint (orange, yellow, red, brown). Press the hand, with fingers spread, onto a sheet of white paper. When the painted paper has dried, draw a jagged outline around the handprint with a fall-colored crayon and then color the white areas inside the outline with a different fall-colored crayon. Cut out the leaf and the fall foliage is ready to display!

Sharon Hackley
Kingman, AZ

Eight-Legged Look-Alikes

Send your spider enthusiasts into a spin with this adorable arachnid! Use black tempera paint to cover both sides of a small-size paper soup bowl. Set the bowl aside to dry. To make the spider's legs, accordion-fold eight 1" x 8" black paper strips. Also cut out and decorate two colorful construction-paper eyes. When the painted bowl is dry, attach the eyes and legs to it as shown. Knot one end of a long length of elastic thread. Thread the unknotted end of elastic through a needle; then poke the needle through the center of the bowl so that the knot remains inside the bowl. Display the three-dimensional spiders where they can spin and sway in the cool October breezes.

Cindy Schumacher—Gr. 1
Prairie Elementary School
Cottonwood, ID

Scarecrows From Spoons

Here's an art project that turns students' thoughts of harvest into spoonfuls of creative fun. Use craft glue to attach a wooden spoon (serving side up) to a 12" x 18" piece of light-colored tagboard. When dry, draw a scarecrow face on the spoon with a marker. Then use construction paper scraps, wallpaper scraps, yarn, glue, and other desired materials to embellish the spoon with scarecrow-like hair and clothing. Last, draw and color a background scene such as a pumpkin patch or a cornfield. Caw! Caw!

Ann Marie Stephens
George C. Round Elementary
Manassas, VA

Paper Plate Jack-o'-Lanterns

Serve up plenty of holiday enthusiasm with these jolly jack-o'-lanterns! To make a jack-o'-lantern, sketch large facial features on the bottom of a thin, white paper plate; then carefully cut out the features. (Assist students as needed with this step.) Sponge-paint the bottom of the plate orange. Also sponge-paint the bottom of a second paper plate yellow. When the paint has dried, glue the orange plate atop the yellow plate. Staple a green paper stem and green curling-ribbon vines to the top of the plate. Happy Halloween!

Tall "Tail" Turkeys

Will the turkey with the tallest tail feathers please step forward? To make one of these gobblers, use red, yellow, brown, and orange fingerpaints to paint an eight-inch square of tagboard. To make the turkey's body and head, use brown paper to cover one and one-half empty toilet-tissue tubes. When the painted tagboard is dry, trim it to create a set of tail feathers. Then glue the paper-covered tubes to the feathers. Cut out two eyes, a beak, and a wattle from construction-paper scraps and glue the cutouts in place. Attach construction-paper feet, and this gobbler is ready to strut its stuff! For a fun follow-up, have each child write a very tall *tale* about his tall-tailed turkey!

Laura LaPerna—Grs. K–2
Tedder Elementary
Pompano Beach, FL

Indian Corn Napkin Rings

Add the perfect touch to any Thanksgiving table with colorful Indian corn napkin rings. Cut a supply of empty toilet-tissue tubes and paper-towel tubes into two-inch sections or rings. To make a napkin ring, tear individual two-inch squares of brown, yellow, red, black, orange, blue, and purple construction paper into small pieces. Then, in a mosaic pattern, glue the torn paper pieces on a two-inch ring. When the glue dries, tuck a napkin inside. Happy Thanksgiving!

Elizabeth Searls Almy
Greensboro, NC

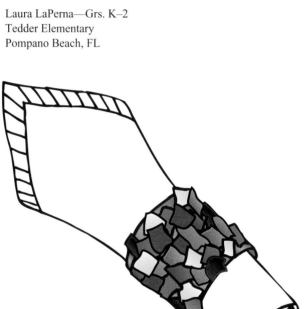

Mosaic Placemats

Students will be delighted to add these placemats to their Thanksgiving dinner plans. Cut a supply of one-inch squares from brown, yellow, red, green, orange, and purple construction paper. To make a placemat, trace a large cornucopia-shaped template onto a 12" x 18" sheet of white construction paper. Arrange and glue brown paper squares to cover the horn-shaped basket; then arrange and glue the colorful paper squares to create an assortment of fruit shapes spilling from the basket. Use markers to add a holiday greeting; then sign and date the back of the project. For durability laminate the resulting placemat or cover it with clear Con-Tact® covering.

Betsy Ruggiano—Gr. 3, Featherbed Lane School, Clark, NJ

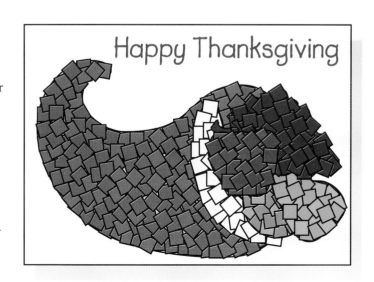

Happy Thanksgiving

Snowflake Snow Pal

You can sum up these snow pals with one word: unique! To make the body, fold a nine-inch white circle in half three times and make a series of desired cuts. Then unfold the paper and glue a four-inch white circle (head) to the top of the body. Add desired facial features. Next cut out a paper scarf and hat for the snow pal. Use markers or crayons to brightly color the clothing cutouts, creating a striped or checkered pattern if desired. Glue the clothing to the project and the snow pal is ready to display. Very cool!

Mary Napoli—Gr. 1
Swiftwater, PA

Star of David

Brighten your Hanukkah festivities with the glow of this colorful Star of David. Prepare a tagboard tracer of the triangle pattern on page 49. Position the top point of the tracer near the top of an eight-inch square of yellow construction paper. Trace inside and outside the shape, and then flip the tracer so the top point is near the bottom of the yellow paper. Adjust the tracer as needed to make a six-pointed star; then trace inside and outside the tracer. Color each section of the resulting star a shade of blue or green. Then cut out the star, leaving a narrow border of yellow around the outer edge. Glue the cutout to dark blue paper. Cut out the shape again, this time leaving a narrow border of blue. Happy Hanukkah!

Elizabeth Searls Almy
Greensboro, NC

Creative Checks

Check this out! Here's a holiday art project that encourages creativity and requires minimal supplies! Begin with a 7" x 10" sheet of 1/2-inch graph paper. Using the lines as your guides, lightly sketch (in pencil) the outline of a desired holiday shape. Color the interior of the shape with markers or crayons; then use a black crayon to outline the shape and desired elements within the shape. Next choose two colors, and alternate between them to color each of the remaining squares on the page. When the page is completely colored, mount it onto a 9" x 12" sheet of colorful construction paper. "Check-tacular!"

Doris Hautala
Washington Elementary School, Ely, MN

Pretty Poinsettia Greetings

Pretty-as-can-be poinsettias are perfect for delivering heartfelt holiday greetings. To begin, make a tagboard tracer for each leaf and bracht pattern on page 49. Trace two A shapes on green felt. Trace the B and the C shapes on red felt. Cut out the four resulting shapes; then cut a slit in shape C as indicated on the tracer. Also cut three to five tiny circles from yellow felt or Fun Foam™.

To assemble the poinsettia carrier, fold the thin cutout (B) in half and carefully push its folded end through the slit in cutout C. When a small loop forms under the project (Figure 1), separate the two red brachts and glue the yellow dots to the center of the resulting bloom (Figure 2). Glue one end of each green leaf beneath the bloom as shown. Design a colorful and heartfelt greeting on a quarter page of blank paper; then roll the paper lengthwise into a tight tube and poke it through the loop of felt underneath the project. Seasons greetings!

Amy Barsanti—Gr. 3
Pines Elementary
Roper, NC

Figure 1

Figure 2

Kwanzaa Windsock

Herald the arrival of Kwanzaa with a striking windsock fashioned from traditional holiday colors.

Materials:
one 6" x 18" strip of black construction paper
one 2" x 18" strip of red construction paper
one 2" x 18" strip of green construction paper
six 16" strips of black crepe paper
one 36" length of black yarn
glue

Steps:
1. Glue the red and green strips to the black paper as shown.
2. When the glue has dried, roll the project into a cylinder and glue the overlapping edges together.
3. Glue one end of each crepe paper strip underneath the green rim.
4. Punch two holes opposite each other near the top of the black rim.
5. Thread each end of the yarn length through a different hole and securely tie.

> **More About Kwanzaa Colors**
> *Black* represents African-American people, *red* symbolizes the struggles of the people, and *green* stands for a happy future.

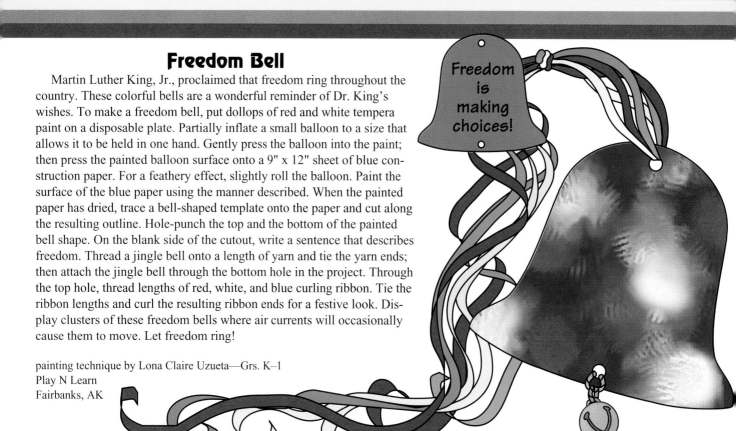

Freedom Bell

Martin Luther King, Jr., proclaimed that freedom ring throughout the country. These colorful bells are a wonderful reminder of Dr. King's wishes. To make a freedom bell, put dollops of red and white tempera paint on a disposable plate. Partially inflate a small balloon to a size that allows it to be held in one hand. Gently press the balloon into the paint; then press the painted balloon surface onto a 9" x 12" sheet of blue construction paper. For a feathery effect, slightly roll the balloon. Paint the surface of the blue paper using the manner described. When the painted paper has dried, trace a bell-shaped template onto the paper and cut along the resulting outline. Hole-punch the top and the bottom of the painted bell shape. On the blank side of the cutout, write a sentence that describes freedom. Thread a jingle bell onto a length of yarn and tie the yarn ends; then attach the jingle bell through the bottom hole in the project. Through the top hole, thread lengths of red, white, and blue curling ribbon. Tie the ribbon lengths and curl the resulting ribbon ends for a festive look. Display clusters of these freedom bells where air currents will occasionally cause them to move. Let freedom ring!

painting technique by Lona Claire Uzueta—Grs. K–1
Play N Learn
Fairbanks, AK

Freedom is making choices!

Happy New Year!

Ring in the Chinese New Year with this impressive class-created dragon! In a large open area that has a washable floor, display a length of white bulletin-board paper. If you plan to have eight student groups working on the project, visually divide the length of paper into seven equal sections and label each one with a different numeral from one to seven. On another length of bulletin-board paper, sketch a large dragon head. Label this section "8." Assign a small group of students to paint each section. Provide the same colors of paint for each group and encourage student creativity. When the paint has dried, cut out the dragon head and trim one end of the long paper length to resemble a dragon tail. For added interest, make a wavy cut along each side of the resulting dragon body. Then glue the dragon head to the dragon body. Display the impressive project in a school hallway. To add a 3-D effect, incorporate a few bends in the dragon. Totally hot!

Phoebe Sharp—Gr. 1
Gillette School
Gillette, NJ

A Gingerbread Glyph

Try as you might, you won't find a more unique gingerbread project than this one! Make available the following colors of construction-paper scraps: pink, blue, white, orange, red, green, yellow, purple, and black. Each student also needs a large paper cutout of a gingerbread pal, glue, scissors, crayons or markers, a pencil, and a copy of "Gingerbread Decorations" on page 50. A student completes page 50 by following the provided instructions; then she uses the resulting code to make hair, buttons, stripes, and facial features to glue on her gingerbread cutout. Display the completed projects and an enlarged version of page 50 on a bulletin board titled "A Gingerbread Who's Who."

Bonnie Hansen—Gr. 1
Ashton Elementary
Sarasota, FL

Snowpal Snack Bag

What goes thumpity, thump, thump—poppity, pop, pop? A snowpal snack bag that's filled to the brim with popcorn!

Materials:
one resealable sandwich bag
one 5" x 6" piece of blank white paper
one 5" x 8" piece of black construction paper
green, orange, and black construction paper
　scraps
two blue ³/₄" dot stickers
eight red ³/₄" dot stickers
scissors
crayons
glue
popcorn

Directions:
1. Slip the white paper inside the sandwich bag.
2. Cut a hat shape from the black paper.
3. Cut two holly leaves from green paper and add desired crayon details. Glue the leaves to the hat and add three red dot stickers (holly berries).
4. On the front of the bag, run a trail of craft glue approximately one-half inch below the seal. Firmly press the hat atop the glue.
5. Cut out an orange carrot-shaped nose and two black eyebrows.
6. Attach facial features to the bag as shown.
7. When the project is dry, open the bag and pour popcorn behind the white paper.

Melanie Miller
Nashport, OH

Gift of Love

This handcrafted valentine keepsake is sure to win the heart of a loved one!

Materials for one frame:

6 tongue depressors
two 1" x 3" strips of red felt
one 5½" square of red felt
one 5½" square of
    white poster board
1 student photo
assorted colors of Fun Foam™
crayons
scissors
craft glue

Steps:

1. To make the wooden frame, lay two tongue depressors parallel to each other and about 4½ inches apart. Squeeze glue near the ends of each wooden stick and then connect the sticks with two more depressors. Allow to dry.
2. To make the frame stand, write, date, and sign a valentine greeting in the center of the poster board square. Glue a tongue depressor to the left edge and the right edge of the programmed square. Allow to dry.
3. Trim the photo as desired, and glue it in the center of the felt square. Then squeeze a trail of glue around the perimeter of the felt and press the wooden frame atop the glue. Allow to dry.
4. To connect the frame to the stand, glue the felt strips to the back of the frame and then to the frame stand as shown. Lay flat to dry.
5. Cut out desired decorations from the Fun Foam and glue them on the wooden frame.

Heather Graley—Gr. 3
Eaton, OH

Step 4

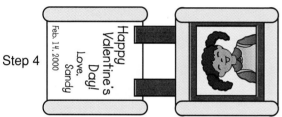

The Valentine Express

For speedy delivery of valentine wishes, "choo-choo-choose" the Valentine Express! Collect a class supply of clean and empty half-gallon milk cartons and then cut away the top and one side panel of each container. If desired, prewrap each child's container in red, pink, or white paper and brad four tagboard wheels in place. (Or assist students as they complete these steps.) Then set aside plenty of time for each child to personalize his boxcar to his heart's desire! Display the completed projects in alphabetical order (by student name) atop a bookshelf or table. It's full steam ahead for a happy Valentine's Day!

Karen Nelson—Gr. 2
Smith School
Helena, MT

Presidents' Windsock

Herald the arrival of Presidents' Day with these bright and breezy windsocks!

Materials for one windsock:
template of President Lincoln's profile
template of President Washington's profile
star-shaped template
one 12" x 18" sheet of blue construction paper
three 2" x 18" strips of red construction paper
one 9" x 12" sheet of black construction paper
one 9" x 12" sheet of white construction paper
four 16-inch strips of red crepe paper
four 16-inch strips of white crepe paper
one 36-inch length of yarn
pencil
glue
scissors
hole puncher

Steps:

1. Glue the red paper strips to the blue paper as shown.
2. Trace each presidential profile on black paper.
3. Cut out and glue each profile to the project.
4. Trace several stars on the white paper.
5. Cut out and glue the stars to the project.
6. When the glue has dried, roll the blue paper into a cylinder (keeping the decorations to the outside) and glue the overlapping edges together.
7. Alternating colors, glue the crepe-paper strips inside the lower rim of the project.
8. At the top of the cylinder, punch two holes opposite each other.
9. Thread each end of the yarn length through a different hole and securely tie.

adapted from an idea by Doris Hautala—Gr. 3, Washington Elementary, Ely, MN

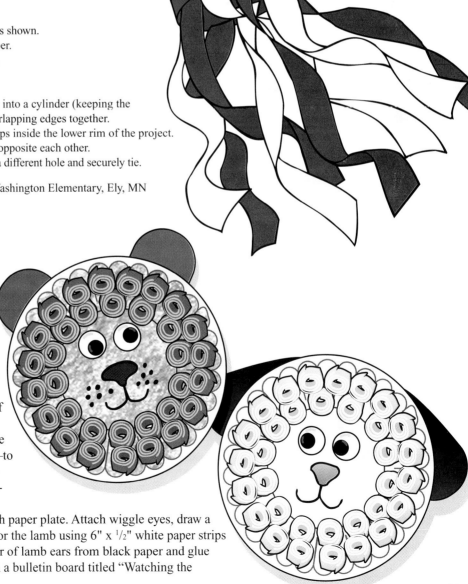

Lions and Lambs

You've heard the old saying, "March comes in like a lion and goes out like a lamb." That makes March the perfect time to get *wild* and *woolly* with these adorable critters! To make a lion, color or sponge-paint a 6-inch paper plate yellow or light brown. Attach wiggle eyes and use a permanent marker to draw a nose and mouth. To make the lion's mane, begin with a supply of 6" x 1/2" brown paper strips. One at a time, wrap a paper strip around a pencil; then slide the strip off and glue it—standing on edge—to the rim of the plate. When the mane is completed, cut a pair of lion ears from brown paper and glue them in place.

To make a lamb, begin with a white 6-inch paper plate. Attach wiggle eyes, draw a nose and mouth, and fashion a woolly coat for the lamb using 6" x ¹/₂" white paper strips and the technique described above. Cut a pair of lamb ears from black paper and glue them in place. Showcase the furry friends on a bulletin board titled "Watching the Weather" (see page 14).

Kite Weaving

Creating this wonderfully woven kite is a breeze! Search through a discarded magazine to find two colorful pictures, each of which is at least six inches square. Trace a six-inch square template onto each magazine picture and cut on the resulting outline. Next cut one picture into ¹/₂-inch strips. Set the strips aside. Fold the other magazine picture in half. Then use a pencil and a ruler to draw parallel lines from the fold. The lines should be 2¹/₂ inches in length and spaced about ³/₄ inch apart. Next cut on the lines; then unfold the paper and weave the magazine strips through the resulting slits. When all the strips are woven, glue the ends of each strip in place. Glue the completed weaving to a six-inch construction-paper square. To create a kite tail, hole-punch one corner of the kite and thread a two-foot length of curling ribbon through the hole; then tie the ribbon and curl the ends.

Elizabeth Searls Almy, Greensboro, NC

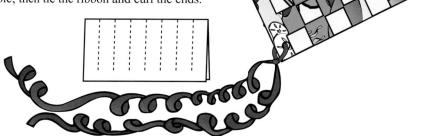

A Lovable Lion

Whether March comes in like a lion or not, you're sure to get a roaring response to this project! To make a lion, color or paint a thin, nine-inch white paper plate yellow or light brown; then add facial features. To make the lion's mane, glue three-inch lengths of brown yarn and yellow yarn (in an alternating fashion) around the entire plate rim. Then cut a pair of lion ears from brown paper and glue them in place. No "lion"! That's a fine-looking animal!

Catherine Strickland—Gr. 2
Myers Elementary School
Gainesville, GA

Pot o' Gold Bank

If you can't catch a leprechaun and his loot, collect your own with this pot o' gold bank!

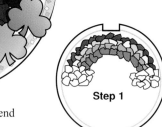

Step 1

Materials for one bank:

2 clear plastic dessert plates	glue
1 green construction-paper copy of the shamrock patterns on page 51	craft glue (for bank assembly)
	scissors
red, yellow, green, blue, white, and black construction-paper scraps	glitter
	coins (optional)

Steps:

1. **To make the back of the bank,** cut a 1¹/₂-inch rectangle from the rim of one plate. Position the plate with the opening at the top; then, in collage fashion, tear colorful paper pieces and glue them on the top half of the plate to create a rainbow. Glue torn white paper pieces to each end of the arch to resemble clouds.

2. **To make the front of the bank,** invert the other plate; then tear black paper pieces and glue them onto the lower half of the plate to resemble a pot. Cut out the shamrock shapes; then place a dot of glue in the center of each shamrock and place the shamrocks near the base of the pot. For a 3-D effect, curl the shamrock leaves.

3. **To assemble the bank,** squeeze a trail of craft glue around the rim of the plate from Step 1. Then align the plate from Step 2 atop the glue, making sure the artwork from both plates is correctly positioned.

4. **For a bit of added sparkle,** squeeze a trail of glue around the rim of the top plate and sprinkle it with glitter. When the glue is dry, shake off the excess glitter and, if desired, place a coin or two in the bank for good luck!

Step 2

Elizabeth Searls Almy

Extraordinary Eggs

Inspire uniquely decorated Easter eggs using this combination technique. To begin, trace an egg shape onto art paper. Inside the egg outline, randomly drip thinned tempera paint; then blow through a drinking straw to transform the paint drips into desired shapes. When the paint is completely dry, use a colored pencil in a contrasting color to completely fill each unpainted area within the egg outline. Cut out the egg shape. Display the egg and others like it on a seasonal bulletin board. Or mount the cutout on a slightly larger piece of contrasting construction paper and trim the construction paper to create a narrow border. The project can be used as a booklet cover for student work, or it can be hole-punched and suspended from a length of monofilament line. "Egg-ceptional"!

Mary Grace Ramos—Gr. 2
Pinewood Acres School
Miami, FL

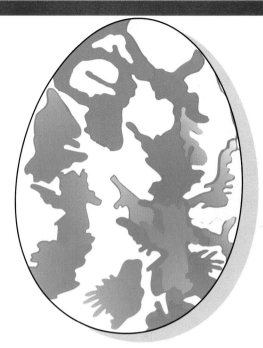

Touchable Tulips

Students will want to reach out and touch these terrific springtime tulips! To make the three-dimensional vase, roll a 4$\frac{1}{2}$" x 6" piece of construction paper into a cylinder and glue the overlapping edges together. When the glue dries, secure the seam of the vase near the bottom of an 8" x 11" sheet of colorful construction paper. Next trace a tulip-shaped template onto a colorful party napkin three times. Cut out the shapes. With the napkin design facedown, use a small drop of glue to attach a cotton ball to the center of each tulip cutout. Next squeeze a thin trail of glue around the perimeter of each cutout. Turn over each tulip and secure it above the vase as shown. Cut out green paper stems and leaves and glue them in place. Mount the completed project atop a 9" x 12" sheet of contrasting construction paper.

Elizabeth Searls Almy
Greensboro, NC

Debonair Ducks

Create a pond full of majestic male mallard ducks in a matter of minutes! Start with one-half of a paper plate. Use brown tempera paint to sponge-print the outside of the plate; then set the plate aside to dry. Trim a 4$\frac{1}{2}$" x 6" piece of dark green construction paper to resemble a duck's head and neck. Create an eye on the duck head and glue a thin, white paper ring to the mallard's neck. Cut a duck bill from a three-inch square of yellow construction paper and attach it to the duck head. Then glue the duck head to the duck body as shown. Display these dapper ducks paddling across a large paper pond. Quack! Quack!

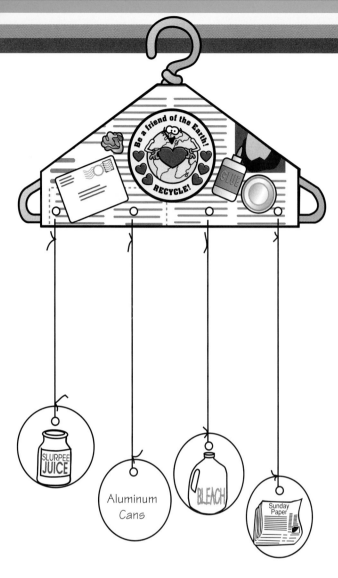

Earth-Friendly Mobile

Just in time for Earth Day—a mobile with important messages about recycling!

Materials for one mobile:

metal hanger

crayons or markers

2-page spread of newspaper, folded twice

scissors

glue

copy of patterns on page 52

hole puncher

four 4" white construction paper circles

small recyclable items

four 1' lengths of string or twine

Steps:

1. Lay the hanger on the folded newspaper with the neck extending off the paper. Fold down the top corners of the paper and bring the lower edge upward, folding the lower corners over the top of hanger (see below). Flip the hanger and glue.
2. Color the patterns on page 14 and cut them out. Glue one pattern on each side of the wrapped hanger.
3. Illustrate a different recyclable item on each circle. Hole-punch the top of the circle; then flip it over and describe the item on the back.
4. Punch four holes along the bottom of the wrapped hanger. Use the string lengths to attach the illustrated circles to the hanger.
5. Glue small recyclables to the newspaper-covered hanger as desired.

Jeri Daugherity
Mother Seton School
Emmitsburg, MD

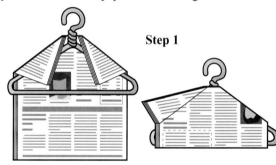

Step 1

Handmade for Mom

Delight moms and other significant women in your students' lives with handcrafted tokens of love! Paint the palm side of a child's hands a desired color. Keeping his thumbs aligned and his fingers spread, he presses his painted hands onto a 9" x 12" sheet of white construction paper. When the paint dries, he uses markers or crayons to draw and color the body and antennae of the resulting butterfly, and to write a desired greeting. Next he colors a copy of the poem on page 52, cuts it out, and glues it on the back of his project. He adds desired decorations with markers or crayons; then he writes the date and signs his name. If desired, laminate the projects for safekeeping before students deliver them to their loved ones.

Paula Stewart—Art, Grs. 1–5
Nathanael Greene Academy
Siloam, GA

Underwater Mobile

Make a splash with this aquatic art project! Draw and brightly color a large fish on a six-inch square of drawing paper. Cut out the fish, color its blank side, and hole-punch the top of the cutout. Using circle templates, trace and cut out a seven-inch and a six-inch circle from blue or green construction paper. Make a spiral cut to the center of each circle, pull each resulting spiral upward, and hole-punch its center. Tie one end of a length of ribbon or string to each cutout; then tie the loose ribbon ends to a plastic drinking straw. Tie one end of a fourth ribbon length near the center of the straw. Suspend the completed mobile and watch the colorful fish swim in the springtime breezes.

Carolyn Williams—Gr. 2, North Augusta Elementary
North Augusta, SC

spiral cut

Flashy Fireflies

You'll attract lots of attention with a display of these flashy fireflies. To make the beetle's body, trim to round the corners of a 2" x 7" strip of green construction paper. Use a green crayon or marker to divide the body into three sections: the head, the thorax, and the abdomen. Cut a small notch in the rounded end of the head; then color and round the resulting eyes as desired. Cut a wing from each of two 3" x 4$\frac{1}{2}$" strips of yellow paper and each of two 3" x 3$\frac{1}{2}$" pieces of waxed paper. Glue the narrow ends of the yellow wings to the firefly's thorax; then glue the narrow ends of the waxed-paper wings to the yellow wings. To complete the bug, glue clear sequins or glitter to the end of its abdomen. Mount the completed projects on a bulletin board covered with black paper. For added appeal, use sturdy tape to attach a strand of clear Christmas-tree lights to the display. Periodically, under close supervision, illuminate the lights for a breathtaking display!

Michele Baerns—Gr. 2, Sevierville Primary School, Sevierville, TN

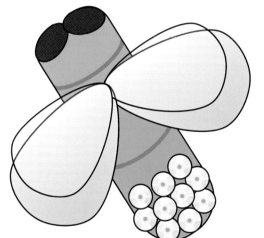

Nifty Notepads

Keep these student-made notepads in mind as end-of-the-year gift-giving occasions approach. To make a 16-page notepad, cut four pieces of blank paper into fourths. You will also need a 4$\frac{1}{2}$" x 7" strip of tagboard and a 4$\frac{1}{2}$" length of decorative bulletin-board border. Stack the blank paper atop the tagboard rectangle and align the lower edges. Staple the top of the paper stack to the tagboard; then fold the extending strip of tagboard forward over the stapled paper. Securely staple the tagboard flap in place. Next glue the strip of decorative border atop the tagboard flap. If desired, have each student add a colorful border or small artwork to the pages of his resulting notepad. The back of each notepad can also be signed and dated. You can count on a special someone being pleased as punch to receive this handmade gift.

Nancy Compton—Gr. 3 Teacher's Aide
Burkhart Elementary
Indianapolis, IN

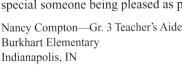

45

Magnetic Note Holder

Here's a gift-giving idea that's perfect for Father's Day! Use the hammer pattern on page 51 to create a template; then trace the hammer shape onto a piece of white poster board. Also trace the hammerhead onto black construction paper two times. Cut out the shapes. Glue one black hammerhead cutout to each side of the poster-board cutout. While the glue is drying, use colorful markers to decorate both sides of the handle. Attach a two-inch strip of magnetic tape to the back of the project. Then turn the project over. Write "#1 Dad" in white crayon on the hammerhead, and use craft glue (or a hot glue gun) to attach a wooden clothespin to the handle as shown.

To create notepaper, press a finger onto a brightly colored stamp pad before pressing it onto 4" x 5" sheets of blank white paper. Use colorful fine-tipped markers to transform each fingerprint into a personalized work of art. Then stack and clip the decorated papers to the note holder. How nice!

Linda C. Buerklin—Substitute Teacher
Monroe Township Schools
Williamstown, NJ

Rainbow Jellies

Make a splash with this seaworthy jellyfish project! Each child needs a gallon-size, clear, plastic food-storage bag; a twist-tie; and eight to ten $1^{1}/_{2}$" strips of tissue paper in a variety of lengths and colors. Align one end of the tissue-paper strips and hold that end of the stack in one hand. Hold the bag in your other hand. Blow air inside the bag to slightly inflate it; then quickly slip the aligned strip ends inside the bag, pinch the bag closed, and secure it with the twist-tie. To suspend the project, carefully tape a length of monofilament line to the bag. Easy to make, extremely colorful, and no poisonous punch—it's a perfect jellyfish!

Michele Converse Baems, Sieverville Elemntary, Sieverville, TN

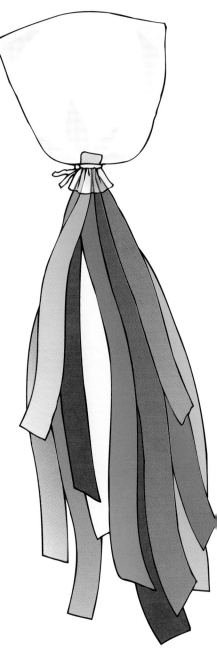

Geometric Wonders

If you know the right moves, delightful geometric designs can be made in a jiffy! To begin, use tape to secure a sheet of white paper to a slightly larger piece of corrugated cardboard. Next use a pushpin to hold one corner of a desired geometric tagboard template in place. Trace around the shape with a colored pencil; then, keeping the pushpin in place, slightly rotate the shape and retrace its outline with a different colored pencil. Continue rotating and tracing the shape, using as many or as few colors of pencils as desired. When the shape has been completely rotated, the drawing is complete. Remove the paper from the cardboard, crop the colorful design, and mount it on a slightly larger piece of construction paper. These colorful creations will be popping up all over the place!

Valerie Smith, Exton, PA

Rainbow Swimmers

Make a colorful splash with these fancy fish! Begin the project by making a simple fish pattern divided into six horizontal sections. Cut out a white construction paper copy of the fish pattern and a supply of tissue-paper squares in the following rainbow colors: red, orange, yellow, green, blue, and purple. Glue the appropriate color of tissue-paper squares in each section, overlapping the squares as you go, until the cutout is completely covered. (If desired, use diluted glue and a paintbrush to adhere the tissue-paper squares.) After the glue dries, trim excess tissue paper from the edges of the cutout, then use a black marker to draw desired details on the fish. What a catch!

Gina Marinelli—Gr. 2
Bernice Young Elementary School
Burlington, NJ

Star-Spangled Sparklers

These festive sparklers are the perfect addition to a patriotic celebration! Glue two red, two white, and two blue 2" x 6" construction-paper strips to a paper towel tube, alternating the colors as shown. Next tape half-inch silver paper strips (cut from wrapping paper) to the inside rim of one end of the tube. Embellish the tube with star-shaped cutouts or foil stickers. Hip, hip, hooray for the red, white, and blue!

Melissa A. Stanek—Grs. K–6
Better Beginnings
Oneonta, NY

Bug Bungalows

Your youngsters will go buggy over these clever creature carriers!

Materials for one bungalow:
one cardboard cylinder (precut with a 2" square opening) and its lid
one 3" square of clear plastic
construction-paper scraps
various art supplies such as pom-poms, yarn, felt, and sequins
one 12" length of curling ribbon
masking tape
glue
scissors
pencil, pen, or other fine-tipped tool for punching holes

Steps:
1. Position the plastic over the square opening in the container and securely tape it in place.
2. Use glue and construction-paper scraps to cover the remainder of the container, then attach other desired decorations.
3. Use the fine-tipped tool to poke tiny ventilation holes in the lid. *(Assist students as needed.)*
4. To make a handle, poke two small holes in opposite sides of the lid. *(Assist students as needed.)* Thread the curling ribbon through the holes and securely tie the ends. Pull the handle upward and snap the lid on the container.

To use the bungalow, remove its lid and carefully collect an insect guest to observe. (Assist students in choosing harmless bugs.) If desired, place some grass, twigs, and soil from the insect's environment in the container. Then snap on the lid. After a short while, return your guest to its original habitat.

Elizabeth Searls Almy
Greensboro, NC

Patterns

Use with "Pretty Patchwork Apples" on page 32.

Patterns

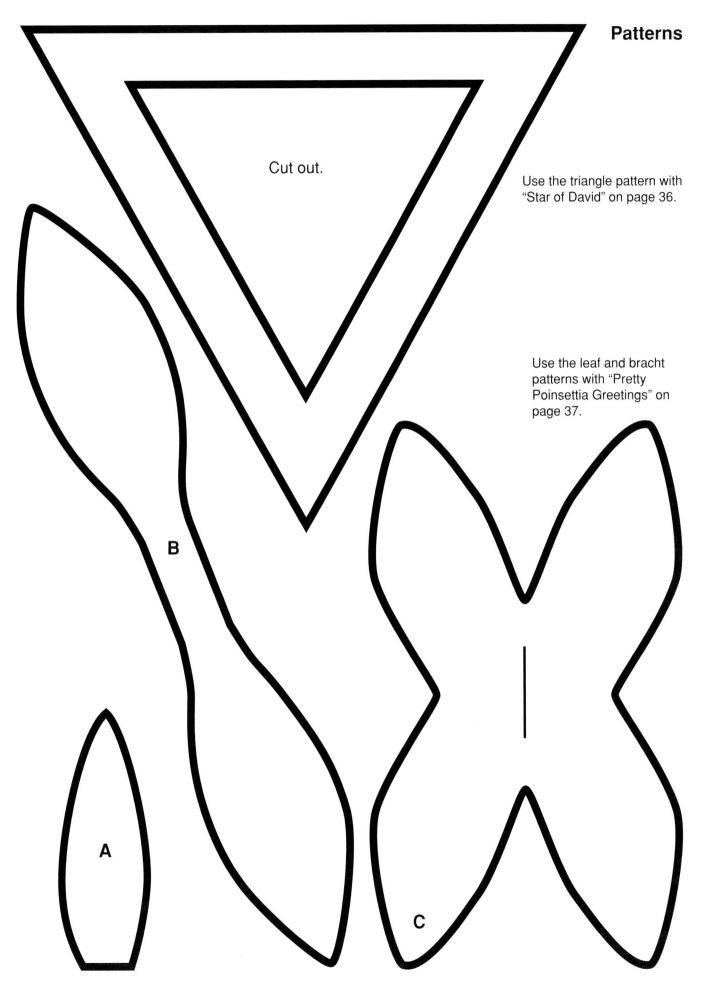

Cut out.

Use the triangle pattern with "Star of David" on page 36.

Use the leaf and bracht patterns with "Pretty Poinsettia Greetings" on page 37.

B

A

C

Name _____

Gingerbread Decorations

Circle each answer that describes you.
Then follow the directions to make decorations for your project.

Which Am I?

girl = pink
boy = blue

Cut out two eyes from
the color you circled.

How Old Am I?

6 = orange
7 = red
8 = green
9 = yellow

Cut out a nose (△) from
the color you circled.

How Many Brothers?

0 1 2 3 4 5 more

For each brother, cut
out one white stripe for
each arm.

How Many Sisters?

0 1 2 3 4 5 more

For each sister, cut out
one white stripe for
each leg.

When Is My Birthday?

January	=	white
		blue
February	=	red
		pink
March	=	green
		yellow
April	=	yellow
		purple
May	=	pink
		green
June	=	blue
		green
July	=	red
		white
		blue
August	=	yellow
		red
September	=	blue
		red
October	=	orange
		black
November	=	yellow
		brown
December	=	red
		green

Cut out hair from the
colors you circle.

What Do I Like to Do?

read = (··) blue

watch TV = △ white

play
outdoors = (··) red

play
indoors = [··] black

use a
computer = (··) orange

draw
pictures = △ purple

write
stories = (··) green

dance = [··] yellow

Make one button for
each circled item.

What Pet Do I Like Best?

dog =
cat =
fish =
bird =
other =

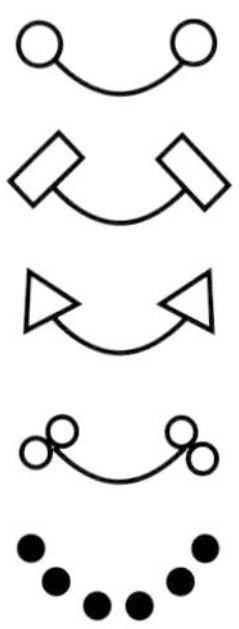

Draw the mouth that
matches your answer.

Note To Teacher: Use with "A Gingerbread Glyph" on page 39.

Patterns
Use the hammer pattern with "Magnetic Note Holder" on page 46.

Use the shamrock patterns with "Pot o' Gold Bank" on page 42.

Poem and Patterns

Use the poem with "Handmade for Mom" on page 44.

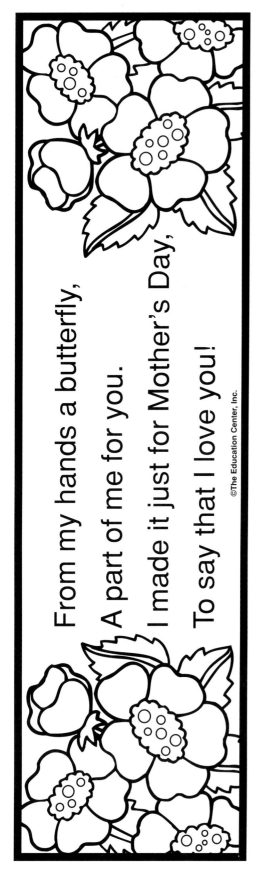

From my hands a butterfly,

A part of me for you.

I made it just for Mother's Day,

To say that I love you!

©The Education Center, Inc.

Use the patterns with "Earth-Friendly Mobile" on page 44.

Learning Centers

WANTED
JED T. TUCKER for

jed t. tucker is wanted for
rustling cattle from the
bucking Bronco Ranch. the
cowpoke is also believed to
have robbed Miss Kitty Copper
last thursday at the Silver
Spur Store? he was last
spotted near the town of
wichita falls, texas. he is most
likely headed for the state of
oklahoma. sherrif sam slaney
is offering a big reward to
anyone who helps in the
capture of Jed t. tucker.

Learning Centers

Domino Sums

This partner center adds up to lots of fun! Make several domino mats like the ones shown. Designate a different sum on each mat. Laminate the mats for durability; then store the laminated mats and a set of dominoes at a center. Each partner chooses a domino mat. If individual domino shapes are shown, the student covers each shape with a domino that equals the mat's designated sum. If a trail of domino shapes is shown, the student covers the shapes with dominoes that—when added together—equal the sum shown on the mat. When a student completes his mat, he asks his partner to check his work. Then he chooses a different mat to complete. The partners continue working in this manner until center time is over or they have each completed all the domino mats.

Ruth G. Trinidad—Gr. 1, 28th Street School, Los Angeles, CA

Clip It!

Students will think this initial-consonant center is a snap! Cut out pictures from discarded workbooks or magazines, and glue each one on a colorful card. At the bottom of each card, label the picture—replacing the initial consonant with a blank. Then, for self-checking, write the full word on the back of the card. Laminate the cards for durability and store them in a resealable plastic bag. Next program a spring-type clothespin for each letter of the alphabet. Place the clothespins and the bag of cards at a center. A student removes the cards from the bag. One at a time he reads each card, clips a clothespin onto the card to complete the word, and flips the card to verify that the word he spelled matches the word written on the back. Then he removes the clothespin and completes the next card. Plan to make similar centers to reinforce final consonant sounds, vowel sounds, blends, and more! It's a snap!

Melinda Casida—Gr. 1, Crowley Elementary, Visalia, CA

Shapely Creations

This hands-on activity familiarizes students with a variety of shapes—and at the same time, challenges students to think creatively. Place a set of attribute blocks, pencils, crayons or markers, and a supply of blank paper at a center. A student creates a desired picture by arranging the attribute blocks on a sheet of blank paper. When he is satisfied with his work, the student uses a pencil to trace around each block before he removes it from his paper. Then he colors his shapely creation!

Peggy Seibel—Gr. 2
St. Mary's School
Ellis, KS

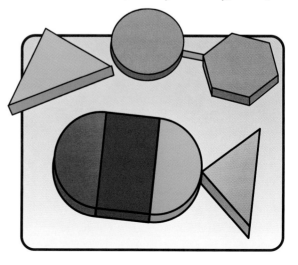

Monster Math

Students will have a monstrously good time at this math center! Create a simple "Draw a Monster" form that lists several monster features. Duplicate five copies of the form. Number each form and program it with desired math facts. Mount each programmed form on a slightly larger piece of construction paper and laminate it. Place the laminated forms, drawing paper, scrap paper (for math calculations), crayons or markers, and pencils at a center. A student chooses a "Draw a Monster" form. As he draws his monster, he refers to the form to find out how many arms, feet, noses, and so on his monster should have. Then he colors his creation. Wow! Math has never been more fun!

Sr. Margaret Ann Wooden
St. Joseph's School
Martinsburg, WV

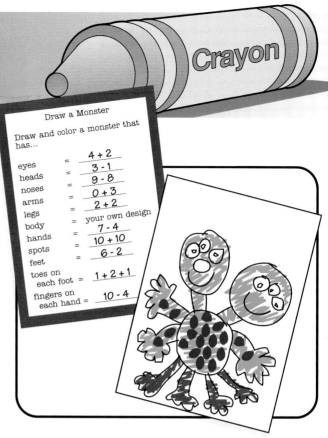

Draw a Monster

Draw and color a monster that has...

eyes	=	4 + 2
heads	=	3 - 1
noses	=	9 - 8
arms	=	0 + 3
legs	=	2 + 2
body	=	your own design
hands	=	7 - 4
spots	=	10 + 10
feet	=	6 - 2
toes on each foot	=	1 + 2 + 1
fingers on each hand	=	10 - 4

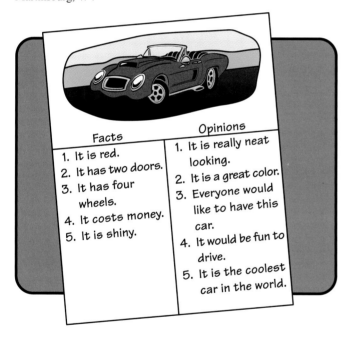

Facts	Opinions
1. It is red.	1. It is really neat looking.
2. It has two doors.	2. It is a great color.
3. It has four wheels.	3. Everyone would like to have this car.
4. It costs money.	4. It would be fun to drive.
5. It is shiny.	5. It is the coolest car in the world.

Picturing Facts and Opinions

Students report facts and opinions at this picture-perfect activity. Place scissors, a ruler, glue, pencils, discarded catalogs and magazines, and a supply of drawing paper at a center. A student cuts out a desired picture and glues it near the top of her paper. Below the picture she draws two columns and labels them "Facts" and "Opinions." Next she studies the picture and lists five facts and five opinions about it. If desired, ask each child to confirm with a classmate that her facts are facts and her opinions are opinions before she submits her work. The end result is a much clearer understanding of fact and opinion!

Joyce Hovanec, Glassport Elementary, Glassport, PA

Top Ten Favorites

Here's a center that's sure to make your students' top ten list of writing activities! On each of several cards, write a different category, such as games, foods, books, and outdoor activities. Place the cards at a center along with pencils and a supply of writing paper. A student chooses a category card, titles his paper "[Student's name]'s Top Ten [category]," and lists his ten favorites for that category. Invite students to write top ten lists for as many categories as time allows. Later, sort the lists by categories and compile each collection into a class book for your youngsters' reading enjoyment.

places to visit

foods

ways to make friends

animals

Ben's Top Ten Places to Visit
1. Waterland Wave Park
2. Grandma's house
3. the park near my house
4. the museum
5. the beach
6. Tommy's house
7. the state fair
8. the zoo
9. the library
10. the toy store

Guide-Word Sandwiches

Celebrate Sandwich Day (annually November 3) and provide guide-word practice with this appetizing center. To create a sandwich project like the one shown, cut two bread slices, a cheese slice, a lettuce leaf, a tomato slice, and one or two lunch-meat shapes from construction paper. Write a guide word on each bread slice. On each sandwich stuffer write an entry word that comes between the two guide words. Program the front of each bread slice and the back of each sandwich stuffer with the same symbol. Create a desired number of sandwich projects, making sure that the guide-word pairs do not alphabetically overlap. Laminate the cutouts for durability; then place the bread slices in one resealable plastic bag and the sandwich stuffers in another. Store the plastic bags in a lunchbox at a center. To assemble each sandwich, a student finds two bread slices with matching symbols; then she uses the guide words to identify the appropriate sandwich stuffings. To check her work, she flips the sandwich stuffers. Now that's a center activity students can really sink their teeth into!

Diane Gonzalez—Gr. 1, Carteret School, Bloomfield, NJ

Thanksgiving Math

Create a cornucopia of story-problem practice! Cut a large cornucopia shape from brown poster board and several fruit and vegetable shapes from colorful construction paper. Number the food cutouts and program them with Thanksgiving-related word problems. Next add desired details to the cutouts and program the back of each food shape for self-checking. Laminate the cutouts for durability; then use Velcro® to attach each food shape to the cornucopia. Place the cornucopia, pencils, and a supply of blank paper at a center. A student removes one food shape from the cornucopia, solves the story problem on his paper, and flips the food shape to check his work. When he has solved all the story problems, he refastens the foods to the cornucopia. Happy Thanksgiving!

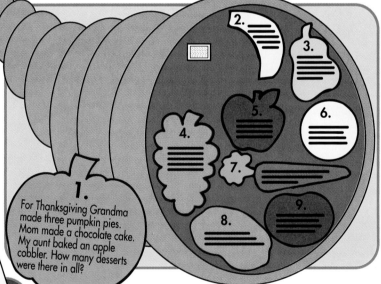

1.
For Thanksgiving Grandma made three pumpkin pies. Mom made a chocolate cake. My aunt baked an apple cobbler. How many desserts were there in all?

Surprising Stories

These story bags are packed with writing inspiration! Gather picture cards from a discarded Memory game or make picture cards by attaching stickers to tagboard rectangles. Then, for each picture card, program a corresponding word card. Laminate all the cards. In each of several resealable plastic bags, sort four picture cards and their matching word cards. Store the resulting story bags, pencils, and a supply of paper at a center. A student chooses a story bag and matches each picture card to a word card. Then she writes a story that includes the four pictured items. Just imagine the surprising stories that will result!

Beth Jones—Gr. 2, Stevensville Public School
Stevensville, Ontario, Canada

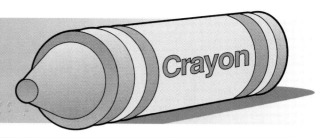

Winter Wonderland

Beat the wintertime blues with this critical-thinking center! Place a winter item—such as a sled, a scarf, a ski, a snowshoe, or a ski boot—at a center and create a list of questions about the chosen item. Place the questions, a supply of writing paper, pencils, and materials needed to answer the questions at the center. A student answers each question on her sheet of paper; then she asks a classmate to verify her work. Too cool!

Mary Jo Fesenmzier, Lake Geneva, WI

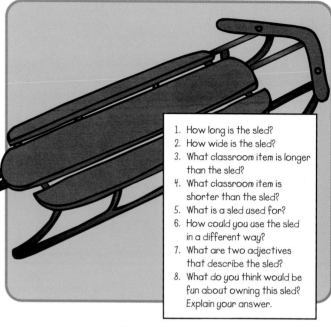

1. How long is the sled?
2. How wide is the sled?
3. What classroom item is longer than the sled?
4. What classroom item is shorter than the sled?
5. What is a sled used for?
6. How could you use the sled in a different way?
7. What are two adjectives that describe the sled?
8. What do you think would be fun about owning this sled? Explain your answer.

Star Puzzlers

This star-studded skill review is a bright idea! Duplicate the patterns on page 63 onto yellow construction paper—one copy for each star. To review math facts, program each star's center with a different answer; then program each set of star points with corresponding math facts. Laminate and cut out the patterns; then use a permanent marker to program the backs of the cutouts for self-checking. Store the cutouts in a resealable plastic bag at a center. A student assembles the stars, then flips the cutouts to check his work.

Maricela Perez—Gr. 2
Anthon Elementary School
Uvalde, TX

Stocking Stuffers

Students consult a dictionary to determine if the items named at this center are appropriate stocking stuffers. Number ten cards and label each one with the name of an object that appears in a student dictionary and may be unfamiliar to students. Create an answer key for self-checking and tuck it inside a holiday stocking. Suspend the stocking at a center and place the cards, writing paper, pencils, and a student dictionary there. A student numbers his paper and looks up each word in the dictionary. If the object will fit in the suspended stocking, he writes "yes" on his paper. If it will not, he writes "no." Then he checks his work against the answer key. To reprogram the center, replace the set of word cards and provide a corresponding answer key. Happy holidays!

adapted from an idea by Mary Jane Farrar—Gr. 1
Viscount Montgomery Public School
Hamilton, Ontario, Canada

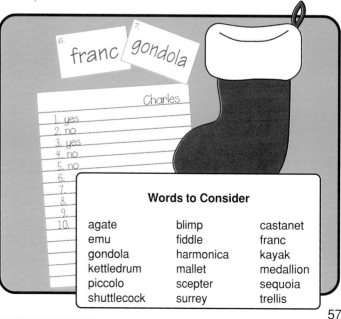

Words to Consider

agate	blimp	castanet
emu	fiddle	franc
gondola	harmonica	kayak
kettledrum	mallet	medallion
piccolo	scepter	sequoia
shuttlecock	surrey	trellis

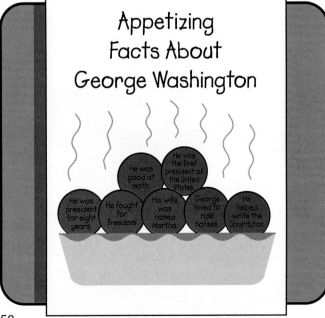

Fact-Family Fun

Now you can deliver fact-family practice at a moment's notice! Place a container of dominoes, drawing paper, and pencils at a center. A student folds a sheet of paper in half twice, unfolds the paper, and letters the four resulting boxes from A to D. To complete each box, he selects and illustrates a domino. He writes the two numbers from the domino as an addition fact and supplies the answer. Then he writes the three remaining number sentences in this fact family. Now that adds up to a whole lot of family fun!

Trudy White—Gr. 2
Mayflower Elementary
Mayflower, AR

Sweet Talk

This center gets to the heart of quotation marks! Stock a center with candy conversation hearts, heart-shaped writing paper, glue, pencils, scissors, pink construction paper, and red crayons. A student selects a candy heart and then she writes and punctuates a spoken sentence on her paper that incorporates the candy heart. After she carefully punctuates the sentence, she traces each punctuation mark with red crayon. Next she glues her work onto pink paper and trims the paper to create a narrow border. Students will ask to repeat this activity in a heartbeat!

Debra S. Sietsema—Gr. 2
Allendale Public Elementary School
Allendale, MI

Presidential Pie

Researching George Washington is as easy as pie at this center! Provide nonfiction books about Washington along with a two-inch circle template, glue, scissors, crayons or markers, and the following construction paper: 2" x 9" gray, 6" x 9" red, 9" x 12" yellow. A student traces five or more circles on red paper, writes a fact about Washington in each one, and then cuts out the shapes. He trims a strip of gray paper into a pie pan shape and colors a pie crust on it. Then he glues the cutouts on yellow paper as shown and adds desired details and a title. Or ask each child to contribute one cherry-shaped fact to a class pie pan that is displayed on a bulletin board at the center. Isn't research delicious?

Kristi Wood—Gr. 1
Woodridge Elementary
Stone Mountain, GA

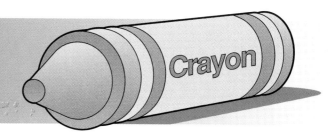

Centimeter Snakes

Legend has it that St. Patrick drove all the snakes from Ireland. So perhaps March is the perfect month for students to measure some colorful centimeter snakes! Cut 15 strips of paper into different centimeter lengths. Carefully round the corners of each strip; then number the strips and decorate them as desired. Design and laminate an answer key that can be attached to the bottom of a cylindrical container. Tape the key to the bottom of the container; then store the centimeter snakes inside. Place the container, a centimeter ruler, a supply of paper, and pencils at a center. A student numbers her paper from 1 to 15; then she removes each snake, measures it, and records her centimeter measurement on her paper. When all of the snakes have been measured, she turns the can over and checks her work. Snakes alive! Measurement is fun—and that's no blarney!

Rita Yanoff—Gr. 2
Sussex Christian School
Hope, NJ

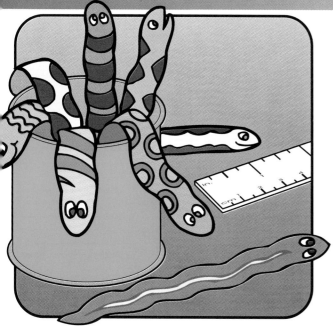

Memory Game

This easy-to-make partner center is sure to receive rave reviews! Collect 28 metal lids from frozen concentrate cans (orange juice, grape juice, etc.), or cut out 28 circles from the same color of tagboard. You will also need 28 stickers—2 each of 14 different varieties. If desired, design this Concentration-style memory game around a chosen theme like the weather, dinosaurs, or the desert. Attach a thematic sticker to the bottom of each lid. Store the lids in a container at a center. To play the game, a pair of students arranges the lids sticker-side down. Then, in turn, each child turns over two lids. If these lids have identical stickers, the child keeps the lids and turns over two more. If the stickers on the lids do not match, the child turns them sticker-side down and his partner takes a turn. The child with the most lids at the end of the game wins.

Diane Benner—Gr. 2
Dover Elementary
Dover, PA

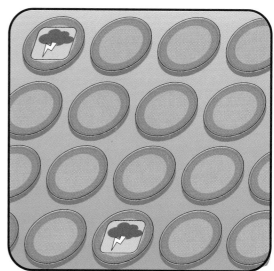

Guide Words Galore

Guide-word practice becomes a real "shoe-in" at this sorting center. Suspend a plastic shoe organizer at a center. Number and label each pocket with a different pair of guide words. Make sure the guide-word pairs do not alphabetically overlap. For each pocket, label one shoeprint cutout with an appropriate entry word. Program the back of the cutout with the matching pocket number. Laminate the shoeprint cutouts for durability, if desired; then store them in a shoebox at the center. A student sorts the cutouts into the shoe organizer. When all the shoeprints have been sorted, he turns each one over to check his work. Now that's some fancy footwork!

Margaret-Ann Rhem—Gr. 3
Western Branch Intermediate
Chesapeake, VA

Egg Carton Multiplication

Do your students need "eggs-tra" practice with multiplication facts? Try this! Number 12 sticky dots with desired factors and press one sticky dot into each egg cup of an egg carton. Place the prepared carton, two pom-poms, paper, and pencils at a center. A student drops the pom-poms inside the egg carton, closes the lid, and gently shakes the carton. Then she opens the carton and on her paper writes (in the form of a multiplication problem) the factors where the pom-poms landed. Then she solves the fact, closes the carton, and repeats the activity until she's written and answered a designated number of facts.

adapted from an idea by Amy Barsanti—Gr. 3
Pines Elementary School
Plymouth, NC

Hot off the Press

Publishing stories is in the cards at this writing center. Stock the center with index cards, markers, pencils, and clear tape. A student lays two index cards side by side, making sure the left-hand card shows lines and the right-hand card does not. Then he tapes the two cards together. Next he flips the left-hand card on top of the right-hand card and titles and decorates the resulting book cover. He opens the book, writes on the lined card, and illustrates the blank card. Then he flips the illustrated card, tapes a blank card to the right of the lined card, and continues writing and illustrating his tale. He continues in this manner until his tale is told!

Amy Emmons—Grs. K–3
Enon Elementary
Franklinton, LA

ABC Egg Basket

Hatch plenty of alphabetical order practice at this seasonal center. Tuck cellophane grass and six different-colored plastic eggs in a basket. For each egg, label four color-coded construction paper cards (e.g., purple cards for a purple egg) with different words to alphabetize. Store each card set in its corresponding egg. Place the basket of eggs, paper, and pencils at a center. A student selects an egg and writes its color on her paper. Next she cracks open the egg, arranges the cards in ABC order, and copies the alphabetized words. Then she returns the cards to the egg, and the egg to the basket. Provide an answer key for self-checking, if desired.

adapted from an idea by Dawn Schroeder—Gr. 1
Kluckhohn Elementary
LeMars, IA

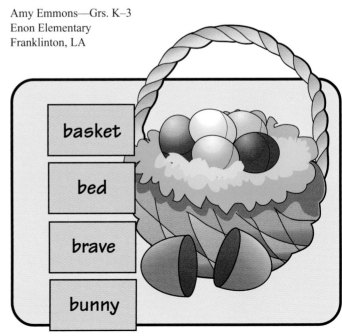

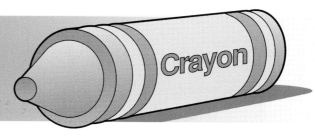

A Real Deal!

You've heard of a two-for-one sale; well here's a two-for-one center! To reinforce money skills *and* problem-solving skills, clip a supply of coupons from discarded magazines and newspapers; then attach each coupon to a 3" x 9" strip of construction paper. Choose a coin combination that equals the face value of the featured coupon and attach one sticky dot to the strip for each coin in the combination. Code the backs of the strips for self-checking; then laminate the strips for durability. Place the coupon strips and a supply of coin manipulatives at a center. A student chooses a coupon strip; then he determines a combination of coins that equals the face value of the coupon and provides him with one coin for each dot on the strip. To check his work, he flips the strip over. The student continues in this manner until he has completed each coupon strip. One center—two skills. Now that's a real deal!

Pat Rutland—Gr. 2
Stockdale Elementary
Stockdale, TX

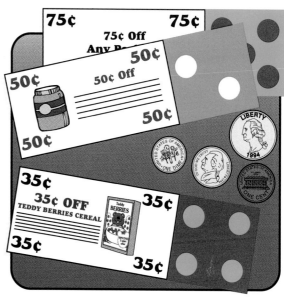

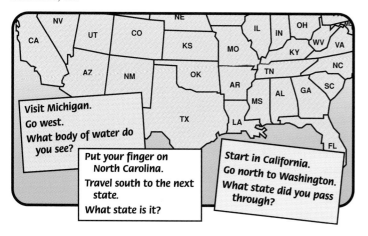

Where in the World?

Oh, the places students can go at this versatile mapping center! Refer to a desired map or a globe as you program each of several cards with directions that lead to a different location. Program the cards for self-checking and laminate them for durability if desired. Place the cards and the corresponding map or globe at a center. A student follows the directions on each card to find its mystery location; then he flips the card to check his work. Feature a different set of direction cards each week and you'll have a year-round center that really takes you places!

Laura Mihalenko—Gr. 2
Harry S. Truman Elementary School
Parlin, NJ

What's the Code?

Keep your students hopping with a secret code center! To make the Code Toad shown, enlarge the pattern from page 64 onto a sheet of tagboard. Glue 26 sequentially numbered library pockets to the toad shape and write each letter of the alphabet near one end of a 3" x 5" card. Laminate the toad and cards for durability; then cut them out. Use an X-acto® knife to slit open the pockets. Slide an alphabet card inside each pocket and display the resulting Code Toad at a center along with a message for your youngsters to decode, pencils, and paper. In addition to decoding your message, students will enjoy writing their own coded messages. To change the code, simply reposition the cards. For an instant math center, feature a series of coded math problems (like "A + Z + C = ____") for students to solve. The possibilities are endless!

Vicki Neilon—Gr. 2
Antietam Elementary School
Lake Ridge, VA

Proofreading Pals

Here's a partner center that clearly strengthens proofreading skills! On lined chart paper, write a paragraph that contains a predetermined number of mistakes like misspelled words and missing or inappropriate capital letters and punctuation marks. Display the paragraph—covered with clear acetate—at a center along with student directions, a dictionary, a corresponding answer key, several wipe-off markers, a container of baby wipes, and a trash can. A student pair proofreads the paragraph and uses wipe-off markers to make the necessary corrections. Once the edit is completed, the students check their work against the provided answer key; then they use a baby wipe to wipe the acetate clean so that the center is ready for another pair. Each week feature a different paragraph at the center. The message is clear—a proofreading center builds editing skills!

Sharon L. Brannan—Gr. 2
Holly Hill Elementary, Holly Hill, FL

Fraction Creatures

These fun creatures familiarize students with fractions—and at the same time, challenge students to think creatively. Place a large supply of one-inch construction-paper squares in assorted colors, black fine-tipped markers, a supply of 12" x 18" sheets of drawing paper, and glue at a center. A student folds a sheet of paper in half and in half again; then he unfolds his paper. At the top of each resulting quadrant, he writes a fraction with a denominator of four or less and a color word that describes some of the paper squares at the center. Each quadrant must be labeled differently. Then, in each quadrant, he uses the available supplies to create a creature that represents the quadrant's programming. For example a creature created in a quadrant labeled "²/₃ blue" would be made with three paper squares—two of them blue. Fractions have never been more fun!

Belinda Darnall Vose—Gr. 1
Evergreen Elementary
Ocala, FL

Sentence Structure Delivery

Here's a delivery that reviews sentence structure and rock-related facts! Cut 25 rock shapes from gray paper. Write "1" near the top of five cutouts and then write each word in Fact 1 (see "Rock Facts") on one of these cutouts. Prepare the remaining facts in a similar manner. Laminate the cutouts for durability; then cut them out and store them in a toy dump truck. Place the truck, writing paper, pencils, and an answer key at a center. A student unloads the paper rocks and sorts them by number. Next, she arranges the rocks in each set to make a fact sentence and copies the sentence on her paper. When she has written all five facts, she uses the answer key to check her work.

adapted from an idea by Sarah Mertz—Grs. 1–2, Owenton, KY

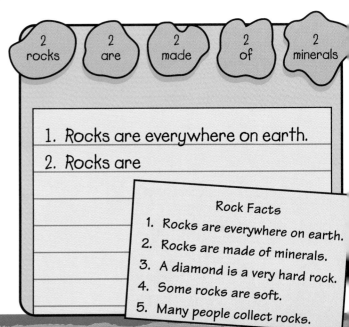

**Assembled
Pattern**

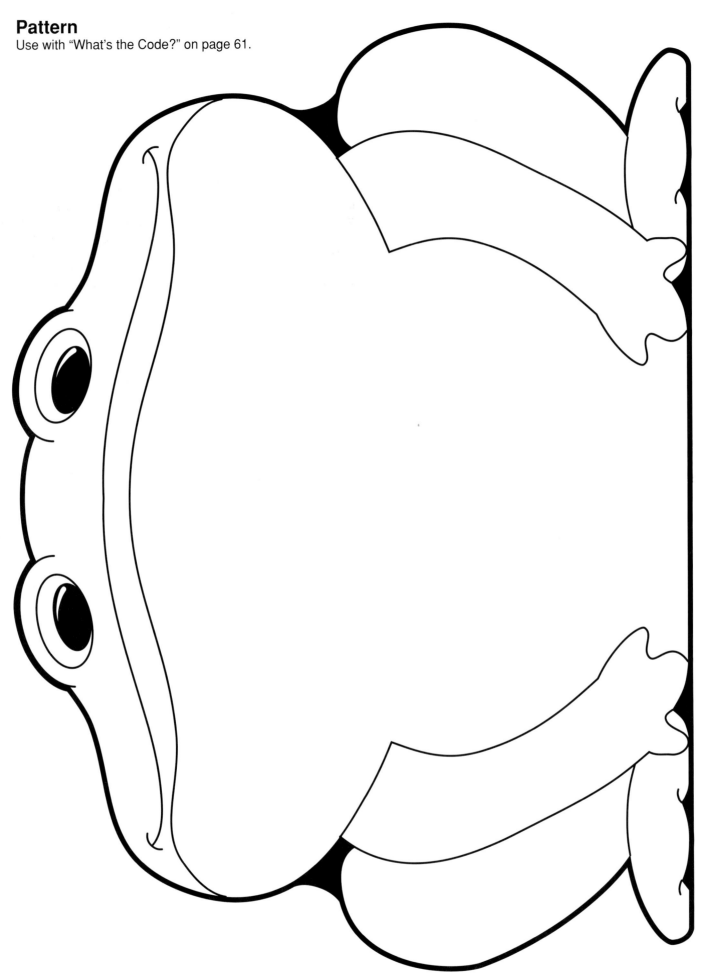

Write On!

Who Said It's January?

The sky did when it
sent a flurry of snow.

The mittens did when
they got ready to be worn.

The icicle did when it
formed outside our house.

The carrot did when it
became a snowman's nose.

The fireplace did when
it cracked and popped.

Write On!

Ideas and Tips for Teaching Students to Write!

Dear Class,
Hi! My name is Lindsay. This summer I went to the lake with my family. I took my first boat ride ever! It was lots of fun. We ate chicken and brownies.

Summer Snapshots

Summer memories become picture-perfect with this back-to-school writing project. Have each student illustrate a favorite summer event on one side of a large white index card. Encourage her to illustrate the entire side of the card so that her work resembles a postcard photograph. On the opposite side of the card have her write a note to the class in which she introduces herself and describes the illustrated event. While the students are working, ask each child to sign the front or back of a large index card titled "Summer Snapshots." Invite each child to share her project with the class. Then collect the cards and hole-punch the top left-hand corner of each one (including the autographed card). Secure the cards on a metal ring for further reading enjoyment.

Sharon MacQueen—Gr. 3, St. Zachary School, Des Plaines, IL

Who's There?

This get-acquainted writing activity induces plenty of grins and giggles! Begin by sharing a few of your favorite knock-knock jokes or reading aloud selected jokes from *1000 Knock Knock Jokes for Kids* by Michael Kilgarriff (Ballantine Books, 1990). Then challenge each child to use his first or last name to write knock-knock jokes. For the best results, display a format like the one shown for students to copy and complete. Be sure to set aside time for students to share the jokes they've written with their classmates— or even another class. Knock, knock. *Who's there?* Ima. *Ima who?* Ima sure your youngsters will love this writing experience!

Jill Hamilton—Gr. 1, Schoeneck Elementary, Stevens, PA

HA! HA! HEE! HO! HO! HA!

Knock, knock.

Who's there?

_____
(name)

_____ who?
(name)

_____
(punch line)

HEE! HEE! HA! HA! HO! HO!

Abloom With Color

Color words are the key to spouting this big book of blossoms! Ask students to imagine a colorful flower garden or show them a picture of one. Then write a student-generated list of color words on the chalkboard. Working in small groups or pairs, have the students use art supplies like crayons, markers, scraps of tissue paper and construction paper, and glue to create colorful flowers on 12" x 18" sheets of white construction paper. Next ask each group to copy and complete the following sentence about its flower (or dictate for you to write): "[Color word] flower, [Color word] flower, What do you see?" Collect and stack the projects; then add a page to the bottom of the stack that you've programmed "I see a colorful flower garden looking at me!" Compile the pages into a class book titled "Our Big Book of Blossoms." Read aloud the big book and share the final page with great fanfare. Then invite each child to draw and color a flower on the final page to create a must-see flower garden! You can count on this class book's being read time and time again!

To increase the difficulty of this activity, ask students to incorporate additional adjectives in their flower descriptions.

Karen Cook—Grs. K–1, McDonough Primary School, McDonough, GA

Red flower,
Red flower,
What do you see?

For Sale

Drafty house with 13 rooms
and a haunted attic.

This creepy mansion has lots of spiderwebs,
countless hidden passageways, squeaky
doors, and floors that creak. It is a spooky
house that is guaranteed to send shivers
down your spine!

Twigatops
My dinosaur discovery is a
Twigatops. He is very nice. He eats
lots of grass. He looks like a big fat
bush. I wish I had a Twigatops in my
backyard. That would be really cool!
by Gene W.

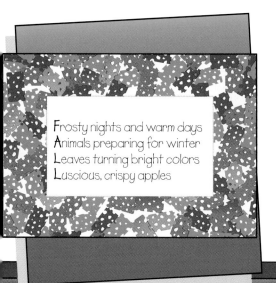

Frosty nights and warm days
Animals preparing for winter
Leaves turning bright colors
Luscious, crispy apples

Haunted Houses for Sale

Strengthen community ties and persuasive writing skills with this "spook-tacular" Halloween activity! To set the stage, read aloud and discuss several real-estate ads. Invite students to explain why some ads appeal to them more than others. Then have students brainstorm the kinds of things that ghosts, goblins, and other Halloween creatures might look for in a house. Instruct each youngster to use these ideas to write and illustrate an ad for a haunted house. Next, invite a local realtor to speak to the class about his career. Allow time during his visit for your young writers to share their spine-tingling work. Then showcase the ads at a display titled "Haunted Houses for Sale."

JoAnne Condelli—Gr. 2 and Carol Masek—Teaching Assistant
Spruce Run Elementary School, Nazareth, PA

"Invent-a-saurus"

Looking for some "dino-mite" writing inspiration? Try this! Have each child cut out a tagboard dinosaur pattern. Then have her take home her cutout and invent a new type of dinosaur by decorating the cutout with a chosen item. For example, a Cottonasaurus might be covered with cotton, a Twigatops adorned with twigs, and a Stamposaurus rex embellished with canceled stamps. Set a date for the dinosaur projects to be returned. Then schedule writing time for students to pen paragraphs about their prehistoric creatures. Display each child's projects together on a bulletin board titled "Priceless Prehistoric Discoveries!"

Mary E. Maurer, Caddo, OK

Picturesque Poetry

Focus on fall with this decorative poetry project. First, have each student completely cover a 9" x 12" sheet of yellow construction paper with red, orange, and green sponge-painting. While the paintings are drying, ask children to brainstorm words and phrases that describe the fall season. Record their ideas on chart paper. Next, have each student write "FALL" on a 5" x 8" sheet of white paper as shown and refer to the student-generated list to write an acrostic poem. Remind students that each line of their poems must start with the corresponding letter in "FALL." Then have each child glue his acrostic in the center of his sponge-painted paper. For an eye-catching seasonal display, mount the completed projects on a bulletin board titled "Poetry Paints a Pretty Picture." This combination of paint and poetry will receive rave reviews!

Amy Erickson—Gr. 1, Montello Elementary School, Lewiston, ME

The sky did when it sent a flurry of snow.

The mittens did when they got ready to be worn.

The icicle did when it formed outside our house.

The carrot did when it became a snowman's nose.

The fireplace did when it cracked and popped.

Who Said It's January?

Reinforce the concept of seasonal changes with this poetry idea. Begin with a discussion of the sights, sounds, and events of January. Make a list of the students' observations. On a length of bulletin board paper, write the title "Who Said It's January?" Model the style of the poem by writing the first line as an answer to the question. (For example, "The sky did when it sent a flurry of snow.") Ask children to create additional lines for the poem, designating a narrator for each line. Write each student's contribution on the bulletin board paper. Conclude the poem with the lines "Who said it's January? Now you know!" If desired, have students add seasonal cutouts to the poem before you display it for all to enjoy.

Patricia E. Buob—Grs. 1–2 Multiage, Central Road School, Rolling Meadows, IL

The best holiday season I remember is the year we went to Disneyland. I saw Mickey Mouse. He looked like Santa. His dog Pluto looked like a reindeer. It was fun!

"Holly-day" Happenings

Create an adorable "holly-day" display with this writing idea! Draw a large holly leaf on white paper, add writing lines, and duplicate one holly leaf for every student. Provide an assortment of story starters, like "My favorite thing about December is..." and "The best holiday season I remember is..." Have each child select a story starter and write a story on his leaf. Then have the student cut out his holly leaf, glue it onto a slightly larger piece of green construction paper, and trim the green paper to create an eye-catching border. Arrange the completed cutouts on a wall or bulletin board in the shape of a giant wreath. Add a few red paper berries and a big, red paper bow for a colorful "holly-day" display!

Loretta W. Lombardi—Gr. 3, Mercer Christian Academy, Trenton, NJ

Winter is having a cold nose.
Marcus

Wintertime Writing

You can count on students' warming right up to this cold-weather writing activity! Ask students to brainstorm words and phrases that remind them of winter. Write their ideas on the chalkboard. Then have each child copy and complete the sentence "Winter is…" on 3" x 5" writing paper, referring to the class-generated list as desired. Next, have him color a white construction paper copy of a mug of cocoa pattern—similar to the one shown—and cut it out. To complete his project, he glues his writing on the mug and a few white pom-pom marshmallows floating in the cocoa. Set aside time for students to share their writing with their classmates over cups of real cocoa!

Fara Singer—Gr. 1, Public School 2 Queens, Jackson Heights, NY

Silly Jill Day

My holiday will be named Silly Jill Day. It will be on January 5. That is my birthday. School will be closed. Everyone will eat fish, french fries, and ice cream. People will act silly and tell jokes all day long!

February 17, 2000

Dear Tooth Fairy,

How are you? I hope you are finding lots of teeth. I have been taking very good care of my teeth. I am brushing a lot. I am eating crunchy foods. I am trying to eat less sugar. I think I will have a tooth for you soon. It just started to wiggle!

Your friend,
Robbie

○ This is Sue Hohbach reporting for Channel 35. The forecast for Bite and Chew looks cloudy. There is a 50 percent chance of orange-juice showers moving in from the West. By noon we should see a heavy downpour of noodles and cheese. The sky should clear slightly before a mist of milk moves our way.

○

Holiday Hoopla

Begin this kid-pleasing writing activity by reviewing with students the history behind a popular holiday celebration like Valentine's Day or St. Patrick's Day. Then have each student contemplate what a holiday designed especially in *her* honor might be like. Ask each child to choose a name for her holiday, decide when it would be celebrated, and select foods and activities for the special day. Then have her write and illustrate a paragraph that names and describes her holiday. Display the completed projects on a bulletin board titled "Hip, Hip, Hooray for *OUR* Holidays!"

Jill Hamilton—Gr. 1, Schoeneck Elementary, Stevens, PA

Dear Tooth Fairy

February is National Children's Dental Health Month, and that makes it the perfect time to write friendly letters to the tooth fairy! After a review of the five parts of a friendly letter, have each child write to the tooth collector. Encourage students to describe in their letters the good dental health habits they are practicing and inform the fairy about any teeth they will soon have ready for her. Display a pillow at the front of the room and have each child tuck his completed letter under it. Before students arrive on the following day, remove the letters and tuck a class supply of sugarless gum under the pillow. Sprinkle glitter around the pillow for added effect. Students will be all grins!

Beth Jones—Gr. 2, Stevensville Public School, Niagara Falls, Ontario, Canada

---

Wacky Weather

There's no shortage of food or fun in Judi Barrett's outrageous weather-related story, *Cloudy With a Chance of Meatballs* (Scholastic Inc., 1978). After reading this story to your students, challenge them to write comical weather reports for other fictitious towns. Each report should include several weather predictions that involve foods and beverages. Since no weather report is complete without a station identification, suggest that each student name a radio or television station as the source of her report. Set aside time for students to read their reports to their classmates. Your classroom will be more fun than the land of Chewandswallow!

Patti Hirsh—Gr. 3, Casis Elementary, Austin, TX

Percy is my pet porcupine. My uncle gave him to me. He is still a baby. He likes to eat carrots. He sits in my lap when we watch TV. When he grows up, he will protect me from bullies. Percy is my perfect pet!
                                        by Trysten

Pet Paragraphs

Paragraph writing is easy to "purr-fect" when pictures of possible pets provide writing inspiration! Each student selects a pet by cutting out a picture of an animal from a discarded magazine. As a prewriting activity, he names the pet and lists details about it. Then he uses his ideas to write a paragraph about his new pet. To assemble his work, he glues his cutout and paragraph on construction paper as shown. Bind completed projects into a class book titled "Perfect Pets and Paragraphs!"

adapted from an idea by Diane B. Rinehard—Gr. 2, Beechgrove Elementary Independence, KY

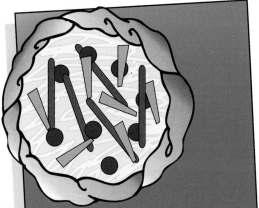

Jessica likes grapes, carrots, licorice, and lemon pudding on her pizza.

Pizza With Pizzazz!

Any way you slice it, this tasty activity teaches students how to use commas in a series! Write a student-generated list of favorite foods. Then write a silly pizza-related sentence on the chalkboard that lists four favorite foods as toppings. For example, "Hope likes ice cream, strawberries, spaghetti, and cream corn on her pizza." Explain that when a sentence contains a list of three or more items, commas are used to separate the items in the list. Ask each child to write several sentences that list silly pizza toppings. Then have her copy her favorite one on provided paper and use construction paper scraps, glue, and crayons to decorate a brown paper circle to resemble the pizza she described. For a 3-D crust, she rolls brown paper towels and glues them around the edge of her pizza. Display the projects with the title "Pizzas With Pizzazz!"

Sharon L. Brannan—Gr. 2, Holly Hill Elementary, Holly Hill, FL

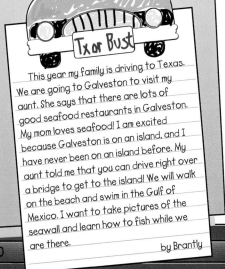

This year my family is driving to Texas. We are going to Galveston to visit my aunt. She says that there are lots of good seafood restaurants in Galveston. My mom loves seafood! I am excited because Galveston is on an island, and I have never been on an island before. My aunt told me that you can drive right over a bridge to get to the island! We will walk on the beach and swim in the Gulf of Mexico. I want to take pictures of the seawall and learn how to fish while we are there.
                                        by Brantly

Fasten Those Seat Belts!

Are your students daydreaming about a vacation? Why not use their dreams as fuel for a writing activity? Ask each child to pretend he is in charge of planning a five-day road trip for his family. Have him pen a story that tells *when* the trip will begin, *who* is going, *where* they are going, *why* they are going, and *what* they will do during the trip. Then have him color a car cutout and glue it to the top of his story as shown. Display the completed projects with the title "Our Seat Belts Are Fastened!"

Cheryl Stein—Gr. 2, Hankinson Elementary School, Hankinson, ND

Reading Skills Roundup

Word-Wall Chant

Find the word;
It is near.
Where's the word?
It's right here!

Say the word.
Clap the parts.
Tap the sounds.
What a start!

Time to spell.
Close each eye,
Do it now—
Don't be shy!

One more time,
Say the word
Loud and clear.
Now let's cheer!

Point and give a cheer.

Say the word.
Clap once for each syllable.
Tap once for each sound.

Spell the word aloud.

Say the word.

Give a cheer.

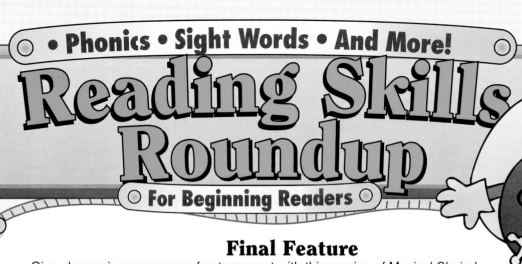

• Phonics • Sight Words • And More!
Reading Skills Roundup
For Beginning Readers

PHONEMIC AWARENESS

Final Feature

Give phonemic awareness a front-row seat with this version of Musical Chairs! Prepare a word list for each of several final consonant sounds. Intersperse the words on each list with words that have different ending sounds. Have youngsters form a circle of chairs with one less chair than students. To play a round, announce a final sound. Then slowly read the corresponding list as students walk around the circle. When a youngster hears a word that does not end with the featured sound, he quickly tries to sit in a chair. The student who is unable to find an empty chair repeats the last word called and identifies its ending sound. Then play resumes. When all of the words on the list have been called, continue the activity with a different word list. For older students, spotlight vowels, blends, or digraphs.

hen
pin
happen
begin
per
again
even
children
make

LaDawn Rhodes, Shelton Park Elementary, Virginia Beach, VA

RIMES

Roll and Write

With just a roll of a die, this small group activity gives word-family lessons a new twist! Each small group needs a die that you've programmed with different rimes like -ot, -ip, -an, -ell, -ug, and -ap. Each group member needs a piece of paper and a pencil. To play, one student in each group rolls the die and announces the rime. Then each group member writes on his paper a word that contains the rime. Next each child shares the word that he wrote with his group. Repeat this procedure until each group member has rolled the die. No doubt youngsters will be on a roll with this fun phonics activity!

Joy O'Gwen—Gr. 1, Oak Street School, Basking Ridge, NJ

not
bug
map
sip
dot

Word-Wall Chant

Find the word;
It is near.
Where's the word?
It's right here!

Say the word.
Clap the parts.
Tap the sounds.
What a start!

Time to spell.
Close each eye.
Do it now—
Don't be shy!

One more time,
Say the word
Loud and clear.
Now let's cheer!

Point and give a cheer.

*Say the word.
Clap once for each syllable.
Tap once for each sound.*

Spell the word aloud.

Say the word.

Give a cheer.

SIGHT WORDS

Word-Wall Chant

Looking for a motivating way to teach or reinforce sight words? Then try this catchy word-wall chant! Display the chant shown near your class word wall. Choose a student to point to a selected word on the word wall. Then lead the class in the chant, pausing for students to follow the provided directions. Next, if appropriate, have each child enter the word in a personal dictionary or practice writing it on scrap paper. Now that's a reading idea to cheer about!

adapted from an idea by Lynn L. Caruso—Gr. 1
Littlebrook Elementary, Princeton, NJ

Vowel Review

What's in the cards? A quick and easy short-vowel review for the whole class! Give each student five cards and have her label each one with a different short vowel. Call out a word that has a short-vowel sound. Have each youngster silently identify the vowel sound and then hold up her corresponding vowel card. Quickly scan the raised cards to determine the youngsters' accuracy. Ask a student who is holding the correct card to announce the vowel. Continue in a like manner with a desired number of other short-vowel words.

Dianne Neumann—Gr. 2
Frank C. Whiteley School
Hoffman Estates, IL

Mystery Words

Here's a case for your young word detectives to crack—the case of the mystery blend words. Give each student a card bearing a different noun that has a beginning blend, cautioning her not to reveal the word to her classmates. Ask her to write at least three clues for the word. Then have each student, in turn, read aloud her clues. After each clue, she invites her classmates to identify the mystery blend word. The first classmate who correctly identifies it takes the next turn (or, if she has already taken a turn, she selects another youngster who has not). What a nifty way to get students hot on the trail of blends!

adapted from an idea by Cindy Ward
Yellow Branch School
Rustburg, VA

1. It is shiny.

2. It comes in different colors.

3. It is used to decorate things.

glitter

Wipeout!

Students are sure to flip over this sight word game! Prepare two identical class sets of sight word cards. Divide students into small groups of equal size. Give each youngster a word card from the first set and have him place it faceup in front of himself. Place the second set of cards in a large bag.

To play, remove a card from the bag and read it aloud. The child who has the word flips over his card. Play continues in this manner. When all members of a group have turned their cards facedown, they stand and call "Wipeout!" To win the round, each child in the group reads aloud his word for verification. Next, have the students exchange word cards as you return your set of cards to the bag. Play as many additional rounds as desired. Out-of-sight!

Kathryn Levy—Gr. 1, Jacksonwald Elementary School, Reading, PA

Left or Right?

-IGHT

Word List

fight	sight
tight	might
side	find
light	lightbulb
boat	rise
bright	read
sky	twilight
fly	frighten
night	nighttime

This class word-family game is right on! Prepare a word list that includes several *-ight* words. Instruct students to arrange their chairs in a large circle and then be seated. Tape a wrapped candy or a sticker (with its backing in place) under one chair. To begin play, read aloud a word from your list. If a student agrees that the word has the *-ight* word family (rime), he gives a thumbs-up. If he does not, he gives a thumbs-down. Reveal the correct response. If it is thumbs-up, students stand and move two chairs to the right. If it is thumbs-down, they stand and move one chair to the left. Continue in this manner until you have read the first half of the word list. Then momentarily stop the game and instruct each child to look under the chair in which he is seated. If he finds a prize taped there, he removes the prize and the chair, and becomes the word caller for the last half of the game. Before continuing the game, tape another prize to the bottom of one chair within the circle. With this lively game, students' word-family skills will move right along!

Sara Harris—Gr. 2, West View Elementary, Knoxville, TN

On a Roll

BLENDS AND DIGRAPHS

Blend and digraph skills roll along at this partner center! Label each side of a blank cube with a different blend or digraph. Label three sides of a second blank cube "1" and three sides "2." Place the dice, blank paper, and pencils in a center. One partner divides a sheet of paper into six columns and labels the columns with the blends and digraphs written on the letter cube. Then, taking turns, each partner rolls the cubes and names a word that begins with the blend or digraph rolled and has the number of syllables shown. Her partner lists the word in the appropriate column and records the number of syllables. When each partner has taken a designated number of turns, the twosome totals the number of syllables in each column to discover which blend or digraph has the highest (lowest) syllable count.

Now that's an idea that adds up to loads of learning!

adapted from an idea by Karyn Karr—Gr. 1
Cleveland Elementary School
Cedar Rapids, IA

bl	fr	sh	cr	gr	bl
blue (1) bluebird (2)	friendship (2) freedom (2)	ship (1)	crayon (2) cream (1)	green (1)	chain (1)

"Sound-sational" Review

VOWELS

Here's a lively class activity that boosts vowel *and* listening skills! Program a class set of cards with long- and short-vowel words. Randomly distribute the cards to students. Announce a vowel sound and a direction that features the sound, such as "short *a:* clap" or "short *i:* wink." Each student who has a word with the designated vowel sound follows the direction. Then ask each of these students, in turn, to read her word aloud. Feature each remaining vowel sound in a like manner. For more practice, have each child trade cards with a classmate, and then repeat the activity.

adapted from an idea by Kathy McLenaghan—Gr. 1, St. Paul's Catholic School, Leesburg, FL

Literature-Related
Units

The Custodian
From the
Clown Town Circus

Cazet Dorado

Frog Jones
W. Melrose Ave.
Buffa, MD 21204

Road
10001 Ivy Trad Road
Riversdale MD 00012

Officer Buckle and Gloria
Written and Illustrated by Peggy Rathman
(G.P. Putnam's Sons, 1995)

"Don't swim right after eating," "Don't sit too close to the television," "Don't run with a pen in your mouth," "Don't eat paste." No doubt your youngsters will have heard these admonishments once or twice in their young lives. But, if your youngsters think parents and teachers are safety-conscious, wait until they meet Officer Buckle. In this Caldecott Medal-winning tale, an earnest—but boring—police officer is upstaged by a dynamic dog and her invigorating imitations. Once Officer Buckle realizes what has happened, he doesn't want to continue with the safety lectures he's been giving. In the end, though, Officer Buckle realizes that it's important to "always stick with your buddy." So if you're looking for a fresh alternative to integrate with your safety lessons, here's a tip: Don't miss this hilariously funny book.

ideas by Stacie Stone

Meet Author and Illustrator
Peggy Rathmann

Peggy Rathmann was born and raised in St. Paul, Minnesota. After graduating from high school, Rathmann attended several colleges and changed her major repeatedly. Eventually Rathmann received her degree in psychology, but she also took many art courses along the way. Rathmann wanted to teach gorillas sign language, but after taking a class in signing, she realized she'd rather *draw* gorillas! When Rathmann was 37, her brother enrolled her in a class on illustrating and writing children's books. She took the class over and over again. During the first few weeks of those classes, the first versions of each of her books was created. However, Rathmann says her books take years to write. She reworks them time and time again and says that she gets many of her ideas from things that have happened to her. *Officer Buckle and Gloria,* Rathmann's latest book, earned her the 1996 Caldecott Medal. Rathmann says of the award, "This is the greatest gift anyone ever gave me." Rathmann lives with her husband, John, in San Francisco, and is the author-illustrator of *Good Night, Gorilla* (Putnam, 1994) and *Ruby the Copycat* (Scholastic Inc., 1991).

Officer Buckle Says...

Undoubtedly your students will love the humorous illustrations in this book. After the initial reading, revisit the book and take time to examine the detailed pictures that often include safety tips. And you won't want to miss the safety tips printed on the inside front and back covers, either. Select several safety tips to discuss and ask students what consequences might result should the safety tip not be observed. Then challenge students to brainstorm other safety tips and print their ideas on the chalkboard.

Afterward have students assist you in creating this safety-centered bulletin board. Duplicate the star pattern on page 78 on yellow construction paper to make a class supply; then program each one with a safety-tip number. Give each student a star pattern and ask him to select and print a safety tip from the class-generated list on his star. Invite each student to draw and color a picture of Gloria demonstrating the consequences of not following the safety tip before he cuts out the star. Staple the completed stars to a bulletin board entitled "Safety Tips From Officer Buckle and Gloria." Keep a supply of numbered star cutouts handy so that students can write and illustrate other safety-related tips on them. Staple these stars to the bulletin board too. Who knows—maybe your safety-conscious students will beat Officer Buckle's record of 101 safety tips!

Safety Tip #4
Never slide down a slide backwards
by Kevin

Safety Tip #16
Never jump off a swing.
by Diane

Adventures With Officer Buckle and Gloria

Ask students to brainstorm specific situations in which people should exercise caution and follow safety rules. Students' responses may include: while bicycle riding, while riding the bus, while working in the kitchen, and while swimming. Talk with students about safety measures that need to be taken before and during each of the named activities. Then divide your class into groups of five students each. Have each group select an activity from the list; then briefly review safety measures that need to be taken for that activity.

Afterward have each group write its own Officer-Buckle-and-Gloria adventure. Give each group member a quart-size resealable plastic bag and a 6½" square of white construction paper. Have one member from each group write the title "Officer Buckle and Gloria [name of activity]" and then draw a corresponding picture on his paper. Have the remaining group members write and illustrate related safety facts on their paper squares. To assemble the booklet, each group member turns his plastic bag so that the zippered portion is facing left, inserts his work, and seals the bag. Stack the pages with the title page on top and staple the project along the left-hand side. Allow each group to share its completed booklet.

A Terrific Team

Like peanut butter and jelly—Officer Buckle and Gloria go together. Discuss with students how Officer Buckle's safety lectures were just not the same without Gloria and how Gloria, by herself, was not very entertaining either. Guide students to understand that Officer Buckle and Gloria had a *partnership*. Then ask students to name activities that are done with partners. List their responses on the board. Then, on a 12" x 18" piece of white construction paper, have each student copy and complete the phrase "It takes two to…," using the class-generated list for assistance if needed. Then have students use markers or crayons to draw pictures of Officer Buckle and Gloria engaging in the named activities. Allow volunteers to share their pictures and sentences with their classmates; then compile the students' work into a class big book titled "It Takes Two."

For a fun extension, allow each student to pick a partner; then have them complete their daily assignments and activities together. Students will likely agree with tip #101—always stick with your buddy.

Pins With Panache

These perfectly pleasing pins will help your students spread safety messages. To make a pin, have each student bring a clean plastic lid from home (lids from frosting, cream cheese, sour cream, and margarine containers will work well). Using her lid as a template, have each student trace a circle shape onto a piece of white Con-Tact® paper. Next have each student use permanent markers to decorate her circle shape with a safety-related message and illustration. Then she cuts out her circle shape, peels away the paper backing, and firmly presses the decorated circle in place atop the lid. Hot-glue a clasp to the back of each pin. (Clasps are available at craft stores.) Help each student attach her pin to her shirt. If desired allow students to make extra pins for school personnel such as the principal, bus drivers, and cafeteria workers to wear.

Star Pattern

Use with "Officer Buckle Says…" on page 76.

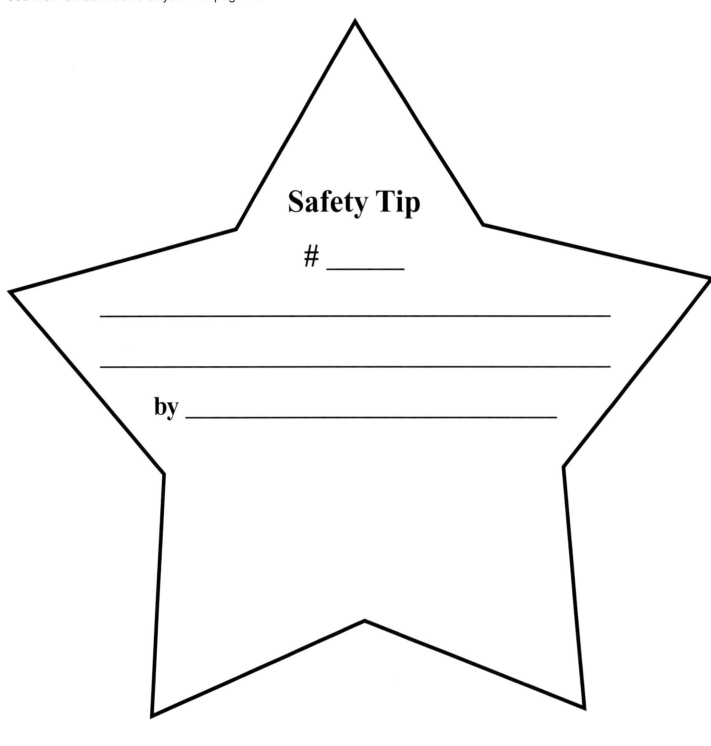

Safety Tip

_____

_____

_____

by _____

Play It Safe

Finish each safety tip:
   Unscramble the word.
   Write the word on the line.

Color Officer Buckle. Cut on the dotted lines.
Write your name on the booklet cover.
Staple the booklet pages to the cutout.

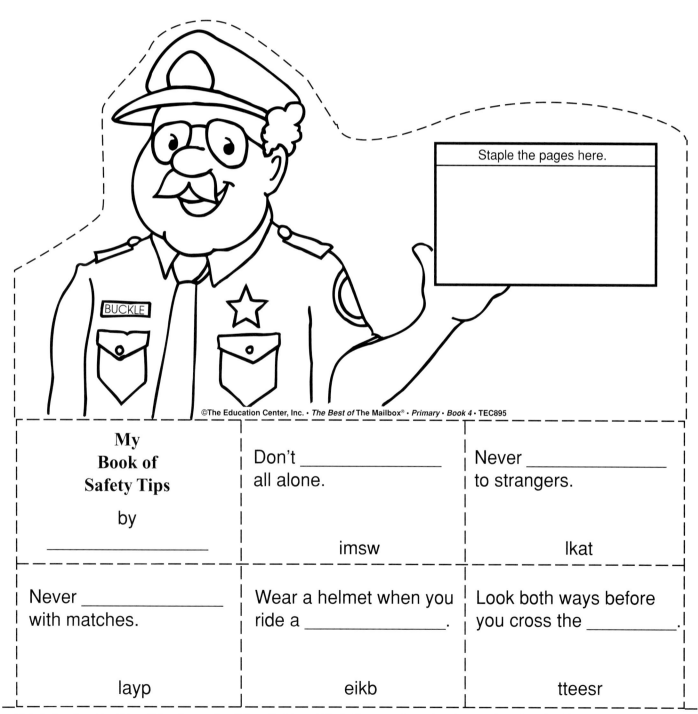

Staple the pages here.

©The Education Center, Inc. • *The Best of* The Mailbox® • *Primary • Book 4 •* TEC895

| **My Book of Safety Tips** by _____ | Don't _____ all alone. imsw | Never _____ to strangers. lkat |
| Never _____ with matches. layp | Wear a helmet when you ride a _____. eikb | Look both ways before you cross the _____. tteesr |

Note to teacher: Use this activity after reading *Officer Buckle and Gloria*. For a sturdier project, have each student glue his completed cutout to a 9" x 5" piece of construction paper.

The Mouse and the Motorcycle

Written by Beverly Cleary

What happens when an inquisitive mouse befriends a medium-size boy who owns a nifty mouse-sized motorcycle? Plenty! Beverly Cleary's heartwarming tale of friendship and suspense is sure to appeal to your students who—at one time or another—have probably wished they could talk with animals, too!

ideas by Stacie Stone Davis

Clevell Harris

Mouse Tales

There are plenty of journal-writing opportunities throughout this delightful chapter book—and what better place for youngsters to complete their writing activities than inside mouse-shaped journals! To make a journal, a student stacks several sheets of circular writing paper on top of a gray construction-paper circle; then he staples the stack at the top. Next he folds the project in half by aligning the bottom half of the stack with the top half of the stack. To decorate his journal, the student glues two construction-paper mouse ears, a pink pom-pom nose, and a wiggle eye in place. For the mouse tail, he bends a pipe cleaner as desired and tapes one end of it inside the cover, near the fold. Then the student uses a crayon to draw a mouth and write his name. Have students pen their thoughts about the story characters, make story predictions, summarize chapters, or create new Ralph-related adventures in their journals. It won't take long for students to determine that Ralph isn't just an ordinary mouse!

A Late-Night Spin

In chapter 5 Ralph takes Keith's motorcycle for a late-night spin, and quite an adventure unfolds. At the conclusion of the chapter, have students recall the events that took place that night. Then divide students into groups of six and challenge each group to write a late-night adventure featuring the motorcycle-riding mouse. To do this give each group a copy of the story frame on page 82, a pair of scissors, a 9" x 12" sheet of construction paper, pencils, and glue. Ask one member of each group to cut along the dotted lines on the reproducible and distribute the resulting paper strips, keeping the title strip and one additional strip for himself. Next instruct the students to complete the sentences on their strips. Then have each group sequence its story strips and glue them on the construction paper—beginning with the title strip and ending with strip number six. Allow time for the group members to read the story they wrote; then invite one member of each group to read his group's story to the rest of the class. Without a doubt, Ralph will have his share of wacky adventures—and there's a good chance that your youngsters will request this writing activity again!

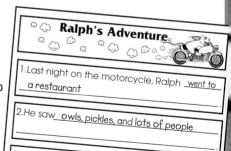

Ralph's Adventure

1. Last night on the motorcycle, Ralph _went to a restaurant_

2. He saw_ owls, pickles, and lots of people_

3. He heard _cows mooing and chickens crowing_

4. The funniest thing that happened to Ralph was _when he rode his motorcycle into the bathroom_

5. The scariest thing that happened to Ralph was _when he rode his motorcycle off the edge of a chair_

6. Ralph knew his adventure was over when

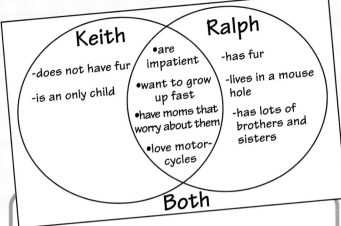

Keith
- does not have fur
- is an only child

Both
- are impatient
- want to grow up fast
- have moms that worry about them
- love motor-cycles

Ralph
- has fur
- lives in a mouse hole
- has lots of brothers and sisters

Forming Friendships

Ralph the mouse and Keith have more in common than a love of toy motorcycles! As a follow-up to chapter 9, draw and label a Venn diagram on the chalkboard that resembles the one shown. Then, under your students' direction, list the similarities and differences that they observe in the two characters. Next have the students evaluate the diagram and offer explanations about why they think the two get along so well.

To extend the activity, ask each youngster to think about a friend with whom she enjoys spending time. Then have each student create a Venn diagram on a sheet of paper that she can use to compare herself to her friend. After the diagrams have been completed, ask each student to determine why this friendship is special. Invite interested students to share their findings with the class.

A Mighty Fine Machine

Vroom! Vroom! Here's an art activity that's sure to get your students' creative wheels turning! Ask each child to choose a favorite motorcycle-related event from the story. Then have each student cut a picture of a motorcycle from a discarded magazine. Ask each student to glue his motorcycle cutout to a sheet of drawing paper and use crayons or markers to draw Ralph riding it. Next the student draws and colors scenery around the motorcycle-riding mouse that depicts the story scene he selected. Finally the student writes a sentence on a paper strip that describes his artwork. Display each illustration with its corresponding caption on a classroom bulletin board titled "Mouse on the Move!" Vroooooom!

Awesome Accomplishments

In chapter 12 Ralph puts his life on the line to find an aspirin for his sick friend. And in chapter 13, he is considered a hero for his brave acts. Ralph feels especially proud when Keith praises him for being a smart and brave mouse. Ask students to think of times when they have felt especially proud. Then challenge each child to describe and illustrate the accomplishment for which he feels most proud. Ask each student to title his work so that it resembles Beverly Cleary's title and includes his accomplishment or deed (like "Ashley and the Spelling Bee" or "Samuel and the Snake"). Collect the completed projects. Next title a sheet of poster board "Look What We've Done!", add a decorative border, and laminate the poster. Display the poster at students' eye level in the hallway outside your classroom door. Each day showcase two or three different stories on the poster. Continue featuring stories until every student's work has been on display. Who feels proud now?

Riding With Ralph

Put each youngster in the driver's seat with this review activity! Pair students and give each twosome a copy of the gameboard on page 84, a penny, and two game markers. Instruct the student pairs to play the game by following the provided directions.

To extend the activity and expose students to more than one classmate's book-related ideas, have the students play the game with a variety of partners. To do this, have the students trade partners on your signal. (For easy management establish a rotation system.) After several rounds of play, serve the students a snack of peanut-butter sandwiches or cookies in honor of Ralph.

There's More!

If your youngsters enjoyed *The Mouse and the Motorcycle*, they'll also enjoy the sequels: *Runaway Ralph* and *Ralph S. Mouse*. There's no doubt that Ralph returns as mischievous and brave as ever!

Ralph's Adventure

1. Last night on the motorcycle, Ralph _____

   _____

   _____ .

- -

2. He saw _____

   _____

   _____ .

- -

3. He heard _____

   _____

   _____ .

- -

4. The funniest thing that happened to Ralph was _____

   _____

   _____ .

- -

5. The scariest thing that happened to Ralph was _____

   _____

   _____ .

- -

6. Ralph knew his adventure was over when _____

   _____

   _____ .

Note to teacher: Use with "A Late-Night Spin" on page 80.

Name_____

Summer Fun

Oh no! The story Keith wrote for school is mixed up.
Cut out and read the story events.
Glue them in order on the notebook paper.

	My Summer Vacation by Keith Gridley
○	
○	
○	

Story Events

I gave Ralph my toy motorcycle to keep.

We checked into a hotel.

Ralph found me an aspirin.

I brought Ralph a peanut-butter sandwich.

My parents and I traveled to California.

I let Ralph the mouse ride my toy motorcycle.

I found a mouse in the wastebasket.

Then I got really sick.

Bonus Box: If you were Keith's teacher, what would you think about his summer vacation story? Write your comment at the top of the story.

WHEEEEEE

Note to teacher: Use this activity after completing the book.

Vrooooooom!

START

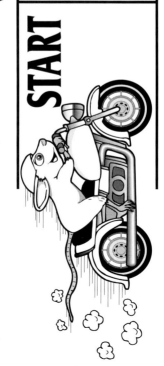

What is one way that you are like Keith?		
Which story character do you like the best? Why?	What is one way that you are like Ralph?	**Trapped!**  **Miss One Turn** → Do you think Ralph is honest? Why or why not?
	Should Ralph have gone home with Keith? Why or why not?	What do you think is the funniest part of the story?
If you saw a mouse, would you talk to it? Why or why not?	What is one way that you are not like Ralph?	What do you think is the scariest part of this story?

Directions for two players:
1. Place your game markers on START.
2. In turn, flip a penny and move:
   HEADS = 1 space
   TAILS = 2 spaces
3. Answer each question in the box.
4. The first player to reach FINISH wins.

Do you think Keith is responsible? Why or why not?		What is one way that you are not like Keith?
What would you like to say to Beverly Cleary about this book?	If you could ask Ralph one question, what would it be?	Why do you think Ralph and Keith became such good friends?
If you could change one part of the story, what would you change?	Would you tell a friend to read this book? Why or why not?	
	FINISH	

84

©The Education Center, Inc. • *The Best of The Mailbox®* • *Primary* • *Book 4* • TEC895

Note to teacher: Use this activity with "Riding With Ralph" on page 81.

Literature From the Black Lagoon
Using Mike Thaler's Books in the Classroom

Guaranteed to generate miles of smiles, loads of laughs, and plenty of enthusiasm for reading, Mike Thaler's outlandish lagoon series is perfect for launching the school year. Introduce youngsters to Thaler's zany books with these fun ideas and watch back-to-school jitters disappear in a flash!

by Amy Erickson

Meet the Author

Author of more than 80 humorous children's books, Mike Thaler has been tickling readers' funny bones for nearly 40 years. Thaler was born in Los Angeles, California, in 1936. He began his career in New York City by drawing cartoons for adults. He later ventured into children's literature. Recognized as one of the most creative people in his field, Thaler is dedicated to motivating youngsters to read and to promoting an imaginative use of language. In fact, his favorite motto is "The most powerful nation in the world is IMAGINATION."

The Black Lagoon Series

Written by Mike Thaler & Illustrated by Jared Lee

Thaler's Black Lagoon books are entertaining accounts of one boy's apprehension about meeting school staff members. The lad (whose name is Hubie) is so worried that he imagines all sorts of frightful, implausible situations. Thaler's wacky sense of humor and tongue-in-cheek writing style might seem a bit insensitive at first, but keep reading! Each book concludes with Hubie discovering that the actual staff member is much nicer and friendlier than he could ever have hoped. Readers young and old will identify with Hubie's runaway fears and delight in Thaler's hilarious storytelling.

Books in the series are:

The Teacher From the Black Lagoon (Scholastic Inc., 1989)

The Principal From the Black Lagoon (Scholastic Inc., 1993)

The Gym Teacher From the Black Lagoon (Scholastic Inc., 1994)

The School Nurse From the Black Lagoon (Scholastic Inc., 1995)

The Cafeteria Lady From the Black Lagoon (Cartwheel Books, 1998)

The Librarian From the Black Lagoon (Scholastic Inc., 1997)

Order books on-line. www.themailbox.com

First-Day Introductions

No doubt youngsters will arrive on the first day of school with plenty of questions about you and their new classmates. Get introductions rolling and set minds at ease with this follow-up activity to *The Teacher From the Black Lagoon.* To prepare, cover an empty cube-shaped box with colorful paper. Label each side with a different topic, such as hobbies or favorite food. For younger students, add a corresponding picture for each topic.

Inform students that in *The Teacher From the Black Lagoon,* a young boy named Hubie has so many questions about his new teacher that he imagines all kinds of frightful things about her. At this point, poll the students to find out how many of them have questions about you! Then read aloud this amusing book about first-day jitters. At the book's conclusion, gather students in a circle on the floor. Tell them that instead of having their imaginations get the best of them (like Hubie!), you've planned an activity that will help them get to know you, and each other, better. Then roll the prepared cube and respond to the topic that you roll. Have each student take a turn in a similar manner. Repeat as desired. Conclude the activity with a short question-and-answer session to address any remaining concerns.

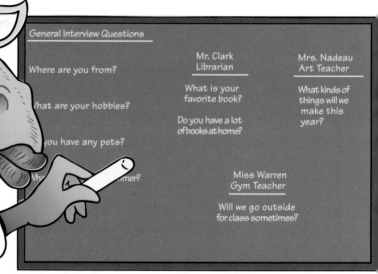

Pleased to Meet You!

Tell students that not only does Thaler's wary main character fear that his teacher comes from the Black Lagoon, he suspects that other staff members do too! To establish this, read aloud another title or two from the series. Then ask youngsters how suspicions like Hubie's could be put to rest. Lead them to conclude that the best way to alleviate fears about staff members is to get to know them! Have students identify general questions that would help them get acquainted with the school staff. Write these questions on the chalkboard. Also write the name and position of each staff member who has agreed to visit your classroom and be interviewed. Invite the class to brainstorm additional questions for each of these people. Next, group students and assign each group a staff member to interview. Instruct each group to compile a list of interview questions and decide which group member will ask each one. Require that all members be involved.

Conclude each interview by photographing the visitor. Then ask students to dictate what they learned about this staff member as you write the information on chart paper. Later copy the information onto booklet-size paper. Compile the student-generated paragraphs and the corresponding staff photographs into a class book. The resulting who's who of staff members is sure to be a favorite!

I Heard That...

From the nurse who vaccinates students kebab-style to the gym teacher who has youngsters running laps around the world, the Black Lagoon series is filled with rumors of absurd situations and comical exaggerations. After students have heard a few of Thaler's tales, they'll be ready to conjure up (and resolve) their own amusing and implausible rumors.

To begin, a child draws a line five inches from each end of a 4½" x 12" strip of white construction paper. Then she chooses a staff member and writes this person's name and title between the two lines.

Next she aligns the left end of the paper with the line on the left, flattens the paper, creases the fold, and writes "I heard that…" on the resulting flap. She opens the flap, completes the sentence with an outlandish rumor, and adds an illustration, being careful to stay to the left of the line. In a similar manner, she makes a flap on the right end of her paper. She labels this flap "I found out that…" Then she opens the flap and completes and illustrates a truthful sentence about the featured staff member. Showcase the youngsters' grin-inducing work on a bulletin board titled "Really Ridiculous Rumors!"

The Staff From the Black Lagoon

So just exactly what is a lagoon? Gather your youngsters' ideas, then reveal that it is a shallow body of water similar to a pond. Ask students why they think Thaler chose to have the school staff come from a *black* lagoon. Lead them to realize that a black lagoon creates a creepy and mysterious mood. Then invite youngsters to name locations that would set a silly mood for staff-related stories. Write their ideas on the chalkboard, and have each child write and illustrate a silly tale about an imaginary staff member from one of these locations.

To create a cover for his story, a student folds in half a 12" x 18" sheet of white construction paper. Next he colors a copy of the schoolhouse pattern on page 88 and cuts it out. Then he carefully cuts along the dotted lines and folds back the resulting doors along the fine lines. Keeping the doors of the schoolhouse open, the student glues the cutout to the front of his folded paper as shown. He illustrates his character in the open doorway, and adds a title, his name, and other desired decorations to the cover before stapling his story inside. No doubt this creative-writing activity will receive high marks from your young authors!

Who Else Lurks There?

Are there other mysterious characters lurking around in the black lagoon? Sure! Ask students to name school-related staff whom Thaler has not yet featured in his Black Lagoon series. Write their suggestions on the chalkboard. Ideas might include a custodian, substitute teacher, vice-principal, teacher assistant, secretary, and school bus driver. Then have each child write and illustrate a story about one of these people. To do this, give each child a copy of the booklet project on page 89 (for a larger booklet, photocopy the page at 125% onto 11" x 17" paper). Have each child complete the cover by writing the title of her main character on the line and then drawing and coloring a picture inside the box. For best results, suggest that students study the covers of the books in the Black Lagoon series before they complete their illustrations. Then have each child finish and illustrate the sentence on each booklet page. To assemble her booklet, she cuts on the bold lines, stacks the pages in sequential order, places the cover on top, and staples along the left edge. The Black Lagoon will definitely be teeming with activity!

Pattern

Use with "The Staff From the…" on page 87.

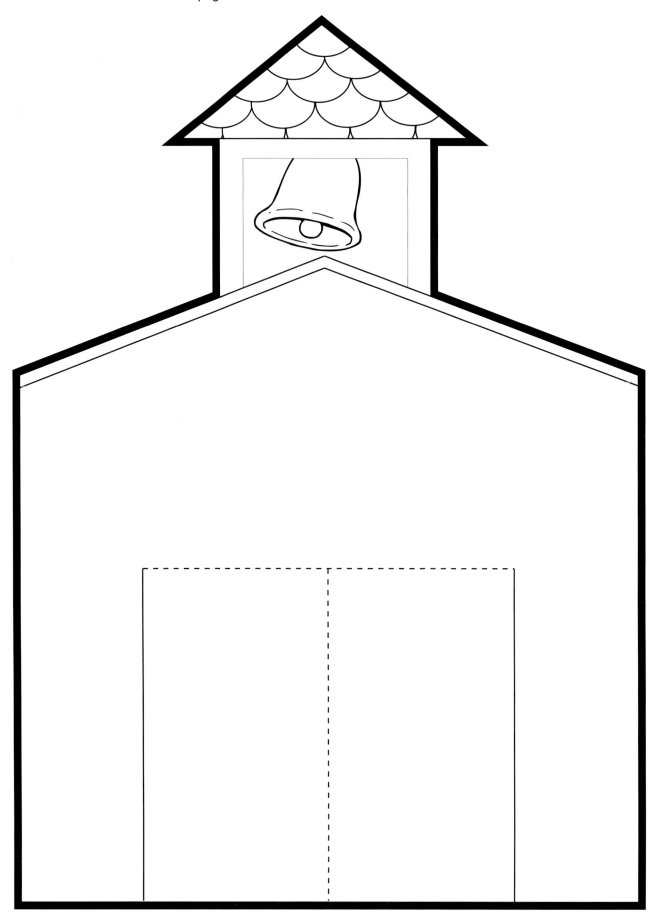

The ______________ from the **Black Lagoon** by ______________	I heard ______________ 1
I thought ______________ 2	I saw ______________ 3
I believe ______________ 4	I now know ______________ ©The Education Center, Inc. 5

Note to teacher: Use with "Who Else Lurks There?" on page 87.

The Underground Railroad

Former slave Harriet Tubman became the driving force of the Underground Railroad—a network of hiding places and forest trails that led slaves to free northern states and eventually into Canada. There were no rails for the runaways to follow, just the North Star and plenty of tracks and trails. Along the way an occasional lantern or quilt signaled a house where safety, shelter, and food awaited them. The books in this collection tell tales of Harriet Tubman and other brave Americans who traveled and conducted along the Underground Railroad.

by Njeri Jones and Deborah Zink Roffino

Minty: A Story of Young Harriet Tubman
Written by Alan Schroeder & Illustrated by Jerry Pinkney
Dial Books For Young Readers, 1996

Tender and emotional watercolor illustrations introduce readers to Minty, a spunky and headstrong eight-year-old who holds a special dream tucked inside her heart. For Harriet Tubman's own escape from slavery, and to engineer the freedom of so many others, she needed ingenuity and countless survival skills. This fictional account of her childhood, which is based on extensive research, suggests ways she may have acquired the skills she needed to free herself, and hundreds of others, from slavery.

It took many, many years before Minty's dream came true, but she never gave up! Minty was about 29 years old and known as Harriet Tubman when she finally made her daring escape from the Brodas plantation. Share this information at the conclusion of the book; then draw the outline of a large sunflower on the chalkboard. Remind students how Minty pretended to be a sunflower when no one was looking. Then use the sunflower sketch to show students how Minty kept her dream alive for all those years. To do this, write Minty's wish—"To Escape!"—in the flower center. Next ask students to recall ways that Minty worked toward her dream. Write these ideas on the petals. When each petal is programmed, help students understand that working toward a dream is the best way to make it come true. Then have each child draw an outline of a large sunflower on a 12" x 18" sheet of drawing paper. Ask each child to write his dream in the center of the flower, how he is working toward the dream in the flower petals, and his name inside a leaf outline. Suggest that each student use crayons to outline his drawing and create desired background scenery. Display the projects on a bulletin board titled "Our Field Of Dreams!"

Be an Astronaut
- I pay attention in school.
- I read books about space.
- I exercise.
- I learn about other astronauts.
- I eat food in little packages.
- I watch space movies.
- I bug my mom to send me to space camp.
- I pretend I'm in space.

More Books About Harriet Tubman

A Picture Book of Harriet Tubman
Written by David A. Adler & Illustrated by Samuel Byrd
Holiday House, Inc.; 1993

Born more than forty years before the Civil War, Harriet Tubman possessed a powerful love for her people and for freedom. This biography touches upon her years as a slave, her perilous escape, her numerous trips as a conductor on the Underground Railroad, and her duties as a nurse during the Civil War. Readers also learn of Harriet's work after the war, which included helping to establish a home in New York State for impoverished Black Americans. Memorable acrylic paintings accent the highlights of Harriet's ninety-plus years.

Harriet Tubman
Written by Margo McLoone
Capstone Press, 1997

Divided into 9 one-page chapters, each with an accompanying full-page black-and-white photograph, this beginner's biography is perfect for the primary classroom. After a brief introduction to the brave conductor, readers are presented with an overview of Tubman's life that focuses on key events and accomplishments. The final page of the book features a brief bibliography, useful addresses, Internet sites, and an index.

Aunt Harriet's Underground Railroad in the Sky

Written & Illustrated by Faith Ringgold
Crown Publishers, Inc.; 1995

Ringgold's celebrated folk art takes readers to the skies for an imaginative blend of fact and fantasy. Flying high among the stars, Cassie and her brother Be Be learn about the Underground Railroad and discover why Black American slaves were willing to risk their lives for freedom. The dream sequence, which is conducted by Harriet Tubman herself, is based on Tubman's dream of flying to freedom.

At the conclusion of this story, ask students to recall events from Cassie's trip on the Underground Railroad. Encourage students to tell what they learned about slavery, Harriet Tubman, and the series of trails and hiding places called the Underground Railroad. Then, in celebration of the Underground Railroad and the freedom that it brought to hundreds of slaves, have your students create a class Freedom Train. First ask students to brainstorm symbols of freedom and describe benefits of living in a free country. List the students' ideas on the chalkboard. Then ask each child to choose one idea from the list to illustrate and write a brief caption about on a 9" x 12" sheet of drawing paper. Next have each child trim two 3-inch squares of black construction paper into circles and glue the resulting train wheels near the bottom of his project. Display the train cars, connected by 1" x 4" strips of black paper (hitches), along a classroom wall. Add engine and caboose cutouts, and this freedom train—packed with precious cargo—is ready to spread the word about liberty and justice for all!

Follow The Drinking Gourd: A Story of the Underground Railroad

Written by Bernardine Connelly
Illustrated by Yvonne Buchanan
Rabbit Ears Books, 1997

This riveting tale recounts one family's treacherous journey along the Underground Railroad. Dependent upon the North Star and other natural landmarks for guidance, the runaways flee through unfamiliar and unfriendly forests. Engaging text and luminous watercolor illustrations hold listeners hostage between fear and hope. A compact disc, featuring a resonant retelling of the tale by actor Morgan Freeman, accompanies the book.

Natural landmarks and constellations guide 11-year-old Mary, her brother, and their mother along the Underground Railroad to freedom. Take this opportunity to familiarize students with the Big Dipper, the Little Dipper, and the North Star. Draw a simple sketch of the project (above) on the chalkboard or on an overhead transparency. Begin by having each child use a white crayon to label the perimeter of an eight-inch black construction-paper circle with the name of the four seasons. To check his work, have each child rotate his cutout counterclockwise at one-quarter-turn intervals to be sure the seasons are in correct order. Next give each child one large and 13 small self-adhesive foil stars. Have students refer to your diagram to position the stars on their projects; then have them use their white crayons to connect the stars to make the two drinking gourds. By turning their star maps, students can see how the constellations appear in the night sky during each season. Remind students to always look to the north to find the North Star!

91

Allen Jay and
the Underground Railroad

Written by Marlene Targ Brill
Illustrated by Janice Lee Porter
Carolrhoda Books, Inc.; 1993

When his father is unable to help, young Allen Jay finds the courage to aid a runaway slave. His family's farm is a stop on the Underground Railroad, and the boy's parents, who are Quakers, are secret conductors. It is 11-year-old Allen Jay's first experience as a conductor. The clearly written narrative, seen through the eyes of the heroic young Quaker boy, is based on actual events of the 1840s. Muted pastel illustrations accentuate Allen Jay's gripping story.

Conductors of the Underground Railroad risked their lives to help others whom they felt were being treated unfairly. At the conclusion of this story, have students contemplate the courage that Allen Jay displayed to lend a helping hand to Henry. Also ask students to express feelings Allen Jay may have felt as he shook Henry's hand and wished him a safe trip to Canada. Encourage your youngsters to practice helpful behavior with this follow-up activity. Ask each child to trace the shape of his hand on a sheet of drawing paper, then cut out the resulting shape and label it with his name. Each time a child lends a helping hand throughout the day, he collects the signature of the person whom he helped. At the end of the day he will have a visual reminder of his helpful ways. Before dismissal, invite student volunteers to talk about how it feels knowing that they have helped others that day. If desired, have each child make and label a new cutout to take home and return the following school day. This project is sure to be popular with your youngsters' parents!

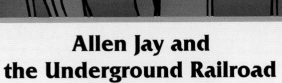

Sweet Clara and
the Freedom Quilt

Written by Deborah Hopkinson
Illustrated by James Ransome
Random House, Inc.; 1995

Based on a true little-known chapter of black history, this powerful picture book tells the story of a young slave girl's plan to map the route of the Underground Railroad. When her last stitch is in place, Sweet Clara has hidden in the squares of her quilt the path that will guide her and many other slaves to freedom. Brightly colored full-page paintings light up the pages of this inspirational tale.

Clara stitches her dreams for the future into a quilt that helps her and others. After reading the story to students and discussing it with them, ask each child to think of a dream that he has for the future that others will benefit from as well. Then have each student illustrate his dream on a six-inch square of white construction paper. Next have each child glue his artwork in the center of an eight-inch square of colorful construction paper that you have punched with a series of equally spaced holes—four per side. To assemble the quilt, divide students into groups of four. Give each group four one-foot lengths of yarn to use to stitch the group's projects into one large square. Provide assistance as needed. Then have one student from each group volunteer to help stitch the resulting projects into a desired quilt shape. Display the completed quilt for all to see. Later, after students have had time to study the quilt, ask each child to reveal which quilt patch he designed and talk about his dream for the future.

Barefoot: Escape on the Underground Railroad

Written by Pamela Duncan Edwards
Illustrated by Henry Cole
HarperCollins Publishers, Inc.; 1997

Near the floor of the deep, dark woods, the bare feet of a young man creep softly in a desperate move toward freedom. On this stretch of the Underground Railroad, Barefoot trusts only the sounds of woodland creatures to assist his flight. The croak of a frog means water is near; the cry of a heron echoes danger. Dark and powerful illustrations create a shadowy nighttime world that is filled with fear and uncertainty.

After an initial oral reading of the story, have students recall the things that Barefoot hears as he presses forward along the Underground Railroad. List these items on the chalkboard. Then read the story aloud a second time so students can listen carefully for additional sound makers. Make any needed additions to the class list, and with your youngsters' help, assign a sound effect to each listed item. Next, under your direction, have the class practice each sound effect. Before each sound is made, ask students how hearing that sound on the trail might have made Barefoot feel. Then encourage students to incorporate these feelings into their sound renditions. Finally read the story aloud one more time, this time arranging for a different small group of students to make each sound effect on the list. This journey along the Underground Railroad will leave a lasting impression!

Item	Sound effect
Barefoot's breath	*(three heavy breaths)*
heron	"skreeeeek, skreeeeek"
Heavy Boots	*(stomp feet three times)*
frog	"ribbit, ribbit, ribbit"
mouse	"nibble, nibble, nibble"
mockingbird	"tra la la, tra la la"
squirrel	"scamper, scamper, scamper"
deer	*(crumpling of paper)*
mosquitoes	"buzz, buzz, buzz"
fireflies	"zing, zing, zing"

Jewels

Written by Belinda Rochelle
Illustrated by Cornelius Van Wright and Ying-Hwa Hu
Lodestar Books, 1998

On a sweet summer's night, rocking on the front porch of her great-grandparents' home, young Lea Mae listens to the story of how her ancestors escaped from slavery. The running, the hunger, the sounds of approaching dogs—and then the mysterious appearance of a small woman who leads Lea's ancestors to safety. Lea's great-grandmother is filled with stories about their heritage—each one a jewel to be treasured forever.

This gentle tale is a shining example of the Black American tradition of storytelling. At the conclusion of the story, ask students if they enjoy hearing stories of long ago. Find out why they think the tradition of passing stories from generation to generation began, and how their lives might be different if the tradition had never been started. Next ask each child to think of a *jewel* from her childhood that she thinks future generations might enjoy hearing and can learn from too! Pair students and have each child tell her story to her partner one or more times. Then invite interested students to share their jewels with the class. In closing, read aloud the final paragraph from the book to remind students that stories must be told to be saved. Encourage students to *save* their childhood jewels and to listen to the stories their family members tell so they can begin saving these jewels, too.

The Chocolate Touch

Written by Patrick Skene Catling • Illustrated by Margot Apple
(Bantam Doubleday Dell Books for Young Readers, 1996)

John Midas is a young boy who is so crazy about chocolate that he isn't interested in eating other foods. He knows his eating habits worry his parents, but he really doesn't understand what all the fuss is about—at least not yet! This highly entertaining tale satisfies young readers and teaches them a memorable lesson about selfishness.

ideas contributed by Stacie Stone Davis

Too Much of a Good Thing?

John quickly dismisses the concerns his parents and doctor have about his candy-eating habits. But do your students think he should be worried? At the conclusion of chapter 2 give each child a quarter-size circle of gray construction paper to represent the coin that John finds. Ask him to write his initials on one side of the cutout and then tape it on a bar graph labeled like the one pictured. Discuss the resulting graph and invite students to share their opinions and the reasoning behind them. Plan to repeat the activity after chapters 6 and 10, each time investigating why students' opinions about John's chocolate-eating habits do or do not change. If desired, give each child a foil-wrapped chocolate coin to eat at the conclusion of each discussion!

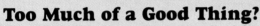

Should John be worried about eating too much candy?

Yes	T.M.	P.C.	A.R.	B.B.	C.E.			
No	N.G.	E.S.	C.H.	J.O.	K.M.	N.B.	R.G.	D.F.

Chocolatey Changes

When his toothpaste and breakfast taste like chocolate, John is convinced something strange and wonderful has happened! Before beginning chapter 4, invite students to describe what they think has happened to John and predict how the chocolatey change might affect his school day. At the end of chapter 4, have students recall the chocolate-related events that have occurred in the story. Then ask a different child to illustrate each one on provided paper. Display the illustrations side by side in chronological order. Conclude each remaining chapter by selecting different students to illustrate the chocolate-related events from the chapter and then display the pictures as described. At the end of the story students will have a clear picture of John's chocolate touch.

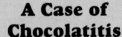

A Case of Chocolatitis

In chapter 10 Dr. Cranium diagnoses John with an unprecedented case of *chocolatitis,* or *Cranium's Disease.* For a fun follow-up to the chapter, instruct each child to write and illustrate a captivating newspaper article that discloses this newly discovered illness. Ask that she include in her article the name of the disease; when, where, and how it was discovered; and the doctor who discovered it. Suggest that she also describe the cause and symptoms of the disease and offer a possible cure for it. Be sure to set aside time for interested students to share their late-breaking news with the class.

Sealed With a Kiss

It isn't until John's mother turns into a lifeless chocolate statue (chapter 11) that he stops thinking only of himself. Help students understand that John's selfish chocolate-eating habits end up hurting the people he loves the most. Then have them name things their parents routinely remind them to do, such as pick up their clothes, wash their hands, brush their teeth, and so on. List their ideas and discuss why having to be reminded to do each action is selfish.

Next have each child make a selfless pledge and seal it with a kiss—a candy kiss, that is! To do this a child chooses a selfless act and describes it on a white candy kiss pattern (page 24). Then he cuts out the pattern, glues it on brown paper, and trims the brown paper to create an eye-catching border. On a paper strip he writes to whom his pledge is dedicated and glues one end of it to the back of his project. Students will be proud to present these sweet pledges of selflessness, and others will be pleased to receive them.

MOM

I pledge to make my bed each morning without a reminder from you. Love, Billy

Candy Bar Book Reports

What's the perfect way for students to wrap up this irresistible chapter book? A candy bar book report, of course! To make a report, a child completes a copy of page 96 by finishing and illustrating the sentences. Then she cuts along the bold lines, stacks the resulting rectangles in sequential order, and staples the left-hand edge of the stack. Next she wraps a 7" x 9" length of foil around her project and folds the foil ends toward the center. To make the outer wrapper, she centers her project atop a 6" x 7" construction paper rectangle, folds the top and bottom edges of the paper toward the center of the project, and secures the overlapping edges with tape. Then she temporarily removes the foil-wrapped pages while she decorates and personalizes the resulting candy bar wrapper. How sweet!

My favorite character in The Chocolate Touch is John Midas. I like this character because I love chocolate, too! I thought he was funny. He taught me something.

Thoughtful Touches

This follow-up activity puts students in touch with their thinking skills! If possible read aloud *King Midas and the Golden Touch* as told by Charlotte Craft (Morrow Junior Books, 1999), and discuss with students the similarities and differences between the two tales. Remind students that John's last name is Midas and invite them to speculate why the author did this. Then challenge each child to write and illustrate a story in which the main character is given a magic touch. What's the catch? The magic touch must be one that will help—not hurt—other people! Publish these one-of-a-kind tales in a class book titled "Thoughtful Touches."

Order books online. www.themailbox.com

95

My favorite character in *The Chocolate Touch* is

_____. I like this character

because_____

_____

_____

1

In this story the problem that needs to be solved is

_____

_____

_____

_____

2

The problem is solved when _____

_____

_____

_____

_____

3

My favorite part of *The Chocolate Touch* is _____

_____

_____

_____

4

Note to teacher: Use with "Candy Bar Book Reports" on page 95.

Too Much Chocolate!

Read each sentence.
Write the missing word in the puzzle.
Use the Word Bank.

Across:

4. Miss _____ is John's teacher.
5. John eats all the _____ because it tastes like chocolate.
9. In the cafeteria, the prongs of John's _____ turn chocolate.
10. John finds a strange coin on the _____.
13. During a test, John's _____ turns to chocolate.
14. John was glad when his _____ touch was gone.

Down:

1. A _____ turns John's mother into chocolate.
2. John spends his coin on a _____ of candy.
3. Spider snatches a _____ from John.
6. John plays a _____ in the school orchestra.
7. Dr. _____ tells John he has a disease.
8. Susan Buttercup is proud of her new _____ dollar.
11. An empty _____ is where the candy store once stood.
12. John knows his chocolate touch is gone when he drinks an ice-cold glass of _____.

Word Bank

pencil
trumpet
sidewalk
kiss
Plimsole
chocolate
Cranium
silver
glove
box
toothpaste
milk
lot
fork

Bonus Box: On the back of this paper write three reasons why this story is fiction.

Note to teacher: Use this activity after completing the book.

Arnold Lobel

Award-Winning Author and Illustrator

Arnold Lobel's endearing characters, insightful story lines, and charming illustrations make his books perfect for classroom use. Step into Lobel's wonderful world of literature with these tried-and-true suggestions.

Meet Arnold Lobel

Arnold Lobel, renowned author and illustrator, was born on May 22, 1933, in Los Angeles, California. Young Lobel often amused his classmates and teachers with his entertaining stories and illustrations. As an adult, Lobel wrote and drew about events in his own life, which he believed to be the key to great storytelling. For Lobel, writing a story required much more patience and perseverance than illustrating one. But he never gave up. When Lobel died in 1987, at the early age of 54, he left a legacy of children's books with lasting and universal appeal.

Mouse Tales
HarperTrophy, 1978

Papa Mouse tells seven entertaining bedtime stories—one for each of his seven mouse boys.

Look high and low, and you won't find a story with more kid appeal than this Lobel favorite! Read aloud "Very Tall Mouse and Very Short Mouse" and then explore each mouse's unique point of view with this categorization activity. Challenge students to recall the items that each mouse greets. List these items on the chalkboard under the appropriate mouse's name. Help students conclude that Very Tall Mouse sees high things and Very Short Mouse sees low things. Next say the provided chant with the class and select a student volunteer to name something that is either high or low. Have the remaining students chorally name the mouse who would be likely to see the item. Confirm the students' response by writing the item on the chalkboard under the appropriate name. Continue the activity in a like manner for as long as desired. "Hello, cloud!"

Tall mouse, short mouse,
They went walking.
Listen to the word
To see who's talking.

Theresa J. Casey—Gr. 1
Chukker Creek Elementary
Aiken, SC

On Market Street
Illustrated by Anita Lobel
Mulberry Books, 1989

A youngster's incredible shopping spree takes him from A to Z in this Caldecott Honor Book.

Take students on a picture-perfect shopping trip that results in a one-of-a-kind class book! After an initial reading of the book, revisit the illustrations so students realize that each shopkeeper is a creation of his or her wares. Next assign each letter of the alphabet to a student. (If necessary, assign some youngsters more than one letter.) To make his booklet page, a student writes his letter at the top of a sheet of drawing paper and a noun that begins with his letter at the bottom. Then he illustrates a shopkeeper who is composed of his or her wares. Bind the students' pages in alphabetical order between construction-paper covers. Title the resulting class book "On [your school's street address]." You can count on this publication suiting your youngsters' literary interests to a T!

Barbara A. Denlinger—Gr. 1
Akron Elementary School
Akron, PA

C

KISS THE COOK

Cookies

Ming Lo Moves the Mountain
Mulberry Books, 1993

Move a mountain? Impossible! Or so it seems until Ming Lo seeks a wise man's advice.

Empower young listeners with this tale's important message. First read aloud the book's title and challenge students to predict how Ming Lo moves the mountain. Then follow up the story by asking students to compare their predictions to the story's outcome. Encourage students to talk about the way Ming Lo feels when he believes he has accomplished the impossible. Next invite students to describe their past achievements and any feelings they associate with them. Lastly have each youngster write about and/or illustrate a dream or an ambition that she has for the future. Display the students' work on a bulletin board decorated with a simple mountain scene and the title "If Ming Lo Can Move a Mountain…"

I would like to travel into outer space. Maybe I will open a business on Mars.

Whiskers & Rhymes
Mulberry Books, 1988

Lobel puts a new spin on some old favorites with this humorous collection of poems. From Clara, little curlylocks, to Beanbag Jim, Lobel's fanciful felines are sure to delight readers of all ages.

If you're looking for a "cat-alyst" to motivate your young writers, this rhyme activity is a "purr-fect" choice! At the conclusion of the book, discuss with youngsters how Lobel's poems are similar to nursery rhymes. Then challenge each child to write an original version of a familiar rhyme. For added fun, have each student publish his work in a cat-shaped book. To make the pages for his book, a student copies each line of his poem on a 2" x 6" strip of paper, then he stacks the pages in sequential order. To make the book's cover, he folds a 9" x 12" sheet of construction paper in half. He tucks the pages inside the folded paper (flush against the fold) and staples them in place. Next he trims the folded paper as shown to create a cat's body and legs, and then he cuts out a cat's head and tail from construction-paper scraps. After he adds eyes, a nose, and whiskers to the feline's head, he glues the cut-outs in place. Meow!

Little Miss Muffet sat under a tree.

The Rose in My Garden
Illustrated by Anita Lobel
Mulberry Books, 1993

Beginning with one delicate rose, this cumulative tale builds until a tranquil garden is transformed into a flurry of excitement.

Memory skills will blossom with this storytelling activity! As you read the story aloud, encourage students to chime in on familiar phrases. After discussing the story's repetitive nature, engage students in telling a cumulative tale. To do this, gather students in a large circle. Introduce the story with the sentence "This is [name of school]." Then have a student volunteer begin the story by completing the following sentence: "I am [student's name], and I like to [verb or verb phrase] in [teacher's name]'s room." The classmate to this student's right repeats the sentence, and then she completes the sentence herself. The next classmate to the right repeats the previous two sentences before she completes the sentence, and this continues until every child has taken a turn. Conclude the story by having the youngsters repeat the introductory sentence in unison. Telling a story has never been more memorable!

Owl at Home
HarperTrophy, 1982

Owl's innocent nature and unique solutions to daily dilemmas will quickly endear him to readers, young and old alike.

Read aloud the five short whimsical stories about Owl; then put your students' critical-thinking skills to the test with a flip-book project. To make the book, a student folds a sheet of drawing paper in half lengthwise and makes two equally spaced cuts in the top layer to create three flaps. He writes "Owl's Problem" on the first flap; then, under the flap, he describes a problem that Owl confronts in the book. He labels the second flap "Owl's Solution." Under this flap he explains how Owl solves the problem. On the third flap he writes "My Solution," and then he writes how he would solve Owl's problem under the flap. Set aside time for students to illustrate their work; then invite them to share how they solved Owl's predicaments.

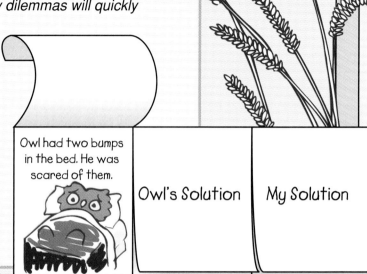

A Treeful of Pigs
Illustrated by Anita Lobel
Greenwillow Books, 1987

With the help of his wife's ingenuity and some seemingly amazing pigs, a lazy farmer learns a valuable lesson about keeping promises and accepting responsibility.

Youngsters will go hog-wild over this investigation into responsibility! As a follow-up to the story, have students compare and contrast how the farmer and his wife handle the duties of pig ownership. (Use a Venn diagram for this step if desired.) Next have students brainstorm responsibilities related to owning pets, and list their ideas on the chalkboard. For a fun follow-up project, have each student visually divide a sheet of drawing paper in half. Ask each youngster to choose a pet responsibility from the class list, then write and illustrate how the farmer would handle this responsibility on the left half of his paper. On the right half of his paper, he writes and illustrates how he would handle the pet-related task. Compile the students' work into a class book titled "A Bookful Of Pets."

Fables
HarperTrophy, 1983

A host of animal characters with surprisingly humanlike qualities is featured in this beautifully illustrated collection of original fables.

What better way to introduce fables to students than with this Caldecott Medal winner? Make a chart similar to the one shown. Explain to youngsters that a fable is a story that teaches a lesson and that most fables have animal characters. Choose one of Lobel's fables to read aloud. Then, under your students' direction, write on the chart the title, characters, and main events of the fable along with a summary of the lesson it teaches. Repeat this procedure for each fable you read aloud until the chart is completed. Then have each student choose a lesson from the chart, and write and illustrate an original fable that reteaches it. Set aside time for each child to read aloud his fable and challenge his classmates to identify its lesson.

Fables

Title	Characters	Main Events	Lesson
The Baboon's Umbrella	Baboon Gibbon	Baboon's umbrella is stuck open. Gibbon tells baboon to cut holes in the umbrella.	Not all advice is good.

Frog and Toad Together
HarperTrophy, 1979

From struggling with the temptation of freshly baked cookies to facing their fears, Frog and Toad do everything together. Their steadfast friendship is portrayed with sensitivity and insight in this timeless Newbery Honor Book.

"A List"

As Toad discovers in this chapter, nothing compares to the satisfaction of completing everything on a to-do list. And there's a good chance your students will agree! To find out, ask each child to list ten things she plans to accomplish during the school day. Then have her tape her resulting to-do list on her desktop. When she completes an item on the list, she draws a line through it. You can count on plenty of smiles at the end of the day when students see how much they've accomplished!

Debbie Erickson—Gr. 2
Sunset Elementary
Whitehall, WI

"Cookies"

In this brief tale, Frog and Toad learn that it takes plenty of willpower to stop eating fresh-baked cookies. Review the steps Frog and Toad take to stop eating cookies. Next divide students into small groups and have each group create a plan to help the amphibians resist eating too much of the cake Toad plans to bake. Require that the plan be a series of steps that build upon each other (like in "Cookies") and that each group member participate in presenting the plan to the class. Your students' creativity and memory skills are sure to be enhanced as these willpower plans unfold.

To-Do List

1. silent read
2. take math fact test
3. go to recess
4. learn about frogs
5. write in my journal
6. eat lunch
7. go to the library
8. ~~~~
9. ~~~~

Days With Frog and Toad
HarperTrophy, 1984

Beginning readers will delight in these five tender stories of friendship that feature the lovable amphibian pals, Frog and Toad.

"The Kite"

This adventure finds Frog and Toad trying to fly a kite—only to have it repeatedly crash to the ground. Despite discouraging remarks from some onlooking robins, the two friends persevere until they succeed. At the end of the story, invite students to describe times they had to try again and again to accomplish a goal. Then have each child make a kite to remind himself of the importance of perseverance. To make his kite, a student cuts out a kite shape and four kite bows from construction paper. (Provide tagboard tracers or duplicated patterns for this step.) On each bow he writes something he accomplished by perseverance, and then he illustrates two of these accomplishments—one on each side of his kite cutout. Next he hole-punches the bottom of the kite shape and threads and ties one end of a length of yarn through the hole to make a kite tail. Lastly he glues the bow cutouts back to back along the kite tail, keeping the programming to the outside as shown. If desired, suspend each child's kite above his desk.

adapted from an idea by Diane Afferton
Afton Elementary School
Yardley, PA

riding a bike

swimming in the deep end

Frog and Toad Are Friends
HarperTrophy, 1979

In this Caldecott Honor Book, Frog and Toad help each other cope with situations that will undoubtedly ring true for readers.

"Spring"

In this funny tale, a fully awake Frog is ready to greet spring, but a very sleepy Toad is not! At the conclusion of the chapter, have students brainstorm words and phrases related to spring. Write their suggestions on the chalkboard; then challenge each child to refer to the resulting word bank as she pens a list poem titled "Spring." For an attractive display, have each student copy her edited poem in the center of an 8" x 11" sheet of white paper and then create a border of colorful springlike art around her writing. Mount each youngster's work on a 9" x 12" sheet of construction paper before showcasing it on a bulletin board titled "Welcome, Spring!"

Janet Gross
Stowe, PA

Spring

Flowers bloom.
Bees buzz.
Ducklings hatch.
Grass grows.
Birds chirp.
Kids play.

Spring

"The Story"

Frog wants to hear a story, and Toad can't think of one to save his soul! Invite students to talk about times they've wanted to tell or write stories and, like Toad, couldn't think of any ideas. Next have students brainstorm remedies for these situations. List the students' ideas on the chalkboard; then, with your youngsters' input, identify the top ten tips for overcoming story block. Use these tips to make a colorful classroom poster for future reference.

Janet Gross

Ten Tips for How to Cure
⮞ **Writer's Block** ⮜

1. Talk about the story with a friend.

2. Daydream about the story.

3. Pretend that you are a part of the story.

"The Letter"

Frog leaps into action when he realizes how much better Toad will feel if he receives a letter in the mail. At the conclusion of this story, give each child a copy of page 104 so she too can write a letter to Toad. Instruct each student to cut along the bold lines, turn her paper over, write her letter on the blank side, and then sign her name "Frog [student's last name]." To prepare her letter for delivery, she folds her paper in half along the thin line; then she writes a return and a mailing address on the provided lines. Next she colors the artwork and tapes the envelope closed. Collect the letters. The next day, have students assume the role of Toad and give each child a letter to read that was written by a classmate. Then have each student respond to her new frog pal on another copy of page 104. Invite students to personally deliver these letters. Now that's a "toad-ally" terrific writing activity!

adapted from an idea by Patricia Heilman—Gr. 1
The Bryn Mawr School For Girls
Baltimore, MD

"A Lost Button"

This amusing tale has the two pals frantically searching for Toad's lost button. For a fun follow-up activity, have each child create a personalized version of the story. To do this, a child makes six construction-paper buttons—each of a different size, shape, color, and/or design. Then he incorporates his props into a story that tells how he loses a button, searches for the button in five locations only to find five buttons that are not his, and eventually finds his button. Next pair students and have each child use his props to tell his partner his story. Then have each student take his props home so he can retell his tale for friends and family members.

adapted from an idea by Marilyn Meyerson
Key School
Annapolis, MD

Frog Jones
W. Melrose Ave.
Balto, MD 21207

Toad
1000 Lily Pad Road
Riverdale, MD 00012

Frog and Toad All Year

HarperTrophy, 1984

Follow the beloved amphibious duo throughout the year with this seasonal collection of Frog and Toad adventures. Recognized as an ALA Notable Children's Book, this collection is too good to miss!

"Ice Cream"

After reading about Toad's mishap with melting ice cream, have your youngsters experiment with the melting process. Divide students into small groups and give each group an ice cube in a small plastic container. Have each group document how long it takes for the ice cube to completely melt. Then repeat the experiment with a second and a third ice cube. Each time, challenge the groups to shorten (lengthen) the melting time. After each experiment, ask every group to explain its strategy and share its results. Wrap up the activity by having students identify elements that influence the melting process.

Beth Jones—Gr. 2
Stevensville Public School
Niagara Falls, Ontario, Canada

More With "Ice Cream"

Frog and Toad like chocolate ice cream the best. Use this delicious idea to find out which flavor is tops among your students and their families. Have each student label one paper ice-cream scoop for each family member, herself included. Then have her take the cutouts home, label each one with the named person's favorite ice-cream flavor, and return the cutouts by a designated date. If desired, also invite students to lightly color the cutouts to reflect the flavors they represent. Then use the cutouts to create a class graph of favorite ice-cream flavors. After each youngster has written and/or shared three statements about the completed graph, serve the class a yummy ice-cream treat.

Phyllis Bowling—Gr. 2
Smithville Elementary
Smithville, MS

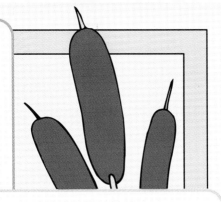

Erin

Strawberry

"The Surprise"

In this humorous chapter, each best friend works selflessly to surprise the other with a kind deed. Lead students to understand that each friend's surprise was a gift from the heart. Discuss the meaning of this phrase with youngsters and then have each student label a colorful heart cutout with another example of a gift from the heart. Mount these hearts on a jumbo paper heart titled "Gifts From The Heart." Display the completed project in a prominent classroom location to remind students of the selfless things that good friends do for each other.

helping with chores

making a get well card

sharing a snack

sharing my jump rope

©The Education Center, Inc. • *The Best of* The Mailbox® • *Primary* • *Book 4* • TEC895

104   **Note to teacher:** Use with "'The Letter'" on page 102.

The Boxcar Children®

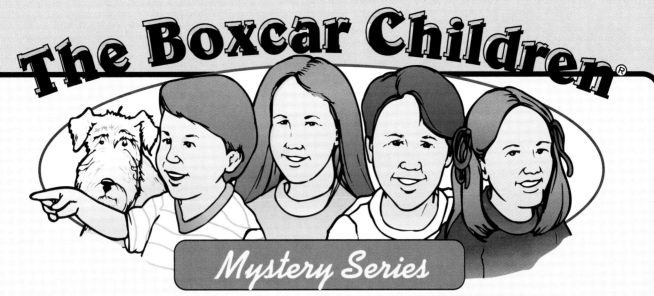

Mystery Series

Created by Gertrude Chandler Warner
Published by Albert Whitman & Company

Delight your students with the escapades of Henry, Jessie, Violet, and Benny Alden! For a rich appreciation of the Alden family, begin your investigation with the first book in the series, *The Boxcar Children*. It is here that the youngsters, who have been orphaned by the death of their parents, temporarily set up housekeeping in an abandoned boxcar. Then, in each of the subsequent books, the children find adventure in another unique setting.

Use this trainload of specially engineered activities to enhance *any* book in the Boxcar series.

Meet
Gertrude Chandler Warner
1890–1979

Growing up across the street from a railroad station, Gertrude Chandler Warner often dreamed of keeping house in a caboose. Early in her teaching career, Warner wrote *The Boxcar Children* based on this dream. Initially librarians opposed the book because they felt the Alden children were having too much fun without proper parental supervision. And this, of course, was one reason why children loved the story so! In 1942, Warner rewrote the story using less challenging vocabulary. This is the version that children enjoy today. Before her death in 1979, Warner authored 18 additional Boxcar adventures. Today the series continues with the help of new authors who steer the Alden children into a variety of settings and adventures!

To learn more about Miss Warner as a child, an adult, a teacher, and a writer, read *Gertrude Chandler Warner and the Boxcar Children* by Mary Ellen Ellsworth (Albert Whitman & Company, 1997).

Cases to Solve

No matter where the Alden children go, they always find themselves in the midst of a mystery! Since there's little doubt that your young gumshoes will want to help solve each case, have them make magnifying-glass booklets in which to record the clues they gather. To make a booklet, cut out a desired number of eight-inch circles from white paper, two from black construction paper, and one from clear plastic. Center a six-inch template atop one black circle, trace around it, and cut on the resulting outline to create a frame. Also trim a 2" x 8" strip of black construction paper to resemble a handle. To assemble the booklet, stack the white circles. Sandwich this stack between the plastic circle (on top) and the eight-inch black circle. Place the frame atop the stack and staple. Glue the handle to the back cover. Have each child personalize the first white page in his booklet. To store the booklet, fold the handle forward, and keep it flush against the front cover. Paper-clip the handle in place, if desired.

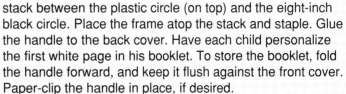

Set aside time at the conclusion of each read-aloud session for students to write any clues they gathered in their booklets. Prior to revealing the ending of the story, invite students to share their ideas of how the mystery will be solved.

adapted from an idea by Katie Robinson—Gr. 3
Limestone Walters School, Peoria, IL

Staying on Track

Keep your students' summarizing skills on the right track with this locomotive display. For each chapter in your upcoming Boxcar mystery, make and label a paper boxcar. (To make a boxcar, glue black construction-paper wheels to the bottom of a 9" x 12" sheet of red construction paper.) Laminate the boxcars and an engine cutout. Use a wipe-off marker to program the engine cutout with the book's title. Mount this cutout on a classroom wall. Then, at the end of each chapter, use a wipe-off marker to write a student-generated summary of events on the corresponding boxcar. Mount the programmed boxcars behind the engine, in sequential order. Use black paper strips to connect the cars, if desired. Leave the train on display until you're ready to read another Boxcar adventure. Then simply wipe away the programming and repeat the activity.

Jill Hamilton—Gr. 1, Schoeneck Elementary, Stevens, PA

A Mystery From A to Z

An alphabetical review of a Boxcar adventure will suit your youngsters to a T! List the letters of the alphabet on the chalkboard. As students brainstorm story-related words and phrases, write their ideas next to the appropriate letters. Next assign each child one letter and ask him to create a page for an ABC version of the featured mystery. To make his page, a student writes his letter at the top of a sheet of drawing paper and then he writes and illustrates a story-related sentence on the remainder of the paper. If desired, have each child use a crayon to trace over his alphabet letter and to underline the word or phrase associated with it. Bind the completed projects in alphabetical order between construction-paper covers and title the book "The ABCs of [book title]." Right down to the letter, this book is sure to be a class favorite.

Kelly A. Lu—Gr. 2, Berlyn School, Ontario, CA

Henry, Jessie, Violet, and Benny spend their summer in a lighthouse.

Showing Character

Use the positive character traits that Jessie, Henry, Violet, and Benny display to encourage similar traits in your students. Title a large boxcar shape "Precious Cargo" and display it on a classroom wall. At the conclusion of each read-aloud session, ask the class to recall the children's positive actions and name the character traits that describe them. Write each trait that is discussed on the boxcar (unless it is already listed there). To encourage your students to exhibit these same traits, place pencils and a spiral notebook titled "Boxcar Guests" near the display. Each time a student experiences one of the listed traits, she makes an entry in the guest book. To do this, she writes her name, the name of each person involved, the date, and a brief description of the positive experience. Read aloud several entries each day and praise the spotlighted individuals for demonstrating and recognizing positive traits!

Another Boxcar Series!

The Adventures of Benny and Watch™ series (Albert Whitman & Company) is written with the beginning reader in mind. Each book in this series stars Benny, the youngest Alden, and his lovable pooch, Watch. Now even the youngest reader can catch Boxcar fever!

Acting It Out

The escapades of the Boxcar youngsters provide excellent opportunities for creative dramatics. As you read aloud the mystery of your choice, keep a list of events that could easily be acted out by small groups of students. At the conclusion of the book, group students and secretly assign each group one event from your list. Allow plenty of time for students to prepare. Then have each group enact its assigned event for the class. At the end of each performance, invite the audience to identify the corresponding part of the story. Then, if desired, have the groups repeat their performances in sequential order as you videotape them. Lights, camera, action!

Jill Hamilton—Gr. 1
Schoeneck Elementary
Stevens, PA

What Memories!

Photographs and mementos capture special events forever, so why not have students make scrapbooks to remember their most recent Alden adventure? Discuss with students the purpose of a scrapbook. Then have each child align two 9" x 12" sheets of construction paper and fold the papers in half. On the cover of the resulting (unbound) scrapbook, write "The Alden Family Scrapbook," followed by the title of the Boxcar mystery. On the chalkboard write a student-generated list of story events. Have each child choose six different events to feature in her scrapbook and illustrate each one on a white 4" x 5" rectangle to resemble a photograph. She glues each picture on a separate scrapbook page and adds a caption. On each page she also illustrates a related souvenir (or she crafts one from scrap paper and glues it to the page). Finally, she punches two holes near the fold of her scrapbook, threads a two-foot length of yarn through the holes, securely ties the yarn ends, and fashions a bow. Be sure to set aside time for youngsters to share the keepsakes they've created!

The Alden Family Scrapbook

The Mystery at Snowflake Inn

Book Report Boxcars

Students will be eager to hop aboard this book report project! Have each child complete a copy of page 108 about a selected Boxcar mystery. Then have him cut around his report on the bold lines and fold back each tab along the thin line. Next demonstrate how to bring the folded edges to the center of the report and then flatten the paper. Have students do the same. Provide assistance as needed.

To make a boxcar cover for his report, a student transforms a 7" x 12" sheet of red construction paper into a boxcar by adding crayon details and attaching construction-paper wheels. He folds his boxcar in half, unfolds it, and cuts along the resulting crease line. Then he aligns and glues each half of his boxcar to the corresponding tab of his folded project. It's full steam ahead for book reports!

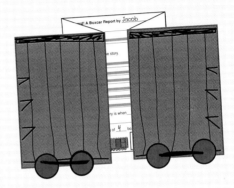

Mystery Writers

The Alden children are not the only ones who visit new places and take part in exciting activities! For this writing activity, students use a school-related event like a field trip or a school assembly as the basis for a Boxcar adventure. Select a recent event and ask students to share their memories of it. List their recollections on the chalkboard. Next have students brainstorm possible mystery plots that could be associated with this occasion. Then challenge each child to write and illustrate a mystery that is based on the school event and that features the Alden family and himself as story characters. No doubt students will be eager to share the adventures they've written, *and* help solve the mysteries their classmates have written, too!

Kari Koebernick—Gr. 3, Enders-Salk School, Schaumburg, IL

A Tasty Addition

If you're looking for a tasty addition to an Alden family adventure, locate a copy of *The Boxcar Children Cookbook* by Diane Blain (Albert Whitman & Company, 1991). From Boxcar Brown Bread to Jessie's Apple Pie, the cookbook contains a collection of recipes based on meals eaten by the family during its mystery escapades.

Glue left half of cover on this tab.

All Aboard! A Boxcar Report by ____________________

Title: ____________________

Setting: ____________________

Here is a summary of the story.

Beginning ____________________

____

Middle ____________________

____

End ____________________

____

The best part of the story is when ____________________

____

____

I give this book a rating of ______ boxcars.

Boxcar Code

1 = OK
2 = good
3 = very good
4 = excellent

Glue right half of cover on this tab.

 Note to teacher: Use with “Book Report Boxcars” on page 107.

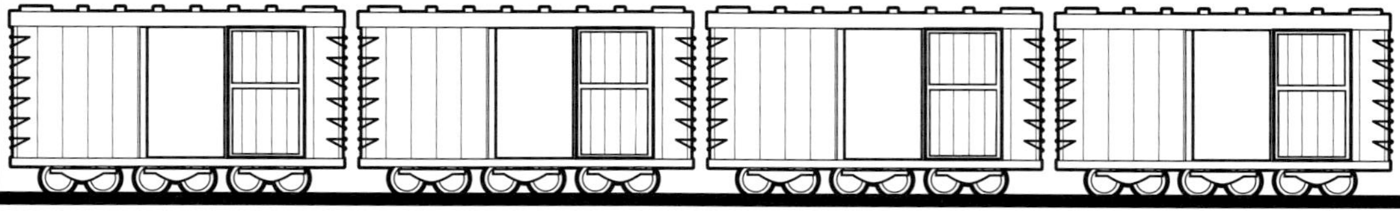

Teaching and Resource Units

Our Class Dictiona

Dawson, Brad (noun) 1. A boy with brown eyes. 2. A boy who loves to play basketball. 3. A boy whose favorite food is pizza. 4. A boy who has a silly sister who drives him crazy. 5. A boy who watches cartoons for one hour every Saturday morning. 6. A boy who wants a dog so badly that he has agreed to take out the trash every day for one whole year.

Getting Ready for a New School Year

Back-to-School Ideas From Our Subscribers

Any way you stack it, the start of another school year is just around the corner! Thanks to our trusty subscribers, we've gathered a blockbuster collection of back-to-school tips and teaching suggestions for your perusal. So whether you're just starting to collect back-to-school ideas or you're looking for a few fresh ideas to add to your tried-and-true repertoire, you've definitely come to the right spot!

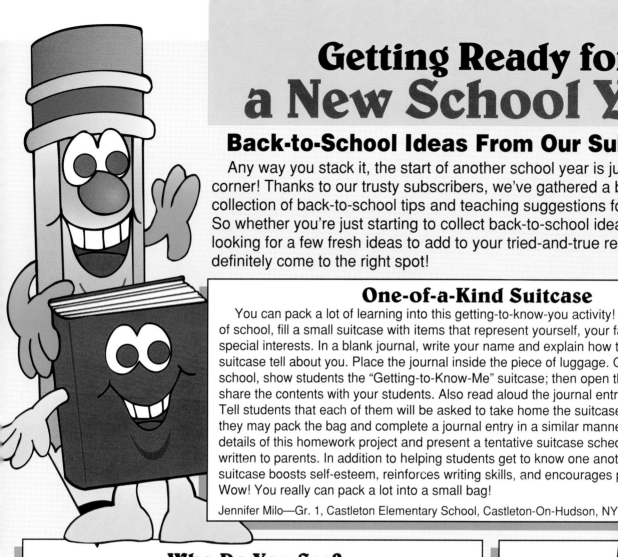

One-of-a-Kind Suitcase

You can pack a lot of learning into this getting-to-know-you activity! Before the first day of school, fill a small suitcase with items that represent yourself, your family, and your special interests. In a blank journal, write your name and explain how the items in the suitcase tell about you. Place the journal inside the piece of luggage. On the first day of school, show students the "Getting-to-Know-Me" suitcase; then open the suitcase and share the contents with your students. Also read aloud the journal entry that you wrote. Tell students that each of them will be asked to take home the suitcase and journal so that they may pack the bag and complete a journal entry in a similar manner. Explain the details of this homework project and present a tentative suitcase schedule in a letter written to parents. In addition to helping students get to know one another better, the suitcase boosts self-esteem, reinforces writing skills, and encourages parent involvement. Wow! You really can pack a lot into a small bag!

Jennifer Milo—Gr. 1, Castleton Elementary School, Castleton-On-Hudson, NY

Who Do You See?

This first-day booklet-making activity helps students learn the names of their classmates. To prepare write each child's name on a paper slip. Place the paper slips in a container along with an extra slip that you have labeled "everyone." You will also need a class supply of the booklet page shown and a copy of *Brown Bear, Brown Bear, What Do You See?* by Bill Martin, Jr. Read the book aloud; then distribute the booklet pages. Have each student write her first name in each blank at the top of her paper and illustrate herself in the box. Create your own booklet page in a similar manner. Next remove a paper slip from the container and write the student name in the remaining blank on your booklet page. (If you draw "everyone," return the slip and choose another one.) Then have each child draw a paper slip from the container and copy the name (or the word) on her paper. With your students' assistance, order the booklet pages—your page will appear first and the student page labeled "everyone" will be last. Bind the pages between tagboard covers. This class-created booklet is sure to provide hours of reading enjoyment all year long!

Char Blundy—Gr. 1
Westwood Elementary School, Portland, MI

Jackson, Jackson, who do you see?

I see ___ Pam ___ looking at me.

Welcome to Third Grade!

Back-to-School Bookmarks

Roll out the reading carpet with these nifty bookmarks. For each student label an apple cutout "Welcome to _____ Grade" and attach a length of 1 1/2"-wide fabric ribbon to the back of the cutout. These easy-to-make bookmarks are sure to motivate students to crack open their books!

Betsy Ruggiano—Gr. 3
Featherbed Lane School
Clark, NJ

Recipes for Success

This motivational display is perfect for the media center or school lobby. Use a plastic checked tablecloth as a backdrop and title the display "[school name]'s Greatest Recipes for Success." Each month every teacher in the school selects a student of the month from her classroom and composes this child's recipe for success on a large provided recipe card. (Each recipe should include the positive qualities that have helped the child succeed.) You will also need an enlarged photograph of each selected student. Trim away the background of each photo and mount the resulting head shot at the display. Decorate each snapshot with chef's attire and attach the child's recipe for success as shown. Look who's cookin'!

Dawn Stefano—Gr. 1 & Roger Lewis—Art Teacher
John Glenn Elementary School, Pine Hill, NJ

Weekly Seat Assignments

Instead of making permanent seat assignments at the beginning of the school year, try this weekly approach. Code each desk location with a number; then make a corresponding set of number cards. Every Monday morning or Friday afternoon, ask the students to randomly select number cards. Then, under your direction, have the youngsters quietly move their desks and/or belongings to their new locations. By changing your students' seating arrangement weekly, you encourage students to work cooperatively with lots of different children.

Jeanette Harrison—Gr. 2, Kingsbury Elementary School
Sumter, SC

Cute Quotes

Kids say the cutest things! This year write the witty comments and sweet compliments that you hear each child say on a personalized notecard or notebook page. At the end of the year, use the material you've collected to make a book of quotes for each youngster's family.

Carolyn S. Kanoy, Winston-Salem, NC

School-Year Scrapbooks

These easy-to-make student scrapbooks will quickly become cherished keepsakes. To make the scrapbooks, bind 12" x 18" sheets of manila paper between slightly larger tagboard covers. The number of pages in each scrapbook should equal one-half of the total number of weeks (full and partial) in the school year. Have each child personalize the cover of her scrapbook; then store the scrapbooks in a designated classroom location. At the end of each school week, a student chooses what she considers to be her best work of that week and mounts it in her scrapbook. On the same scrapbook page, she writes a one- or two-sentence comment about her work and the date. The scrapbooks are perfect tools for evaluating student progress. And, at the year's end, each child has an impressive collection of her best work.

Cindy Sweeney—Gr. 3
Homan Elementary School, Schererville, IN

Pam Crane

The Apple of Your Eye

Here's an activity that makes teaching students to read a grid as easy as eating apple pie! On red bulletin-board paper, draw the shape of a large apple. Then, using a straight edge, draw a desired grid on the apple. You will need one point of intersection per child. (A grid that has five vertical and five horizontal lines creates 25 intersecting points.) Cut out the apple shape and mount it on a bulletin board. Attach letter and number cutouts to label your grid. At each point of intersection, pin a card labeled with a different student's name. Each day write a different coordinate on the chalkboard. The student whose name is at this point on the grid becomes the teacher's special helper or "the apple of the teacher's eye" for the day. Be sure that each child is given a chance for this special privilege. You may also use the same method to randomly select students for a variety of other reasons. To keep students on their toes, periodically relocate their names on the grid. When October rolls around, replace the apple-shaped grid with a pumpkin-shaped one!

Vicki Neilon—Gr. 2, Antietam Elementary School, Lake Ridge, VA

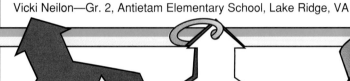

Dawson, Brad (noun) 1. A boy with brown eyes. 2. A boy who loves to play basketball. 3. A boy whose favorite food is pizza. 4. A boy who has a silly sister who drives him crazy. 5. A boy who watches cartoons for one hour every Saturday morning. 6. A boy who wants a dog so badly that he has agreed to take out the trash every day for one whole year.

Schoolhouse Dictionary

Shape up your students' writing and dictionary skills with this back-to-school activity. For each student duplicate the outline of a schoolhouse on a 9" x 12" piece of tagboard (see the illustration). Each student uses markers to draw and color his self-portrait in the box. Below the box, he writes a dictionary listing for himself. To do this the student writes his last name, followed by his first name, and then his middle name if desired. After listing the part of speech in parentheses, he composes five to ten self-describing dictionary listings. Each listing should be numbered. Laminate the completed projects for durability; then cut them out. Bind the cutouts between two slightly larger, red poster-board cutouts. Title the resulting booklet "Our Class Dictionary." Let students take turns carrying this student-created dictionary home to share with their families.

Linda P. Lovelace—Gr. 3
Halifax Elementary
Halifax, VA

Yummy Apple Pizzas

This cooking activity is perfect for the beginning of the school year. In addition to being an easy-to-manage cooking project, it is "apple-lutely" delicious!

Ingredients for 30 pizzas:
three 10-biscuit cans of refrigerated biscuit dough (large, Texas-size biscuits work best)
5 large apples, peeled and sliced
1 1/2 cups mild cheddar cheese, grated
1/2 cup firmly packed brown sugar
1/2 teaspoon cinnamon
2 tablespoons flour
a small tub of margarine

Directions:
Preheat the oven to 350°. In a small bowl, mix together the brown sugar, cinnamon, and flour. To make an apple pizza, place the dough of one biscuit on waxed paper. Use your hands to gently flatten the biscuit. Sprinkle it with grated cheese. Arrange two or three apple slices atop the cheese. Spoon a layer of brown-sugar mixture over the biscuit; then put a dot of margarine on top. Peel away the waxed paper and place the pizza on a lightly greased baking sheet. Bake for 25–30 minutes.

Vicki O'Neal—Gr. 2, Lincoln School, Baxter Springs, KS

Poetry Notebooks

Here's a yearlong poetry plan that culminates with an impressive end-of-the-year celebration. Ask each child to bring to school a three-ring notebook. Each week display a different poem and give each student a copy of the poem for his notebook. During the week incorporate the poem into a variety of activities. Every Friday allow students to pair up with their classmates to practice reading and reciting the poems in their notebook collections. At the end of the year, invite your students' families to school for a poetry celebration. Plan for individuals and small groups to present their favorite poems from the past year. Then serve refreshments that the students have prepared. In just one year, a student can have an impressive poetry collection and a greater appreciation for poetry.

Bev Bell—Gr. 2, Churchill School, Homewood, IL
Linda Johnson—Gr. 1, Rockway School, Springfield, OH

Piece by Piece

Everyone gets a piece of the action with this first-day activity! In advance draw on white paper a large rendering (approximately three feet tall) of the numeral that represents your grade level. Divide the numeral into puzzle pieces—one piece for each child enrolled in your class plus a few extra pieces for students who have not yet enrolled. Cut out the numeral. Then, starting at the top of the cutout, cut apart the puzzle pieces. As you do this, number the backs of the pieces in sequential order. On the first day of school, ask each student to decorate a puzzle piece. When all the pieces are decorated, enlist your students' help in piecing together the number puzzle atop a second sheet of paper. Glue the completed puzzle on the paper. Write "Welcome to Grade" above the colorful number; then invite each child to sign the resulting poster. Display the project for all to admire.

Wendy Bousquet—Substitute Teacher
Scarborough Board Of Education, Scarborough, Ontario
Canada

Paper-Bag Puppets

These adorable puppets encourage parents to get involved in their children's studies. Each student needs two construction-paper patterns like the ones shown, and a paper lunch bag. Show students a puppet that you decorated to look like you. Make sure that students understand how to attach their patterns to the paper bag; then have each child create a puppet that resembles himself. Ask students to share their puppet projects with their parents. With these puppets on hand, parental involvement is almost guaranteed!

Theresa Bernal—Grs. K–2
Summerdale School
San Jose, CA

113

Daily Specials for Spelling Success!

Students will quickly develop a taste for spelling when you begin dishing out this delicious spelling cuisine! Each enticing entree is served with a scoopful of spelling reinforcement and a slice of irresistible fun. There's no doubt that these daily specials are made-to-order for spelling success!

Spelling That Scores

Youngsters will have a ball playing this unique spelling game! Write "1" on two tennis balls, "2" on two others, and "3" on two more. Place all six tennis balls in a paper bag. Divide students into four teams and write each team's name on the chalkboard. Then have each team line up single file facing its name. To begin play, the first player in each line steps up to the chalkboard and the remaining students sit in place. In turn ask each player to write a different word on the chalkboard. If a player correctly spells his word, randomly remove a tennis ball from the bag and bounce it to him. He reads the numeral on the ball and records this number of points near his team's name. If a player misspells his word, his turn is over. Then each first-round player moves to the back of his team's line and a new round of play begins. The team with the most points wins. No doubt this team approach will net world-class spelling skills!

Sue Crosby, Camey Elementary, Colony, TX

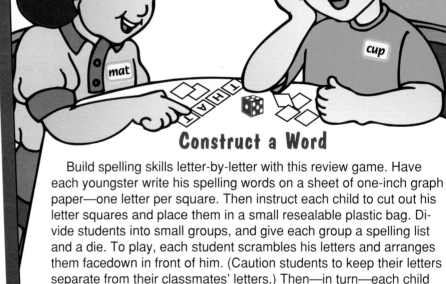

Weekly Special

Reinforce spelling and proper word usage with wearable words! Every Monday use a wipe-off marker to write the spelling words for the week on a laminated poster titled "This Week's Specials." Review the word list with students and encourage them to use the words in class discussions throughout the week. One day each week, reinforce your students' oral usage of their spelling words with self-stick labels. Each time a student correctly uses a different spelling word in a sentence, give her a label. The student programs the label with the corresponding spelling word and attaches it to her clothing. The spelling of these words is sure to stick!

Jill Hamilton—Gr. 1
Schoeneck Elementary, Stevens, PA

Construct a Word

Build spelling skills letter-by-letter with this review game. Have each youngster write his spelling words on a sheet of one-inch graph paper—one letter per square. Then instruct each child to cut out his letter squares and place them in a small resealable plastic bag. Divide students into small groups, and give each group a spelling list and a die. To play, each student scrambles his letters and arranges them facedown in front of him. (Caution students to keep their letters separate from their classmates' letters.) Then—in turn—each child rolls the die, turns over the corresponding number of letters, and forms as many spelling words as possible. He moves the assembled words aside and turns the unused letters facedown. Play continues until one student has spelled each word on the list. Now that's a constructive approach to spelling!

Kyle Welby—Gr. 1, Epstein Hebrew Academy, St. Louis, MO

Spell and Sort

Strengthen alphabetizing and sorting skills with this hands-on spelling activity. Have each student fold a sheet of blank paper in half three times, then unfold the paper and write a different spelling word in each box. Next have her cut apart the boxes and arrange the eight resulting word cards in alphabetical order. Verify each student's work before inviting her to sort her word cards by self-selected categories, such as vowel sounds or number of syllables. To wrap up the activity, have each student name the spelling words in each of her categories and ask her classmates to identify what sorting rule(s) she used. Students will have all sorts of fun with this engaging activity!

Sue Crosby
Camey Elementary
Colony, TX

Roll 'em!

This small-group game adds up to "die-namite" spelling! Give each group a pair of dice. Each student also needs his spelling list, a sheet of writing paper, and a pencil. To play, each group member takes a turn rolling the dice and adding the two numbers shown. The youngster who rolls the greatest sum wins the round and copies two spelling words on his paper. Play continues in the described manner until one student has listed all of his spelling words and is declared the winner. Count on this high-rolling game to be a race to the finish!

Jennifer Von Pinnon—Gr. 3
Eastwood Elementary
West Fargo, ND

Hit or Miss

You'll be right on target with this partner activity! Give each child a copy of the gameboard on page 117 and a sheet of blank paper. Ask each child to program six rectangles on his gameboard with different spelling words, then cover his gameboard with the blank paper. Pair students and tell them that this spelling game is played similarly to Battleship®. Explain that the object of the game is for each student to locate and correctly spell each of the six spelling words his partner has hidden.

To begin, the first player names a set of coordinates. If his partner has a spelling word at this location, the partner says, "Hit," and reads the word aloud. If the player spells the word correctly, the partner draws an X through it indicating that this word has been hit. Then the second player takes his turn. A player's turn is over if a word is misspelled or no word is located (a miss). Play continues until one student hits all six of his partner's spelling words. With this strategic game, students' spelling skills will be shipshape in no time at all!

Dianne E. Hammond—Gr. 3, North School
Londonderry, NH

Buddy Spelling

Double up on spelling practice with a buddy approach. Give each youngster an envelope to personalize. You will also need a colorful supply of paper slips. After a spelling test or writing conference, have each youngster correctly write each word she misspelled on a paper slip, then store the word slip(s) in her envelope. Every few days provide time for students to practice spelling their envelope words with different partners. After a desired number of weeks, have each student choose five to ten words from her envelope. Ask the student to spell these words for you (orally or on paper). Each word that is correctly spelled can be taken home. A misspelled word is returned to the student's envelope. Spelling accuracy will improve on the double!

Pat Urbach—Gr. 1, BA Kennedy, Prairie Du Chien, WI

Bonus Words

Motivate your young spellers with individualized bonus words. Label a large index card for each child. Each week date and program the card with a bonus word that is appropriate for the student's spelling skills. A young-ster may keep his bonus spelling-word card at his desk, or you may store the cards in a central location. Throughout the week provide special bonus-word activities like "When you finish your math paper, use a crayon to write your bonus spelling word three times near the bottom of the page," or "During recess spell your bonus word out loud for everyone to hear!" When you administer your weekly spelling test, ask each child to write his bonus word in a complete sentence. If a student successfully completes this task, give him a foil star to attach near the word on his bonus spelling card. If he is not suc-cessful, encourage him to try again the following week. Each young speller will beam with pride as his galaxy of starred bonus words grows!

Speedy Spelling

Students love the chance to outscore their teacher! And this spelling game provides plenty of opportunities! For each round of play, write a differ-ent spelling word on the chalkboard. Choose one student to oversee an egg timer and ask the remaining students to copy the word from the chalkboard onto their papers. The object of the game is to continually write the spelling word from the moment the egg timer is inverted until the student watching it calls out, "Time!" Then each student speller awards himself one point for every correct (and legible!) spelling for that round and writes his score near his word list. Identify the student who earns the highest score; then, with your youngsters' help, determine your score for the round by tallying the words you wrote on the chalkboard. If the student wins the round, award the class one point. If you win the round, award the teacher one point. When each spelling word has been speedily spelled, determine whom the speedier speller is: you or your students!

Laine Barresi
Central Academy Nongraded
Middletown, OH

Diane Benner—Gr. 2
Dover Elementary
Dover, PA

Spelling
Partner game

Hit or Miss!

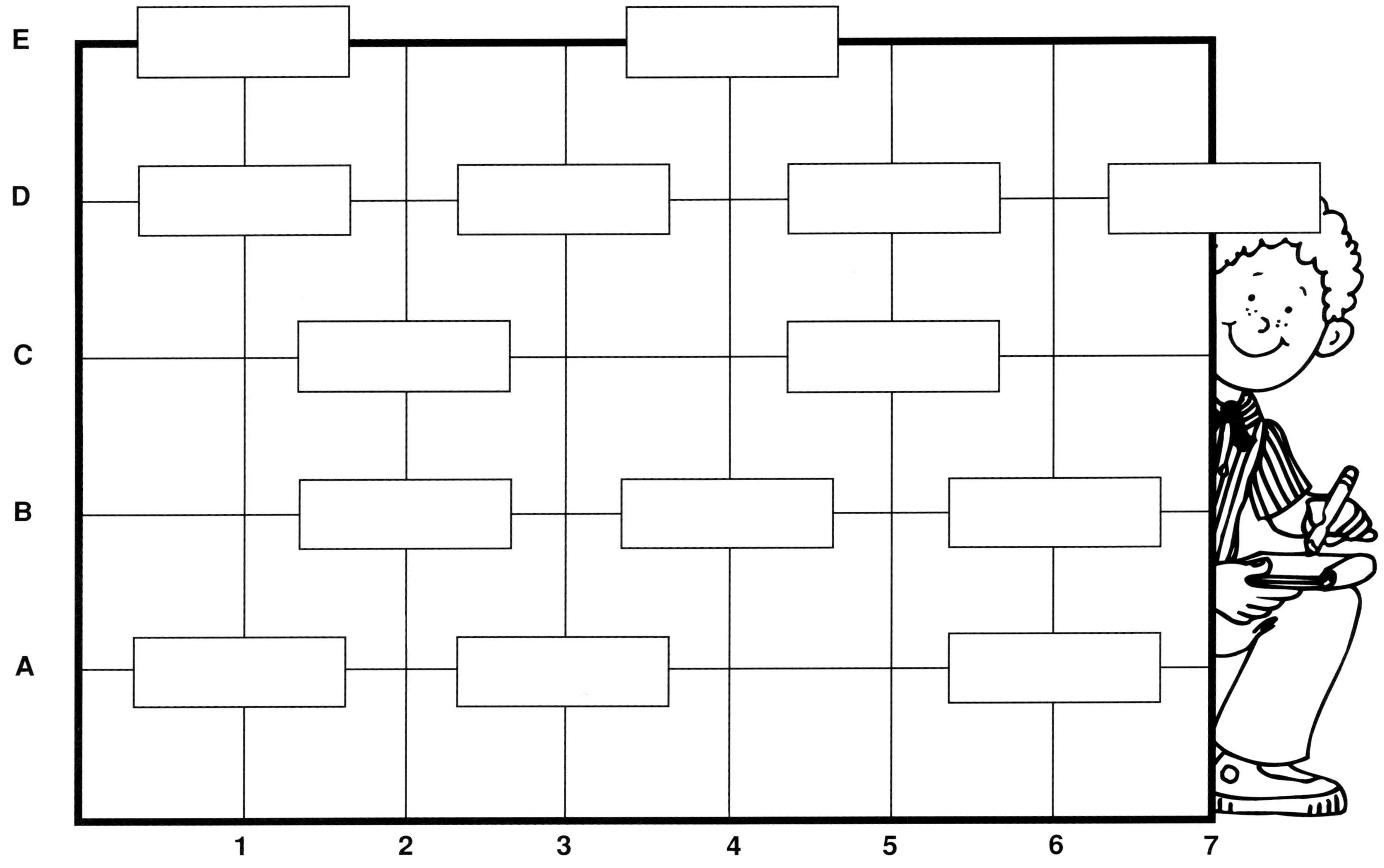

	1	2	3	4	5	6	7
E							
D							
C							
B							
A							

Note to teacher: Use with "Hit or Miss" on page 115.

117

Science With a Song
MAGNETS

Use this collection of activities to explore the fascinating forces of magnetism through music, hands-on experiences, literature, and a whole lot more!

ideas contributed by Michele Converse Baerns and Charles J. Wohl

Sing a Song

Keep students tuned in to major magnet concepts with this little ditty. It's fun to sing and it teaches, too!

What's a Magnet?
(adapt to the tune of "Ten Little Indians")

A magnet is a stone or piece of metal,
North or south pole on each end.
Like poles repel or push apart.
Opposites attract like friends.

Magnets attract things made of iron,
Also cobalt, steel, and nickel;
But not aluminum, brass, or copper,
Paper, glass, or a pickle!

Faye Fowler Haney—Gr. 2, Valley View Elementary, Jonesboro, AR

Sort the Soup

What does a bowl of soup have to do with a study of magnets? Plenty, when the soup recipe calls for marbles, screws, buttons, scrap paper, rubber bands, washers, coins, toothpicks, paper clips, cotton balls, and craft bells! For this science experience, give each pair of students a nonbreakable bowl of magnetic and nonmagnetic soup items, a sorting sheet like the one shown, and a pencil. Ask each twosome to sort the items in its bowl onto the sorting sheet, placing the items that it predicts will be attracted by a magnet under "Yes" and all others under "No." Then give each pair a magnet and have the partners take turns testing their predictions.

To extend the activity, ask each pair to write a recipe for either Magnetic Soup or Nonmagnetic Soup. Encourage students to move around the classroom using their magnets to test and verify possible soup ingredients. Be sure to set aside time for students to read aloud their one-of-a-kind recipes!

Magnets Everywhere!

Realizing how often magnets impact day-to-day activities is an important discovery for students to make and remember. Title a paper-covered bulletin board "Magnets Are Everywhere!" Near the display, place a supply of discarded magazines and a receptacle for collecting cutouts. As students discover items that utilize magnets, invite them to cut out the corresponding pictures and place them in the container. Later, staple the cutouts to the board, overlapping them slightly to create a colorful and informative collage. (Items include electrical appliances, video games, televisions, telephones, radios, vacuum cleaners, computer monitors, floppy disks, audio and video equipment, and airplanes!)

A Field of Force

Every magnet has a field of force called a *magnetic field.* Here's a quick and easy way for students to investigate and feel the force of a magnetic field. As an introduction, hold a magnet high above a collection of paper clips. Ask students why the paper clips are not pulled to the magnet. Then gradually lower the magnet until it pulls the clips to it. Explain that around every magnet there is a field (or area) of magnetic force. When the paper clips are within the magnet's magnetic field, they are pulled to the magnet. Then give each pair of students a magnet to share and a handful of paper clips or other magnetic objects. Allow plenty of time for the partners to investigate the magnetic field of their magnet and feel its force. If the twosomes are using magnets of different shapes and sizes, encourage the pairs to trade magnets for additional investigation.

Seeing the Invisible

This hands-on activity gives students a detailed look at magnetic fields.

In advance:

For every three students, place one teaspoon of iron filings and one-half cup of mineral or baby oil inside a resealable plastic bag. Carefully release any air captured in the bag; then secure the bag's seal with clear packaging tape to prevent all possible spills.

What each trio needs:

1 prepared bag of iron filings
a variety of magnets
8½" x 11" sheet of white paper
1 lab sheet (page 121)
3 pencils

What to do:

Have each child write her name and the question "What does a magnetic field look like?" on her lab sheet. Then have her draw or list the materials that have been provided for this science experience. Next instruct each trio to place one magnet under its white paper, gently tip and tilt its bag to evenly disperse the iron filings inside, lay the bag on the paper directly on top of the magnet, and observe what happens. Have the trios repeat this activity for each of their magnets. Also provide plenty of time for open investigation. Finally, have each student complete numbers 3 and 4 on her lab sheet and then invite students to talk about what they saw and learned.

This is why:

The iron filings are attracted to each magnet along invisible lines of force. Because the filings are so small, the lines of force are clearly illustrated. These lines of force make up the magnetic field. A magnet has a field of force all around it; however, it is always strongest near the ends of the magnet.

Tiny Bits of Matter

While an investigation of iron atoms is most likely beyond the grasp of your youngsters, they will surely be fascinated by how these tiny bits of matter line up in magnetic items. Give each trio of students a sheet of white paper, a strip of magnetic tape (or something similar) and a prepared bag of iron filings from "Seeing the Invisible" on this page. Ask each trio to slide its magnetic tape under the paper so the magnetized side is up and then lay its bag of evenly dispersed iron filings on the paper directly on top of the magnetic tape. Students will see how the bits of iron in their magnetic objects line up. Explain that the atoms in nonmagnetic items do not line up. Allow time for students to repeat the activity using a variety of objects and, if desired, complete individual copies of the lab sheet on page 121.

Making Magnets

Can magnets be made? Believe it or not, yes! To demonstrate *induced magnetism* (a temporary form of magnetism), give each student pair a magnet, a handful of paper clips, and two copies of the lab sheet on page 121. Have each student write his name and the question "Can a magnet be made?" on his paper. Then have him draw or list the provided materials. Next instruct each pair to experiment with its magnet and paper clips before completing the written portion of the activity. Students will discover that when a paper clip is attached to the magnet (or another magnetized paper clip), the magnetic force of the magnet is transferred to it. However, each paper clip immediately loses its magnetism when it is isolated.

Pam Crane

A Delicious Discovery

These cookies are not magnets, but they will—without a doubt—attract plenty of student interest!

North-South Bars
(makes approximately 28 cookies)

Ingredients:
tube of prepared sugar cookie dough
red-tinted icing
blue-tinted icing

Directions:
1. Remove the packaging and then cut the tube of dough in half.
2. Slice the dough lengthwise into 1/4-inch thick slices. Slice each resulting rectangle in half to create two bars.
3. Bake the bar-shaped cookies according to the package directions.
4. When the cookies are cool, have each child decorate a cookie by applying red and blue icing to indicate its north and south poles.

Books About Magnets

Further investigate the force of magnetism with the information and hands-on experiences in these books.

What Makes a Magnet?
Written by Franklyn M. Branley
Illustrated by True Kelley
HarperTrophy®, 1996

Janice VanCleave's Magnets: Mind-Boggling Experiments You Can Turn Into Science Fair Projects
By Janice Pratt VanCleave
John Wiley & Sons, Inc.; 1993

Science With Magnets
Written by Helen Edom
Illustrated by Simone Abel
EDC Publishing, 1992

The Science Book of Magnets
Written by Neil Ardley
Photographs by Dave King
Harcourt Brace Jovanovich, Publishers; 1991

Order books online. www.themailbox.com

Name_____

Investigating Magnets

1. Write the question you are trying to answer. _____

_____

_____

2. Draw or list the materials you will use during your investigation.

```
┌─────────────────────────────────────────────────────────────────┐
│                                                                   │
│                                                                   │
│                                                                   │
│                                                                   │
│                                                                   │
│                                                                   │
└─────────────────────────────────────────────────────────────────┘
```

3. Draw what happened and then write about it.

```
┌──────────────────────────────┐      _____
│                              │      _____
│                              │      _____
│                              │      _____
│                              │      _____
│                              │      _____
│                              │      _____
│                              │      _____
└──────────────────────────────┘      _____
```

4. Explain what you learned. _____

_____

_____

_____

Note to teacher: Use this lab sheet with activities suggested on pages 119 and 120. To use the lab sheet with another science topic, make a copy of the page. Mask out the title and magnet art and then add a desired title and corresponding clip art.

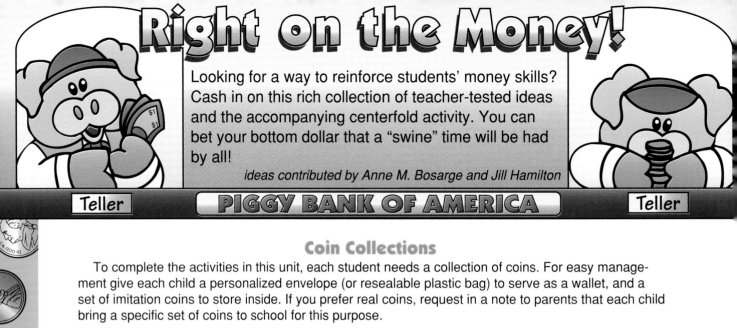

Right on the Money!

Looking for a way to reinforce students' money skills? Cash in on this rich collection of teacher-tested ideas and the accompanying centerfold activity. You can bet your bottom dollar that a "swine" time will be had by all!

ideas contributed by Anne M. Bosarge and Jill Hamilton

Teller   PIGGY BANK OF AMERICA   Teller

Coin Collections

To complete the activities in this unit, each student needs a collection of coins. For easy management give each child a personalized envelope (or resealable plastic bag) to serve as a wallet, and a set of imitation coins to store inside. If you prefer real coins, request in a note to parents that each child bring a specific set of coins to school for this purpose.

Money, Dough, or Moolah?

Get your money unit off to a profitable start with this intriguing activity. Show students a dollar bill and a handful of coins. Ask students what these items are called and write their responses on the chalkboard. Broaden your youngsters' vocabularies by adding to the list some less familiar names for money, like *sawbacks, moolah, greenbacks, bread, bucks, oof, gelt, bits, skins,* and *cabbage.* Then, for added fun, share several money expressions from the provided list and challenge students to determine the meaning of each one.

Money Expressions

"A dime a dozen"
"Your bottom dollar"
"Two cents' worth"
"A penny for your thoughts"
"Time is money."
"Money talks."
"Money doesn't grow on trees."
"Show me the money!"
"A fool and his money are soon parted."
"The love of money is the root of all evil."
"Money can't buy happiness."
"Penny-pincher"
"You look like a million bucks!"
"A penny saved is a penny earned."
"Nickel-and-diming"

Kimberly Richard

Profitable Patterns

If your students need practice identifying coins, this patterning activity is a wise investment! Pair students and give each partner an identical set of coins. In turn each student uses his coin set to create a pattern; then his partner uses his set of coins to continue the pattern. Next the two students work together to state the name and value of each coin in the pattern they created. To increase the difficulty of the task, have each student pair determine the total value of each completed pattern. Wow! Who would have thought coin patterns could be so profitable!

The Banker Says...

Reinforce coin-recognition and listening skills with this variation of the popular game Simon Says. Give each small group a penny, nickel, dime, and quarter for every group member except one. (For example, a group of six students will receive five of each coin.) Ask each group to randomly arrange its coins on a playing surface. Also select one member in each group to be the banker. To play, a banker tells his group to pick up a specific coin. The group members should respond only if the banker's request is prefaced by "The banker says." After the banker has verified the coins that were selected, the coins are returned to the playing surface. A student who chooses an incorrect coin or who responds without the banker's okay sits out for one round of play. After a designated amount of game time, appoint a different banker for each group and resume play. Continue in this manner until each group member has been the banker. Now that's a game plan you can take to the bank!

Pick up a quarter.

Days Of The Week	Number Of Pockets	1¢ Pocket Value	5¢ Pocket Value
Monday	48	48¢	$2.40
Tuesday	60	60¢	$3.00

Pocket Change

Cash in with this daily small-group activity! Give each group a supply of pennies and ask each child to put one penny in each pocket she is wearing. Next have the students remove the pennies from their pockets and determine the cash value of each group member's pockets and the cash value of the entire group's pockets. Then assist the class in finding the total cash value of all the students' pockets. For older students, extend the activity by challenging the small groups to determine similar totals based on a pocket value of five or ten cents. If desired, record this information on a chart like the one shown. Plan to repeat the activity every few days during your study of money. No doubt your youngsters' money skills will grow right along with the number of pockets they are wearing!

Breaking the Bank!

Oink! Oink! This small-group game provides plenty of practice with coin identification. On pink construction paper, duplicate the piggy-bank pattern on page 125 to make a class supply. Laminate and cut out the piggy banks. Also make a spinner wheel (like the one shown) for each group. Divide the class into small groups. Give each group a spinner wheel, a sharpened pencil, and a large paper clip to use as a spinner. Then give each group member a piggy-bank cutout and a predetermined number of coins to place on her bank. (The total value of the coins may vary, but the *number* of coins must be the same.)

To play, each player in turn spins the spinner and removes from her bank the coin that matches the value she has spun. She places this coin in a personal discard pile. If a student spins the pig, she acts like a little pig and puts the coins from her discard pile back in her bank. The first player to empty her bank wins the game!

Dollar Details

Because the dollar bill is used more frequently than any other paper money, it has the shortest life span—only 18 months. During that time, a dollar bill changes hands an average of 400 times! Use "The Dollar Song" and "Dollar Booklet" on this page to reinforce the value of this very popular greenback.

The Dollar Song
(sung to the tune of "Ten Little Indians")

10 little, 20 little, 30 little pennies.
40 little, 50 little, 60 little pennies.
70 little, 80 little, 90 little pennies.
100 pennies make a dollar!

2 small, 4 small, 6 small nickels.
8 small, 10 small, 12 small nickels.
14 small, 16 small, 18 small nickels.
20 nickels make a dollar!

1 tiny, 2 tiny, 3 tiny dimes.
4 tiny, 5 tiny, 6 tiny dimes.
7 tiny, 8 tiny, 9 tiny dimes.
10 dimes make a dollar!

1 big, 2 big, 3 big quarters.
4 big, 4 big, 4 big quarters.
1 big, 2 big, 3 big quarters.
4 quarters make a dollar!

Rebecca Brudwick—Gr. 1
Hoover Elementary School
North Mankato, MN

Dollar Booklet

Here's a great way for students to make some bucks and brush up on their money skills, too! To make a dollar booklet, a student stacks three 8 1/2" x 11" sheets of white paper and holds the pages vertically. He slides the top sheet upward approximately one inch and the bottom sheet downward approximately one inch. Next the student folds his papers forward to create six graduated layers or pages; then he staples the resulting booklet close to the fold. The student writes the title "[Student's name]'s Dollar Booklet" on the cover and labels the bottoms of the booklet pages as shown. To complete his booklet, he illustrates the dollar bill and stamps the appropriate coin impressions on the corresponding booklet pages.

Shari Sullivan Marshall, Crested Butte, CO

dollar bill
quarters
dimes
nickels
pennies

21¢

Money March

Students march toward better money-counting skills with this game plan! To make a trail of coins like the one shown, enlarge the coin patterns on page 125 and duplicate each coin on an appropriate color of paper to make a supply. Laminate and cut out the coins; then tape a path of cutouts on the floor. (Store the extra coins for later use.) Post the cash value of the coin path in a designated location. A student orally adds the coin values as he marches alongside the path. Then he verifies his cash total with the one that you've posted. Modify the coin path every few days, remembering to post its corresponding cash value each time. You can count on improved money-counting skills in no time!

Patterns
Use the coin patterns with "Money March" on page 124.

Use the pig pattern with "Breaking the Bank!" on page 123.

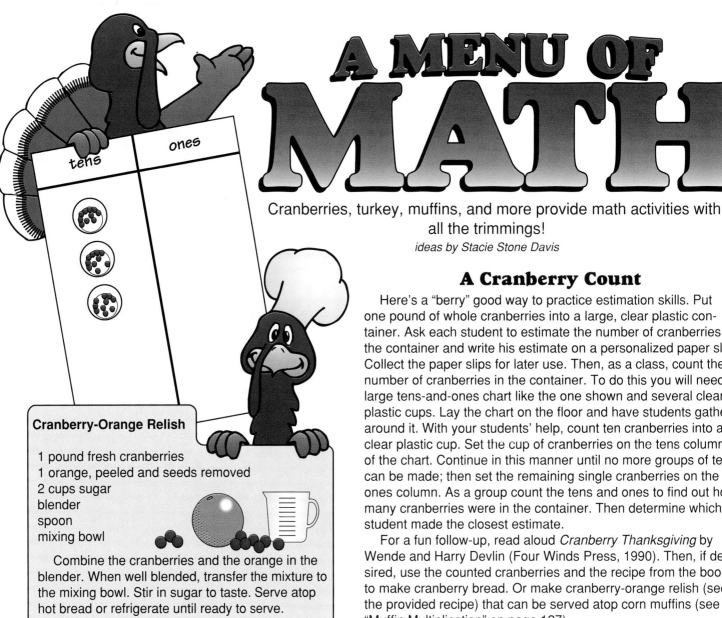

A MENU OF MATH

Cranberries, turkey, muffins, and more provide math activities with all the trimmings!

ideas by Stacie Stone Davis

A Cranberry Count

Here's a "berry" good way to practice estimation skills. Put one pound of whole cranberries into a large, clear plastic container. Ask each student to estimate the number of cranberries i the container and write his estimate on a personalized paper sli Collect the paper slips for later use. Then, as a class, count the number of cranberries in the container. To do this you will need large tens-and-ones chart like the one shown and several clear plastic cups. Lay the chart on the floor and have students gathe around it. With your students' help, count ten cranberries into a clear plastic cup. Set the cup of cranberries on the tens column of the chart. Continue in this manner until no more groups of ter can be made; then set the remaining single cranberries on the ones column. As a group count the tens and ones to find out ho many cranberries were in the container. Then determine which student made the closest estimate.

For a fun follow-up, read aloud *Cranberry Thanksgiving* by Wende and Harry Devlin (Four Winds Press, 1990). Then, if desired, use the counted cranberries and the recipe from the book to make cranberry bread. Or make cranberry-orange relish (see the provided recipe) that can be served atop corn muffins (see "Muffin Multiplication" on page 127).

Cranberry-Orange Relish

1 pound fresh cranberries
1 orange, peeled and seeds removed
2 cups sugar
blender
spoon
mixing bowl

Combine the cranberries and the orange in the blender. When well blended, transfer the mixture to the mixing bowl. Stir in sugar to taste. Serve atop hot bread or refrigerate until ready to serve.

Squash Circumferences

Squash, anyone? This small-group activity helps students compare the circumferences of a variety of squash. Prepare a workstation for each small group that includes a different winter squash (such as *acorn, buttercup, turban, butternut, Hubbard,* or *pumpkin*); three pieces of double-sided tape attached to a wall (or chart); three cards labeled "too short," "just right," and "too long"; scissors; and a supply of uncut string. Assign a group of students to each workstation. One at a time, each group member examines the circumference of the group's squash (at its widest point) and cuts a length of string that he thinks equals that distance. After each student has cut a length of string, have each group member wrap his cut string around the group's squash, then display his string under the appropriate card as shown. Invite each group to report on the accuracy of its estimates; then ask students if they think their estimates might have been more accurate if each group member had tested and displayed his cut string before the next group member took his turn. Discuss the advantages of making an estimate after several pieces of data have been gathered. Then, if desired, rotate the squash and repeat the activity in the manner described.

Muffin Multiplication

Students are sure to enjoy this tasty introduction to arrays! Gather muffin tins in assorted sizes. Then, using a prepackaged mix or a favorite recipe, prepare a large batch of corn muffin batter—enlisting your students' help if desired. Divide students into small groups and give each group a muffin tin, pencils, and scrap paper. Help students see that each muffin tin is an array. Ask each group to determine a multiplication problem (or an addition problem) that its muffin tin represents. Then visit each group, place a paper liner in each muffin tin compartment, and fill the compartments with batter. After the group's muffin tin has been filled, have the group share its array-related problem(s) with the class. Continue in this manner until all the muffin tins have been filled.

While the muffins are baking, challenge each group to locate and list on their papers other classroom arrays, such as windowpanes and desk or cubby arrangements. When the muffins are done, serve them with the cranberry-orange relish prepared in "A Cranberry Count." If desired, invite another class to your corn-muffin feast. While students are enjoying the muffins, read aloud the hilariously funny 'Twas The Night Before Thanksgiving by Dav Pilkey (Orchard Books, 1990).

Time for Turkey!

No doubt many students have heard their moms, dads, grandparents, or other relatives or friends in the kitchen on Thanksgiving Day, anxiously figuring what time the turkey needs to be put in the oven so that it's ready for dinner. Take some of the mystery out of this event with the following gobbling-good activity. Each student needs a clock manipulative with movable hands. Explain that for each pound of a large turkey, the turkey must cook about 15 minutes. Then, with your students' help, make a chart that shows the cooking times for turkeys weighing eight or more pounds.

Afterward ask students to solve problems such as "If a ten-pound turkey were put in the oven at 12:00 noon, what time should the turkey be finished cooking?" or "If a family wants to eat at 5:00 P.M. and they have a 20-pound turkey, what time should the turkey be put in the oven?" Encourage students to use their clock manipulatives for assistance in making the chart and solving the problems.

Pumpkin-Pie Fractions

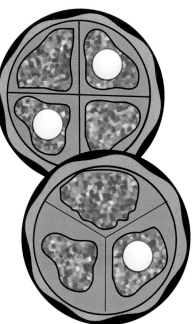

This activity makes reviewing fractions as easy as pie! Under your students' watchful eyes, cut a prepared pumpkin pie into eight equal slices. Put a dollop of whipped cream on one pie slice; then ask students to name how many pie slices have whipped cream. When students volunteer the answer, "One slice," explain that this answer could also be expressed as "One slice out of eight," or "$1/8$ of the pie." Repeat this process until each pie slice is topped with a dollop of whipped cream. If desired repeat the process with other pies that have been divided into halves, thirds, fourths, and sixths.

For a fun follow-up activity, duplicate the patterns on page 128 onto orange construction paper. Give each child one pattern. To make her pumpkin-pie fraction project, a student colors the pie crust brown; then she cuts out the pie pattern. Next she brushes a thin layer of glue on each section of the pie and sprinkles pumpkin pie spice onto the glue. When the project is dry, she shakes the excess spice into a provided container such as a shoebox lid. Next she glues each white pom-pom that she has been given on a pie slice and labels a blank index card to show what fraction of her pie has been topped with "whipped cream." Verify each child's work, and collect the projects and index cards for use at a center. For a fun finale, serve each child a small portion of the sliced pumpkin pie(s) that you used to introduce this lesson.

adapted from an idea by Toni Stewart, Montpelier, IN

A Shopping Extravaganza

Answer Key
For Page 47

1. $3.00
2. $1.55
3. $1.15
4. $2.40
5. $1.90
6. $3.50
7. $1.70
8. $1.90

Culminate your Thanksgiving-related math activities by having each youngster complete the reproducible activity on page 129. Students may complete the activity independently or in small groups. Have money manipulatives available to assist students.

As an extension to this activity, give each student a grocery-store circular that features Thanksgiving-type foods. (Some grocery stores may be willing to donate a class supply of circulars.) Have students use the circulars to solve teacher-created math problems that correspond to the circular. Or challenge each student to plan and determine the cost of a Thanksgiving Day dinner that uses the foods featured in his circular.

Patterns

Use with "Pumpkin-Pie Fractions" on page 127.

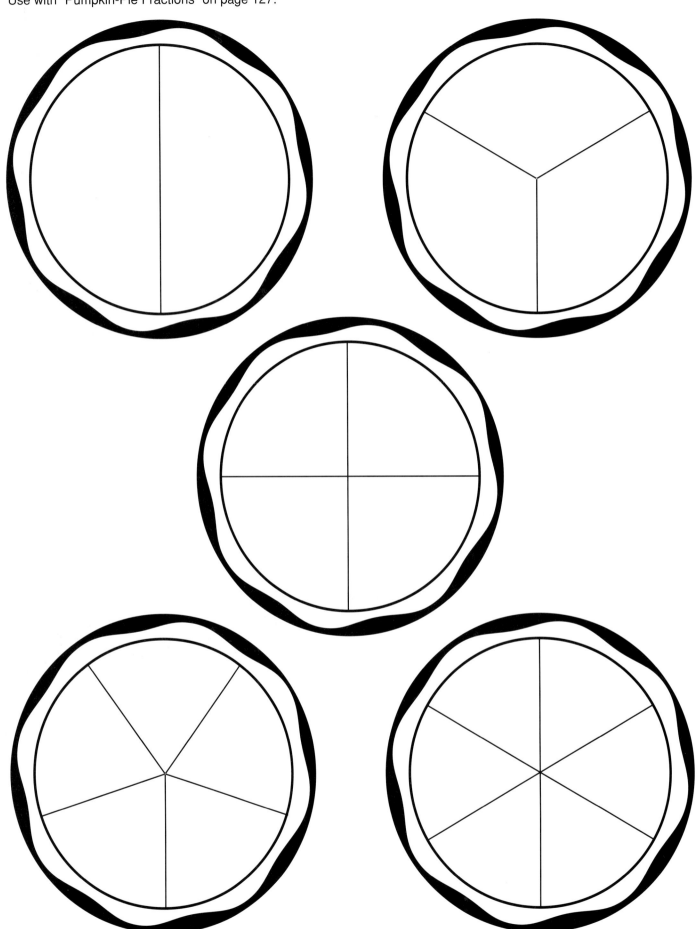

A Gobblin'-Good Sale!

Find the total of each purchase.
Show your work in the boxes.
Write your answers on the lines.

1. two pumpkin pies _____

2. a bunch of celery
   and a box of corn _____

3. a bag of dinner rolls and
   a carton of whipping cream _____

4. a jar of pickles and a bag
   of cranberries _____

5. two boxes of stuffing _____

6. a bag of potatoes and
   a pumpkin pie _____

7. a box of stuffing and
   a bunch of celery _____

8. a bag of cranberries and
   a bag of dinner rolls _____

1.	2.
3.	4.
5.	6.
7.	8.

Note to teacher: Use with "A Shopping Extravaganza" on page 127.

A HARVEST OF READING MOTIVATION

You've planted the seed of reading knowledge and you're busy cultivating your students' reading skills. What more could you use? How about a bumper crop of reading motivation? Implement your favorite ideas from this collection and in no time your budding readers will be blooming with reading enthusiasm!

Literary Door Displays

Get the word out about reading with this schoolwide plan! To begin, ask each class to decorate the outside of its hallway door to spotlight a favorite book. Require that each door decoration include the title of the chosen book. Then, on a predetermined day, ask all teachers to close their hallway doors so that each class of students can take a turn viewing the door displays throughout the school. Students are sure to discover several books that they'd like to read or have read to them! Repeat this schoolwide door-decorating activity as often as you like. To encourage a variety of reading, designate book categories or themes like animal stories, tall tales, fairy tales, nonfiction books, and biographies for future decorating projects.

Andrea Isom Burzlaff—Gr. 3, Coventry School, Crystal Lake, IL
Hope H. Taylor—Gr. 3, Birchcrest School, Bellevue, NE

Books and Backpacks

Boost reading enthusiasm and self-esteem with books and backpacks! Each week distribute a backpack to two or three different students. Help each youngster select and place in his backpack a book from the school or classroom library that he would like to read aloud to others. Also place a copy of a parent note in each backpack that explains the following procedure: On Monday and Tuesday evenings, the student practices reading his selected book aloud to his family members. Also encourage each student to gather (or create) story props and to use the props to enhance his presentation of the book. On Wednesday the backpack (containing the book and story props) is returned to school and the student rehearses his book presentation with you. On Thursday the student presents his book to another staff member, and on Friday he chooses to either give his book presentation to his classmates or to another class of his own choice. You can count on reading enthusiasm to soar right along with your students' self-confidence!

Michelle Dunnam—Gr. 2
Haskell Elementary School
Haskell, TX

Mystery Readers

Mystery readers are a foolproof plan for spreading reading enthusiasm! Throughout the year make arrangements for your students' parents and a variety of other community members to read aloud to your class. If desired, provide each reader with a list of suggested literature and request that each guest confirm in advance his or her reading selection to avoid repetitions. On the day that a mystery reader is scheduled to visit, write the words "Mystery Reader" on the chalkboard. Students will anxiously anticipate the mystery reader's visit. With this plan students are exposed to a variety of books and reading styles, and they quickly discover that books are enjoyed by many people!

Krista K. Zimmerman—Gr. 3
Tuckerton Elementary School
Tuckerton, NJ

Bookish Vests

Your youngsters will be dressed for reading success when they wear these student-decorated vests. For each student sew a simple fabric vest or cut a vest from a large paper grocery bag. Personalize the inside of each child's vest; then store the vests for safekeeping. You will also need a supply of patches cut from iron-on Pellon® (for fabric vests) or construction paper (for paper vests). Each time you wrap up a series of activities that relate to a specific book, have each student decorate a patch that highlights the book. To do this a student uses colorful markers to label his patch with the book's title and author, and then he illustrates her favorite scene from the book. If students are decorating fabric vests, collect the completed patches and iron them onto the vests at a later time. Students can glue the paper patches in place themselves. Your students will love wearing these vests and sharing the attached book recommendations with others.

Sandy Greensfelder—Gr. 1
Naples Elementary
Naples, Italy

Reading Through Your State

Promote a love of literature with a state reading campaign! Create a simple outline of your state that shows each county; then duplicate and distribute a class supply of the resulting map. Or enlarge and post one map for the entire class. The goal of this reading project is for students to read their way through their home state. To do this, allow students to color in one county for every 30 minutes (or other designated time increment) of independent reading. The project is complete when the state map is entirely colored. If desired, plan to share interesting facts about each of your state's counties during the campaign. Once your state reading campaign is finished, challenge students to read their way through the United States—state by state. Wow! Reading really *does* take you places!

Karen Hertges—Gr. 3
C. F. S. Catholic Elementary School
Spillville, IA

Reading Can't Be Beat!

March your students into independent reading with this motivational display. Mount the title "Reading Can't Be Beat!" and several colorful music-note cutouts on a bulletin board. Also make a white construction-paper copy of the bookmark pattern on page 132 for each child. Have each student personalize a bookmark, cut out the shape, punch a hole in the top of the cutout where indicated, and tie a loop of yarn through the hole. Use pushpins to display the bookmarks as shown. When a child finishes reading a book, he writes the title and author of the book on his posted bookmark. When all the spaces on his bookmark are filled, he prepares another bookmark and uses a second loop of yarn to connect his two cutouts. Students will enjoy checking out each others' lists for book suggestions, and you'll have a complete record of each student's independent reading efforts. Now isn't that music to your ears?

Linda Madron—Gr. 1
Mary D. Lang Elementary
Kennett Square, PA

CHECK OUT THESE BO...
The Missing Fossil Myste...
Author: Emily Herman
Title: The Skates Of Uncle Richard
Author: Carol Fenner
Title:
Author:
Title:
Author:
Title:
Author:
Title:
Author:
Name: Zack Pilley

Bookmark Pattern
Use with "Reading Can't Be Beat!"
on page 131.

CHECK OUT THESE BOOKS!

Title: _____

Author: _____

Title: _____

Author: _____

Title: _____

Author: _____

Title: _____

Author: _____

Title: _____

Author: _____

Title: _____

Author: _____

Name _____

Cozy Collectible

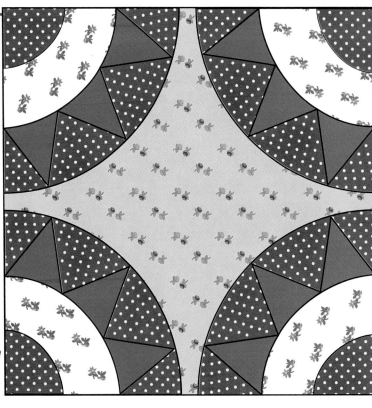

Ideas For Threading Quilts Through Your Curriculum

When the chill of winter seems like it's too much to bear, wrap up in this cozy collection of quilt-related activities. Your youngsters will warm right up to your handiwork—and you can create a colorful pattern of learning!

ideas by Susan Wilson

Class Friendship Quilt

Like quilts, thoughtful comments and compliments make people feel warm and cozy all over. As an introduction to your quilting activities, involve students in creating warm feelings for others by making a class friendship quilt. To begin, have each child trace a seven-inch-square tagboard template in the center of a nine-inch square of drawing paper. Then, using crayons or markers, have each youngster create a colorful design in the resulting border area. Next have each child write his name on a paper slip and deposit it in a designated container. Redistribute the paper slips, making sure that each student receives a name other than his own. Then ask each child to illustrate the classmate whose name he received in the remaining area of his quilt patch. Encourage students to make their drawings look as much like their classmates as possible by using appropriate colors for eyes, hair, etc. Before piecing the quilt together, ask each child in turn to show the class the quilt patch he created and to reveal whom it is, then to say one thing he especially likes about this classmate. Mount the completed quilt patches on a length of bulletin-board paper. Use a marker to draw "stitches" around each project; then attach crepe paper to the outer edges for a quilt border. Display the classy quilt for all to see!

Story Quilting

Remind students that, in addition to providing warmth, quilts are often treasured keepsakes of family memories. Some quilts tell a specific story, some provide information, and others hold numerous family memories. Unlike the real thing, these student-made story quilts can be made in a jiffy—and the results are quite impressive!

To make a story quilt, have each student fold a nine-inch square of drawing paper in half two times, then unfold the paper to reveal four equal-size sections. Then ask each child to choose four favorite parts from a story he has recently read or heard and to illustrate them on his paper. When his illustrations are complete, the child chooses an 11-inch square of colorful paper on which to mount his project. With his paper selection made, he can now use an appropriate color to draw stitch marks along the creases of his paper. Then he centers his project on the colorful paper square, glues it in place, and writes the story title on the bottom of the resulting quilt-patch border. If desired, bind the completed projects into a booklet. Now that's impressive handiwork!

The Josefina Story Quilt

A Cool Experiment

How do quilts provide warmth? Here's a cool way for youngsters to find out! Divide students into small groups and give each group two nonbreakable glasses filled with ice cubes, a cloth napkin, and a quilted pot holder (a mitt works best). Ask each student in a group to take a turn holding both the glasses. To do this she grasps one glass with the cloth napkin and the other with the quilted mitt, then holds both glasses for approximately 30 seconds. After each child has taken her turn, ask questions like "Which material did the cold travel through first?", "Why do you think one material was more effective at keeping the cold out than the other?", and "Which material would make the best covering on a cold winter night?" Help students conclude that the quilted material provides more protection because it has more than one layer. The extra layers keep body heat from escaping, therefore keeping a person warmer. Then give students the opportunity to examine a quilt close-up. Students will discover that a quilt has a top layer, an interlining or filling, and a bottom layer. So that's how a quilt provides warmth!

Patch by Patch

This manipulative center activity is fun for students to make and complete. Use pinking shears to cut a six-inch construction-paper square for each student. Have students label their squares with assigned words from a spelling or vocabulary list, then decorate the squares to resemble the patches of a quilt. Place the completed squares in a sewing basket. Have individual students place the words in alphabetical rows to create a class quilt. Or have a student pair take turns removing words from the basket to have each other spell or define.

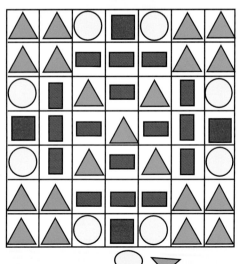

A Quilting Bee

In early America quilting bees were very popular. A group of women and girls would gather together at a friend's home and complete a quilt in one afternoon. Involve your students in a quilting bee with this cooperative group activity. Give each small group a supply of the following shapes cut from one-inch squares of construction paper: yellow circles, red squares, blue rectangles, and green triangles. Each group also needs a seven-inch square of one-inch graph paper. Then challenge each group to create a symmetrical design by gluing the shapes in the graph-paper sections. To make sure that its design is symmetrical, a group may wish to start at the corners and work toward the center, or vice versa. Have each group mount its resulting quilt patch on a nine-inch square and write the name of its quilt-block design on the bottom border of its quilt patch. Then have each group member sign the back of the group's patch and seal the completed project inside a gallon-size resealable plastic bag. To make an impressive quilt-block registry, create a desired cover and seal it inside a plastic bag, too. Then stack the completed projects, place the cover on top, and staple the project along the left-hand side.

Since dinner, singing, and dancing usually followed a real quilting bee, plan a follow-up celebration to your quilting bee activity. Plan to serve cookies and punch, and read aloud *Sam Johnson and the Blue Ribbon Quilt*. Your boys will especially enjoy this tale about a man who forms a for-men-only quilting circle after he is snubbed by the local women's quilting club!

Pretty Patchwork

Who would guess that creating a patchwork could motivate a student to do his best work, keep his desk clean, follow directions, and display positive friendship qualities? Believe it or not—it can! Of course this isn't just *any* patchwork! Give each student a copy of "Patches the Elephant" on page 136 and a construction-paper folder. Have each student glue his paper copy inside his folder for safekeeping, then decorate the outside of his folder as desired. Every day, before dismissal, ask each student to remove his folder from his desk, think about his school day, and color his elephant's patchwork clothing accordingly. You can count on positive behaviors and pretty patchworks, too! (For a fun literature link, read aloud *Elmer* by David McKee [Lothrop, Lee & Shepard Books; 1968]. Elmer is a bright-colored patchwork elephant who is tired of being different from all the other elephants—but not for long!)

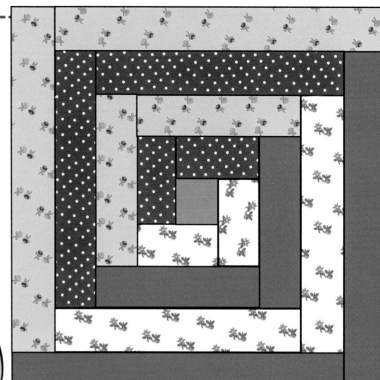

A Peek at the Past

Learning about traditional American quilt-block designs will fascinate your students. *The Quilt-Block History of Pioneer Days With Projects Kids Can Make* by Mary Cobb (The Millbrook Press Inc., 1995) is a brightly illustrated book that shows a variety of quilt designs and provides explanations of them. *Eight Hands Round: A Patchwork Alphabet* by Ann Whitford Paul (HarperCollins Publishers, 1991) is another excellent resource that includes illustrations and descriptions of 26 common patterns found in Early American quilts. Students will learn that quilt blocks were designed for a variety of reasons, including commemorating events in our country's history, honoring important individuals, and reflecting different aspects of pioneer life.

For this journal-making activity, ask each child to design a quilt-block pattern that reflects a special memory of her own. If desired write a student-generated list of special memories on the chalkboard to help students recall important happenings in their lives. Then have each child illustrate her special memory on a seven-inch construction-paper square and mount her work onto a nine-inch construction-paper square. Laminate the completed projects (front covers) and a class supply of nine-inch construction-paper squares (back covers) for durability. Then help each student staple several pages of eight-inch-square paper between her front and back journal covers. The resulting journals can be taken home. Suggest that students describe special events in their journals; then one day they'll have a quilt patch and a journal of memories to share with their own families.

Delicious Designs

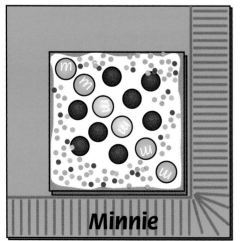

Minnie

For a fun culminating activity, have students make an edible quilt! To create her quilt patch, a student covers a graham cracker square with vanilla frosting. Then—using M&M's®, chocolate chips, red-hot candies, raisins, candy sprinkles, and other edible decorations—she creates a desired design atop her frosted cracker. Next the student writes her name near the lower edge of a plain-colored paper napkin. To create the class quilt, each child centers her decorated graham cracker atop her personalized napkin and places her resulting quilt patch on a designated table along with the quilt patches her classmates have made. After the students have viewed their collaborative work (and a few photos have been taken), let them retrieve their quilt patches and return to their desks to eat their tasty designs.

Quilts
Self-evaluation

Patches the Elephant

At the end of the school day,
think about the day you've had.

Use the color code.

Color a patch on the elephant
for each sentence that is true.

Color Code

red   = I followed directions.
blue   = I did my best work.
yellow = I was a good friend.
green = My desk is neat.

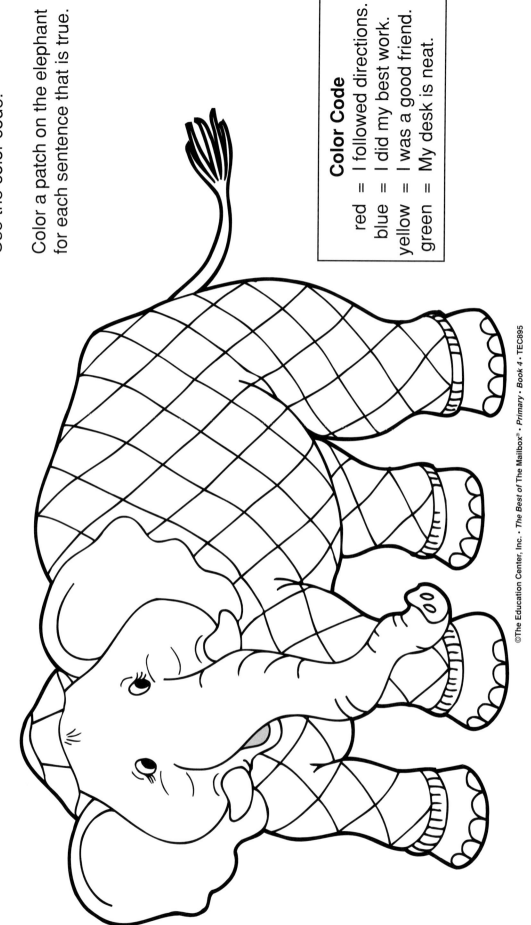

©The Education Center, Inc. • *The Best of The Mailbox® • Primary • Book 4* • TEC895

Animals in Winter

Have you ever seen a snake in a snowstorm? Or a butterfly in a blizzard? Probably not! Animals cope with wintry weather in a variety of ways. Use this cool collection of activities to enhance your study of animals in winter!

ideas by Jill Hamilton

A Cool Beginning

Begin your investigation into animals in winter with this little ditty. Students will enjoy developing motions to accompany each verse, as well as composing additional song verses. Fa-la-la!

Winter's Coming!
(sung to the tune of "Are You Sleeping?")

Winter's coming;
Winter's coming,
Little bear, little bear.
Time to take a long nap.
Time to take a long nap.
Please don't snore!
Please don't snore!

Winter's coming;
Winter's coming,
Snowshoe hare, snowshoe hare.
Time to change your fur coat.
Time to change your fur coat.
White looks nice!
White looks nice!

Winter's coming;
Winter's coming,
Tiny bird, tiny bird.
Time to migrate southward.
Time to migrate southward.
Flap your wings!
Flap your wings!

Winter's coming;
Winter's coming,
Busy squirrel, busy squirrel.
Time to gather acorns.
Time to gather acorns.
Save your food!
Save your food!

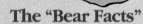

Workers	Sleepers	Tricksters
beavers	groundhogs	snowshoe hares
bees	bears	weasels
pikas	some bats	
deer	frogs	
foxes		

Outwitting Winter

How do animals outwit the most harsh season of the year? In a variety of ways! On a length of bulletin-board paper, draw a three-column chart like the one shown. Lead students to understand that "Sleepers" sleep through all or most of winter, "Tricksters" cleverly camouflage themselves for winter, and "Workers" stay busy all winter long (this category also includes migrators). As students discover how different animals cope with the cold, have them determine as a class which chart heading best describes each animal. Once a decision has been made, write the name of the animal on the chart. You can count on some lively discussions as students attempt to determine the most appropriate column for each animal they study.

The "Bear Facts"

These individual journals are the perfect place for students to record the "bear facts" about animals in winter! On construction paper make student copies of the journal cover on page 142. To make a journal for each child, cut out a duplicated cover, and staple a supply of writing paper between the cut-out cover and a construction-paper back cover of equal size. Have each child personalize a journal and store it in her desk. Also display a variety of books about animals in winter at a center or in your classroom library. As students learn new facts, they write the facts in their journals. Each week set aside time for students to share with their classmates the facts they've discovered. When it's time to wind up your wintry study, students can easily *see* all that they have learned!

Lisa Kelly—Gr. 1
Wood Creek Elementary School
Farmington, MI

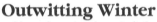

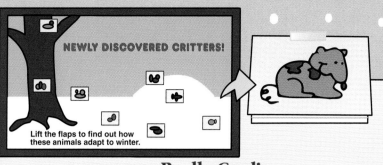

Really Cool!

It's amazing how animals' bodies can help them combat the cold! A *pika* stays warmer because it has a round body, short legs, and small ears. And in addition to a thick coat of fur, a pika also has fur on the bottoms of its feet for warmth! After students have investigated a variety of active winter animals, challenge them to create newly discovered animals that have their own unique ways of adapting to winter. Have each student illustrate his animal on a blank 5" x 7" card, then write how the animal copes with winter on a lined 5" x 7" card. Have each student glue his written description to a large winter scene like the one shown; then have him align his illustration over the description he wrote and use tape to secure the top edge of the illustration to the display. Students will enjoy viewing and reading about these *cool* animals with the extraordinary features!

Hibernation Know-How

Students may initially think that they'd like to *hibernate* through winter! But the thought of missing out on holiday dinners, birthday parties, and other special occasions will probably change their minds! Explain that true *hibernators* (like groundhogs, some bats and squirrels, snakes, frogs, and turtles) fall into a deep sleep and do not awaken (or eat!) until spring. Other animals, like bears and raccoons, also sleep through winter. But these animals sleep more lightly and may wake up on warm winter days and search for food.

Use this fun-to-sing song to teach students about some snoozing animals. For more frosty fun, enlist your students' help in creating additional song verses.

Wintertime Sleepers
(sung to the tune of "There's A Little White Duck")

There's a little brown bear sleeping in a cave,
A little brown bear sleeping in a cave.
He ate and he ate, and he stored up fat.
He may sleep 'til spring; just imagine that!
There's a little brown bear sleeping in a cave.
Sleep, little bear, sleep.

There's a little green frog sleeping in the mud,
A little green frog sleeping in the mud.
She swam to the bottom and she dug right in,
Deep down in the mud where she'll breathe through her skin.
There's a little green frog sleeping in the mud.
Sleep, green frog, sleep.

There's a little groundhog sleeping in a burrow,
A little groundhog sleeping in a burrow.
He crawls from his burrow and he looks around.
If he sees his shadow, he goes back underground.
There's a little groundhog sleeping in a burrow.
Sleep, groundhog, sleep.

Cynthia Payne and Robin Pranga
St. Peters, MO

Cleverly Camouflaged

What do snowshoe hares, weasels, and birds called *ptarmigans* have in common? They all stay active in winter and—turn white! This change of color allows the animals to blend in with their snowy winter surroundings. Making a sliding camouflage card, like the one shown, is a fun and effective way for a student to view this clever winter trick. Give each student a white construction-paper copy of page 140. Instruct each student to color the series of four tree trunks brown, then use brown to color the partial tree trunks and barren trees shown on the smaller card. Next instruct each student to color the remainder of the smaller card, carefully choosing his colors so that the season listed at the bottom of each illustrated column is reflected (for example, the animals would be white in winter and brown in summer). To assemble his sliding camouflage card, the student cuts on the dotted lines and weaves the smaller illustrated card through the trees as shown. By horizontally sliding his smaller card back and forth, the seasons change right before the youngster's eyes!

Peekaboo!

This peekaboo booklet project is sure to make a lasting impression on your youngsters! On the chalkboard write a student-generated list of animals that seek winter shelter underground, at the bottoms of lakes and ponds, in dens, or in caves. Give each child a white construction-paper copy of page 141 and ask him to choose one animal from the list. Then have each student illustrate the animal he chose in the blank space, describe what the animal does during winter on the writing lines, complete the title, and write his name on the provided line. Next have each student cut around his project on the bold lines. Demonstrate how to accordion-fold each end of the project (along the thin lines) as shown in the illustration. Provide assistance with this step as needed.

To make a booklet cover, have each student fold in half a 7¹⁄₂" x 10" sheet of white construction paper, trim the corners of the paper that are not on the fold (cutting through both thicknesses), and unfold the paper. The student then illustrates a desired scene on the resulting oval shape and cuts along the center crease. To complete his peekaboo project, the student aligns and glues each resulting cover to his folded project. Peekaboo!

Elizabeth M. Chappell—Gr. 2
Altura Elementary
Aurora, CO

On the Move!

Some animals survive winter by *migrating* or "traveling to other places in search of food and warmer conditions." When spring comes, these animals return to the homes they left behind. The booklet project on pages 142 and 143 introduces students to five migrating animals. Make student copies of both pages on white construction paper. Distribute page 143. Read aloud each description and invite students to speculate which animal is being described. Then distribute the animal pictures from page 142. Ask each student to color, cut out, and glue each picture in the corresponding box on page 143. To complete the project, a student personalizes the booklet cover, cuts on the dotted lines, stacks the resulting pages beneath the cover, and staples his project together.

Feeding the Birds

Your students are sure to enjoy this unique measurement and graphing project, and so will the birds! In advance nail three disposable, aluminum pie tins to a length of scrap wood (at least three feet long). You will also need three different kinds of birdseed (for example, cracked corn, millet, and black oil sunflower seeds). First ask three students to each measure one cup of a different birdseed and carefully pour the seed into an empty pie tin. Then carefully carry the resulting bird feeder outdoors. If possible position the feeder so that it can be viewed from a classroom window. Before the end of the day, retrieve the feeder and ask three different students to remove and measure the birdseed that remains in each pie tin. Then, on a graph like the one shown, indicate how much of each kind of birdseed *was eaten* that day. The following day, enlist your students' help in refilling each pie tin with one cup of seed, and repeat the process. Encourage students to observe what types of birds and other critters are nibbling on the seeds and to comment on the popularity of the different types of seeds. Continue measuring and graphing the birdseed that is eaten each day for as long as desired. However, make plans to continue feeding the birds (and other visiting critters) until nature's supply of food is once again available.

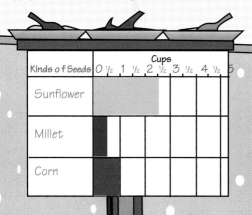

Kinds of Seeds	Cups									
	0	½	1	½	2	½	3	½	4	½	5
Sunflower											
Millet											
Corn											

What About People?

As your youngsters become knowledgeable of how animals adapt to winter, they may start to wonder if they do things differently in winter too! Invite students to describe how winter changes their lives, and list their ideas on the chalkboard. Then use these ideas to make a class book titled "People In Winter." To do this, have each youngster copy a different idea from the class list onto a sheet of white construction paper. Then ask each child to illustrate the idea she copied, suggesting that she include herself in her illustration. If Old Man Winter usually brings snow to your area, have students repeatedly dip the eraser ends of their pencils in white tempera paint and dab a flurry of flakes atop their projects. Laminate the completed book pages for durability; then bind them between two student-decorated covers. Display the resulting book in your class library for all to enjoy.

I wear a hat and a coat to stay warm.

Name _____

Cleverly Camouflaged Critters

(winter)   (summer)   (winter)   (summer)   (winter)   (summer)

Note to teacher: Use with "Cleverly Camouflaged" on page 138.

Glue right half of cover on this tab.

A _____ in Winter

by _____

Glue left half of cover on this tab.

Journal Cover and Picture Cards

Use the journal cover with "The 'Bear Facts' " on page 137.

The "Bear Facts" About Animals in Winter

Name _____

Use the picture cards with "On the Move!" on pages 139 and 143.

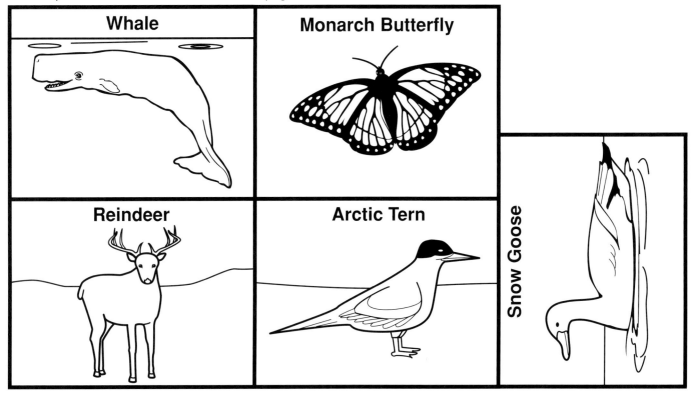

Whale

Monarch Butterfly

Reindeer

Arctic Tern

Snow Goose

Name _____

On the Move!

©The Education Center, Inc.

Glue picture here.

In the winter my food is covered with snow. I must migrate to places where I can find food to eat.

Glue picture here.

I migrate farther than any other bird. I live near the North Pole. Each winter I fly to the South Pole.

Glue picture here.

Snow is part of my name but I still get cold! When winter comes, I fly south to warmer areas.

Glue picture here.

Each fall I gather with many other butterflies just like me. Then we fly south for the winter.

Glue picture here.

My home gets cold in the winter. Sometimes it even freezes! Every winter I swim to warmer waters.

A Man and His Dream

Martin Luther King Jr.

Use these engaging activities to teach students about a remarkable American who dreamed that one day there would be peace and justice for all.

Provide students with a snapshot of the boyhood, adult life, and dreams of Martin Luther King Jr. by reading aloud one or more of the following books:

Happy Birthday, Martin Luther King • Written by Jean Marzollo • Illustrated by J. Brian Pinkney • Scholastic Inc., 1993
A Picture Book of Martin Luther King, Jr. • Written by David A. Adler • Illustrated by Robert Casilla • Holiday House, Inc.; 1991
Martin Luther King Day • Written by Linda Lowery • Illustrated by Hetty Mitchell • Carolrhoda Books, Inc.; 1987

Speaking Out

Dr. King felt that it was his responsibility, or duty, to speak out against violence. Ask students why they think he felt this way. Help them understand that the safety and well-being of the world is everyone's responsibility, and that every person can contribute to making a positive difference. Invite students to share any concerns they have about the world. List their ideas on the chalkboard. Then ask each child to choose one concern from the list and design a poster that speaks out against it. Remind students that when Dr. King spoke out, he always provided peaceful solutions. Ask students to do the same. After each child has presented his poster to the class, showcase the messages around the school.

Festive Timelines

In celebration of Dr. King's birthday (celebrated the third Monday in January), have each child make a festive four-event timeline of his life. To make a timeline, fold a 3" x 12" strip drawing paper in half twice; then unfold the paper to reveal four equal sections. Leaving a half-inch margin at the top of the strip and working in chronological order from left to right, label each section with a different event.

To transform the project into a birthday cake look-alike, accordion-fold the strip and decorate the front of the folded project to resemble a birthday cake. Next cut out four candle flames from scrap paper and glue them to the tops of four $1/2$" x 2" construction paper strips to make lit candles. Unfold the timeline and glue one candle to the top of each section, positioning the candles so that when the project is refolded, each one is visible. Now that's a timeline that's even better than a piece of cake!

Happy Birthday, Dr. King!

In 1929 Martin Luther King Jr. was born in Atlanta, Georgia.

In 1953 Martin got married to Coretta Scott.

In 1963 he gave a speech in Washington, DC, about his dream for the future.

In 1968 Martin Luther King Jr. was killed.

Gifts of Peace

Martin Luther King Jr. dreamed of the day when all people could live in peace. Invite students to describe what *peace* means to them. (*Somewhere Today: A Book of Peace* by Shelley Moore Thomas [Albert Whitman & Company, 1998] is an exceptional book that is perfect for prompting thoughts of peace and reinforcing the concept of nonviolence.) Encourage plenty of discussion and accept all answers. Then, on provided paper, have each child describe and illustrate one gift of peace that she would give the world. Invite each child to share her gift with the class. Then collect the papers and publish them in a class book titled "Our Gifts of Peace."

Footsteps to Follow

When Martin Luther King Jr. graduated from college, he decided to become a minister just like his father. Explain to students that because Martin admired his father so much, he was proud to follow in his footsteps. Ask each student to label a colorful footprint pattern with the name of a person she admires and hopes to grow up to be like. After she cuts out the pattern, have her copy, complete, and illustrate the sentence "When I am older I hope to follow in the footsteps of [name or description of person] because..." Display the completed projects on a bulletin board titled "Footsteps We Hope to Follow."

When I am older I hope to follow in the footsteps of Grandpa Keller because he helps sick kids. He is a doctor.

Keeping the Dream Alive

Dr. King's dream included freedom, peace, and understanding. He dreamed that one day all people would love and help each other. Review Dr. King's dream with the class and challenge students to explain how they can contribute to keeping it alive. Help them realize the impact that their thoughts and actions have on his dream. Next give each child a copy of page 146 and a 6" x 18" strip of red or blue construction paper. To complete the project, a child writes an ending for each sentence and colors the portrait of Dr. King. Then he cuts along the bold lines, positions the pieces on his construction paper in a pleasing manner, and glues them in place. If desired, have each child hole-punch the top of his project, thread a length of curling ribbon through the holes, and tie the ribbon ends. Suggest that each child display his project at home to remind him of the important role that he plays in keeping Dr. King's dream alive!

145

Martin Luther King Jr. Project

A	Man	With	a	Dream
	Martin		Luther	King Jr.

1. Dr. King dreamed that _____

2. He also hoped that _____

3. I can keep his dream alive by _____

4. Learning about Dr. King has taught me _____

'Tis the Season for... Mittens

There's no doubt about it—after you and your students try this cross-curricular unit, you'll be smitten with mittens!

ideas contributed by Vicki Mockaitis Dabrowka and Laura Wagner

WRITING
Warm Up to Winter!

Showcase warm thoughts with this marvelous mitten display! To begin, have youngsters brainstorm ways to keep warm in cold weather, and record their responses on the chalkboard. Then give each student two copies of the blank mitten on page 150. A child cuts out his mittens and places them on his desk so that the thumbs point to each other. On one mitten, he writes and completes the sentence "To warm up on a snowy day…" He illustrates his sentence on the other mitten. Next the youngster glues each mitten onto colored construction paper. He cuts around each shape, leaving a narrow border. Then he tapes one end of a length of yarn at the bottom of each mitten and glues bits of cotton to each cuff. Display the mittens with the title "Warm Up to Winter!" Now that's a handy way to pair writing and illustrating!

To warm up on a snowy day, I drink hot chocolate with marshmallows.

CRITICAL THINKING
"Thumbody" Was Thinking!

Why are mittens designed to keep thumbs free? Challenge students to find out with this hands-on partner activity. First, write on the chalkboard a student-generated list of activities that require the use of hands, such as sharpening a pencil and tying a shoelace. Next give each student pair a mitten and a sock. The twosome chooses three of the activities from the list. Then each partner tries each one—first with the sock on his dominant hand and then with the mitten on his dominant hand. Ask each student pair to share what it discovered. Then invite youngsters to tell why they think mittens have separate thumbholes. Lead students to conclude that thumbs help people grasp objects and make precise movements. When mittens were invented, "thumbody" was really thinking!

PHYSICAL EDUCATION
Snowball Catch

Cooped up inside for recess? Then energize your youngsters with a quiet flurry of activity! Roll together two white socks to create a ball. Ask one student to be the scorekeeper for the first round. Instruct each remaining student to put on a pair of mittens and form a large circle. Explain that for this game, students must be silent—just like falling snow. To play, the students toss the ball to each other as many times as they can without dropping it, while the scorekeeper silently counts the catches. When a student drops the ball, the scorekeeper announces the total number of catches. Then she and the last student who successfully caught the ball switch roles. Continue with additional rounds for a blizzard of fun!

MATH
Mitten Math

Mittens and math go hand in hand with these skill-based ideas!

- **Problem Solving:** Give each student four blank mitten patterns (page 150) to cut out. Have her color two red and two blue. Then ask the youngster to use the cutouts to solve this problem: *How many ways can two red mittens and two blue mittens be lined up on a clothesline? Draw pictures or write a list to show as many ways as you can.*

- **Skip Counting:** Invite students to predict how many mitten pairs are needed for a class supply. Then give each student two copies of the small mitten pattern (page 150) to color and cut out. Each student, in turn, glues her mitten cutouts onto a long paper strip and writes the cumulative total of mittens below her pair. Have students compare the final total with their predictions. Then display the strip throughout the season for a handy skip-counting reference.

2   4   6

LANGUAGE ARTS
A Picture-Perfect Retelling

A mitten unit wouldn't be complete without the traditional tale *The Mitten*. Use Jan Brett's enchanting version for this picture-perfect retelling activity. To prepare, visit Brett's Web site at www.janbrett.com/postcards/1cardpick_mitten.html and print an enlarged picture of each character from *The Mitten*. Then copy a class supply of each one. Next read aloud Brett's *The Mitten: A Ukrainian Folktale* (G. P. Putnam's Sons, 1989) and give each youngster a set of character pictures. A child cuts out each picture, mounts it on construction paper, and cuts it out again. Then he tapes a tongue depressor to the back of each cutout to create a stick puppet. Pair students and have each partner take a turn retelling the story. Then, if desired, arrange for each student to retell the tale for a child in a lower grade.

COOKING
Mouthwatering Mittens

Here's a fitting (and yummy!) recipe for your mitten study. To add an extra special wintry touch, serve with hot chocolate. Mmm!

Mouthwatering Mitten Cookies
For one cookie:
a personalized 5" square of foil
$3/8$" slice of refrigerated sugar-cookie dough*
various cookie decorations (colored sprinkles, mini baking chips, raisins)
ungreased baking sheet

Directions:
1. Working on the foil, gently shape the slice of cookie dough into a mitten shape.
2. Decorate the cookie.
3. Place the project on the baking sheet and bake as directed.

  * One roll of dough makes approximately 24 cookies.

Pam Crane

Mitten Messages

What better way to celebrate individual differences this winter than with warm fuzzies? On white construction paper, copy a class supply of the blank mitten pattern on page 150. Label one for each child. Remind students that everyone has unique skills and talents. Also explain that complimenting a person on his special gifts is often described as giving the person a warm fuzzy. Then, as you distribute the mitten patterns, ask each student to secretly design a warm fuzzy for the classmate whose mitten he receives. (Make sure no child has his own.) To do this, a student writes a positive note about the classmate on the mitten and then he cuts out the shape. Next he colors the blank side of the cutout and decorates it with cotton. Ask each student to secretly deliver the warm fuzzy to his classmate's desk within a designated number of days. You can be sure each recipient will glow with pride and happiness.

SOCIAL STUDIES
Looks Like Mitten Weather!

Compare temperatures across the United States with this graphing activity. Make a class-size graph and label it with the names of several large cities from across the nation and a series of upcoming dates. Help students locate each city on a U.S. map. Next have them predict which cities might have below freezing temperatures for the featured dates. Draw and color a small mitten shape near the name of each selected city.

Each day, have different students use a newspaper or visit a weather Web site such as http://cirrus.sprl.umich.edu/wxnet to determine the temperature in each city. Have them record the temperatures on the graph and then draw and color a mitten shape in each box that shows a below freezing temperature. After the graph is completed, ask students to analyze the data and compare it with their predictions. Then help them draw conclusions about winter temperatures in different parts of the country.

	Jan. 10	Jan. 11	Jan.12	Jan. 13	Jan. 14
Miami, FL	57°F	60°F	58°F		
Topeka, KS	30°F	29°F	35°F		
New York City, NY	20°F	19°F	19°F		
Dallas, TX	45°F	45°F	47°F		
Seattle, WA	29°F	27°F	26°F		

READING
Wintry Reading

Invite students to cozy up to these mitten-related titles!

The Mitten Tree
Written by Candace Christiansen
Illustrated by Elaine Greenstein
Fulcrum Publishing, 1997

Gabby Growing Up
Written by Amy Hest
Illustrated by Amy Schwartz
Simon & Schuster Books for Young Readers, 1998

A Christmas Star
Written by Linda Oatman High
Illustrated by Ronald Himler
Holiday House, Inc.; 1997

The Woodcutter's Mitten: An Old Ukrainian Tale
By Loek Koopmans
Crocodile Books, USA, 1995

Order books online. www.themailbox.com

Mitten Patterns

Use with the ideas on pages 147–149.

Missing Mittens

Oh, no! The kittens have lost their mittens.
Help the kittens find them.
Read the clues.
Color the mittens.

Snowball's mittens have
- stripes
- stars
- no dots

Color them yellow.

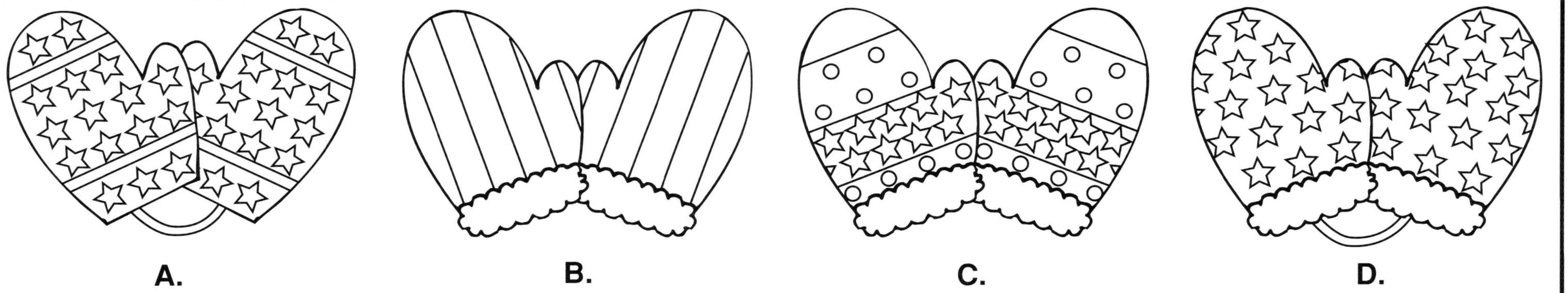

Tiger's mittens have
- stars
- a string
- no stripes

Color them blue.

Puff's mittens have
- a fluffy trim
- stripes
- no dots

Color them red.

D.

C.

B.

A.

Bonus Box: Color the extra mittens any color you choose. On another sheet of paper, write three sentences to describe them. Think about who might own them. Then draw and color a picture of the owner.

The Pioneers
Understanding Pioneer Life

Hungry for land of their own and reaching for the promise of a better life, thousands of frontier Americans journeyed westward. Their bravery, resolution, and daring spirit would forever distinguish America as a nation of courageous trailblazers. Use this sampling of activities and literature suggestions to explore the lifestyle and spirit of our country's first pioneers. Wagons ho!

ideas contributed by Susan K. Wilson

The Pioneer Spirit

The chance for a better life enticed countless frontier Americans to head westward. By the early 1800s, pioneer families were crossing the Mississippi River and the Great Plains to claim fertile land for farming. In 1843, after the first wagon train reached Oregon, thousands more settlers set their sites west of the Rocky Mountains—an area that very little was known about.

Discuss this pioneer spirit with your youngsters. Invite students to describe the characteristics and qualities that pioneers shared. Then ask students how they would feel if their families told them that next month they were moving to a remote island in the West. The island is a peaceful place (there is no violence there) filled with beautiful forests and fertile farmland. Each family will be given a tract of land on which to build a house. The trip westward will be a dangerous one, as it was for the pioneers. And, like the pioneers, each family can take very few of their personal belongings. Encourage students to share their feelings about the planned trip. Would they be willing to sacrifice their belongings? Do they think the advantages of the trip outweigh the risks involved? No doubt early Americans asked themselves similar questions. Not all Americans moved westward. Find out why your students think some early Americans chose to stay in the East.

Preparing for the Trip

After a decision to move westward had been made, the hard work began. Many families held yard sales to sell their belongings. The money a family earned was used to purchase a covered wagon, a team of oxen, and supplies for the trip. A covered wagon was not a traveling house. Instead it was a storage space for all the things the family would need for the long trip west, as well as supplies for a year in the wilderness.

The size and condition of a pioneer wagon depended upon what each family thought was suitable and what it could afford. To give students an idea of how a standard-size wagon box measures up, have each of several small groups of students use chalk and a yardstick to draw a 4' x 10' rectangle on an outdoor blacktop surface. Or use masking tape to create a rectangle of this size on your classroom floor. Students will quickly realize that space was limited inside a covered wagon.

One-of-a-Kind Wagons

Pioneer wagons were as unique as the pioneers themselves—they came in all sizes and shapes. But one thing all wagons had were canvas covers that protected the wagons' contents. Some families painted pictures and/or slogans on their wagon covers so that friends could identify them on a crowded trail.

This art activity gives students an opportunity to design unique covered wagons! To make the box of the wagon, trim a 4" x 9" rectangle of brown construction paper into a desired shape. Position the resulting shape about three inches from the lower edge of a 12" x 18" sheet of light blue construction paper. Glue the shape to the paper, leaving the top edge unattached. Next bring together the short ends of a 9" x 12" sheet of white paper and slide the paper behind the unglued portion of the wagon box. Use a pencil to mark the length of the box on the white paper; then remove the paper and trim it to create an appropriately sized wagon cover. Decorate the resulting wagon cover as desired. Next glue together the short ends of the wagon cover, and then glue the ends behind the top edge of the wagon box. Also glue the wagon cover to the blue paper where the surfaces meet. Use brown paper scraps to create a wagon tongue and other desired wagon decorations. To make each wagon wheel, arrange seven wagon-wheel pasta shapes as shown and glue them in place. To complete the project, use crayons or markers to draw a team of oxen, pioneers, and other desired background scenery.

Nancy MacKenzie, Lafayette, IN

Inside the Wagon

Even though the contents of each family's covered wagon varied, all wagons contained similar items. Remind students that space on a covered wagon was limited before asking them to brainstorm items that most pioneers probably packed. Write their ideas on a length of bulletin-board paper. The student-generated list should include food, tools, spare wagon parts, medicines, cooking utensils, a shotgun, a lantern, and necessary clothing and bedding. Most pioneer families carried at least one trunk of treasured items that would not be opened until the family reached its destination. Fragile items like eggs and beloved pieces of china were often stowed in large barrels of cornmeal or flour to reduce breakage. Some pioneers even packed plant cuttings that could be used to start orchards out West.

Post the student-generated supply list and encourage youngsters to recommend modifications as they learn more about the pioneers. If desired, each week incorporate several of the listed items into the class spelling list. Students can also alphabetize the listed items for extra credit.

Saying Good-Bye

A grand good-bye party was frequently held before a family began its westward journey. Friends, neighbors, and relatives of the family who were staying behind organized the gathering, and often the women would meet secretly to plan a special quilt for the family. The quilt—called an *album quilt*—was created as a colorful reminder of the loved ones left behind. Your students will enjoy making an album quilt for a student, student-teacher, or other special person who is leaving your school or classroom.

To make an album quilt, distribute student copies of page 157. Have each child complete a quilt block by following the directions and then cutting out his quilt block and mounting it on an eight-inch construction-paper square. Glue the completed quilt blocks on a length of bulletin-board paper. Use a marker to draw stitches around the projects. The resulting album quilt will be a cherished keepsake to the person who is moving away.

Wagons Ho!

Most pioneers traveled in groups called wagon trains. The members of each wagon train elected a wagon master (or captain) and promised to abide by the decisions that the master made. Daily responsibilities of the wagon master included determining the order of the wagons and deciding when the wagons would stop. A wagon master usually chose members to scout the area around the wagon train, keeping an eye out for trouble. When meat was needed, the wagon master would ask a few members to hunt for wild game.

During your pioneer studies, arrange student desks in small groups to form wagon trains. Every morning have each wagon train elect a different wagon master until each member of the wagon train has had a turn. Each wagon master may assign a different responsibility to each member of the train. Job titles might include messenger, supply person, paper collector, and line leader.

Pioneer Diaries

How do historians know so much about pioneer life? Thank goodness many pioneers kept diaries in which they described daily happenings and special events. For a fun writing activity, ask your students to keep diaries like the pioneers did. Make a diary for each student by stapling a supply of writing paper between construction-paper covers. Have each child personalize the cover of her resulting diary; then each day provide time for students to write in their diaries. Encourage students to describe daily happenings and special occasions, and remind them that each entry should be dated. At the end of your pioneer study, urge students to reread their diary entries. They may be surprised by what they wrote—perhaps they will even be reminded of events that they might otherwise have forgotten!

Challenges of the Trail

Pioneers faced many challenges along the trail. Perhaps the largest challenge was the environment itself. If pioneers began their journey too early in the year, the ground was soggy and the grass (for feeding livestock) was sparse. If they waited too late, the grass was scorched from summertime temperatures and the mountain passes were likely to have blizzard conditions. In addition to the challenges of day-to-day weather, numerous other hardships and calamities occurred. What happened when a wagon lost a wheel, wagon-train members became sick, or an unexpected attack from a wild animal occurred? On strips of paper write a variety of challenges that the pioneers could have faced. Fold the strips in half and store them in a designated container. Each day ask a different student to remove one strip and read aloud the pioneer challenge of the day. Ask students to consider different ways the pioneers might have handled the challenge. Before the students leave for the day, ask them to share their ideas. Encourage discussion among the students. When possible, relate the pioneer predicaments to your students' everyday lives.

A thunder-and-lightning storm scares the oxen.

A wheel falls off a wagon. There isn't a spare.

The water keg is almost empty.

Pioneer Day

Experiencing a variety of pioneer activities is a fun way for students to learn about pioneer life on the trail. Invite students to wear pioneer-type clothing to school on a designated day. Explain that pioneers wore plain and durable clothes—clothing that could get plenty dirty and last for months! Boys usually wore shirts and pants, and girls wore skirts or dresses. Everyone wore strong and sturdy shoes for walking. To protect their eyes from the sun, boys wore wide-brimmed hats and girls wore bonnets. (No sunglasses allowed—they weren't invented yet!) Then throughout the day, engage students in a variety of pioneer-related activities like the ones included in "Suggested Activities for Pioneer Day." Be sure to enlist your youngsters' help in gathering needed supplies and make advance arrangements for parent assistance.

Jennifer Griffin—Gr. 3, Carroll Elementary
Southlake, TX

Suggested Activities for Pioneer Day
Chores

Everybody worked hard during the long days of traveling west—even the children. The following suggestions offer ways to have your students experience a few chores for which pioneer children were responsible:

Milking a cow: Have students write directions for how to milk a cow.

Fetching water: Have small groups of students transport partially filled buckets of water from "the river" to the "covered wagon."

Food preparation: Enlist students' help in preparing "Lunch on the Trail."

Washing dishes: Have students clean up after lunch.

Collecting firewood: Ask students to collect trash from the playground.

Shaking out blankets: Bring some blankets to school and let each child take a turn shaking out a blanket outdoors.

Make Homemade Butter

Divide students into small groups. For each group, remove the lid from a small clear (and clean) jar. Partially fill the jar with whipping cream and securely reattach the jar lid. (For quicker results, bring the whipping cream to room temperature before you begin.) In turn, have each group member firmly grasp the jar and vigorously shake it for one minute, while his group members watch the clock. Continue in this manner for about ten minutes; then have each group examine the contents of its jar. The students should see several pale yellow clumps (butter) in the liquid. Have students resume shaking the jar in the manner previously described until one large lump of butter is formed. To separate the butter from the liquid, pour the contents of each group's jar into a nonmetal strainer and rinse the butter with cold water until the rinse water is clear. Students may taste the butter at this point, or you may wish to work a little salt into the butter for a better taste. If desired, serve the butter atop cornbread! (See "Lunch on the Trail.")

Lunch on the Trail

After approximately five hours on the trail, most wagon trains stopped for about an hour. The noon meal eaten by most families was leftovers from breakfast, so no cooking was needed. For your pioneer lunch, consider serving baked beans, cornbread (with your homemade butter!), beef jerky, dried-fruit trail mix, and water. This meal gives students an idea of the kinds of foods eaten by pioneers. For a more authentic setting, spread blankets on the classroom floor and invite students to eat their lunches atop the blankets.

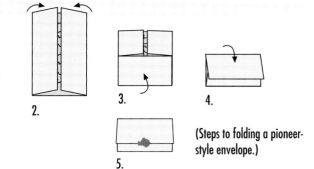

3.

4.

2.

5.

(Steps to folding a pioneer-style envelope.)

Writing a Pioneer Letter

Sometimes pioneer children wrote letters to friends they had left behind. Have each student write a newsy letter to a family member or friend. To do this, provide each student with a sheet of blank paper. Ask students to use pencils to write their letters, since you haven't any quill pens. Then explain that only one side of the paper may be written on. If a student needs more room, he gives his paper a quarter-turn and writes across the lines he's already written—just like the pioneers did! When the letters are completed, demonstrate how to fold a pioneer-style envelope (see the provided diagrams). Have each student address his resulting envelope, then seal it with a length of tape or a sticker. Be sure to point out that a pioneer would have used a blob of candle wax to seal his letter.

Singing Around The Campfire

Sometimes at night, after all the chores had been completed, pioneers gathered around a campfire to sing songs and dance. Usually there was someone in the wagon train who knew how to play a harmonica or a fiddle. For a fun finale to your day, gather students around an imaginary campfire and sing several of your students' favorite songs.

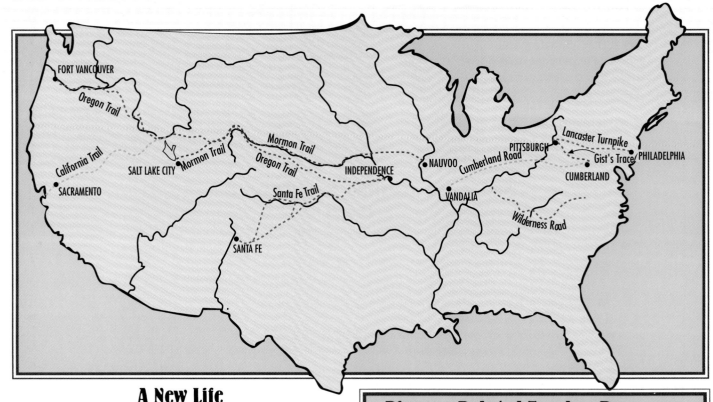

A New Life

Pioneer families rejoiced when they reached their new homesites, even though there was plenty of hard work ahead of them. There was land to clear, a home to build, and crops to plant. Pioneer families worked long and hard, yet they found time to enjoy themselves, too. One way they did this was by planning gatherings that combined their chores with social events. These gatherings were called work-play parties.

Plan to culminate your pioneer unit with a work-play party. On the designated day of the party, have small groups of students work together on a pioneer-related project. Projects might include creating student-made maps of pioneer trails (like the one shown), writing pioneer-related reports, or planning pioneer-related presentations. When the "chores" are done, have each group share the fruits of its labor; then let the party begin! Plan for students to play a favorite class game, socialize, sing a song or two, and enjoy some fresh-baked gingerbread and chilled apple juice.

Pioneer-Related Teacher Resources

A Pioneer Sampler: The Daily Life of a Pioneer Family in 1840
Written by Barbara Greenwood & Illustrated by Heather Collins
Houghton Mifflin Company, 1994
    Details of pioneer family life are described in this account that effectively weaves factual information into a fictional story. A comprehensive index makes this informative volume very teacher-friendly.

Daily Life in a Covered Wagon
Written by Paul Erickson & includes photographs and illustrations
The Preservation Press, 1994
    Join the Larkin family as they set out from Indiana for their new farmstead in Oregon. This first-rate resource is packed with intriguing facts about pioneers and kid-pleasing photographs and illustrations.

The Prairie Schooners
Written & Illustrated by Glen Rounds
Holiday House, Inc.; 1968
    A well-written account of the first wagon trips to the Oregon Territory. Includes a detailed map of the Oregon Trail.

Making An Album Quilt

To make a quilt block:
1. Find the large square in the center of the quilt block.
2. Write your name on the solid line.
3. Draw and color a picture of yourself in the rest of the large square. Show yourself doing something that you like to do.
4. Color the rest of the quilt block. Use two or more different colors.
5. Cut out the quilt block and glue it to a piece of construction paper.

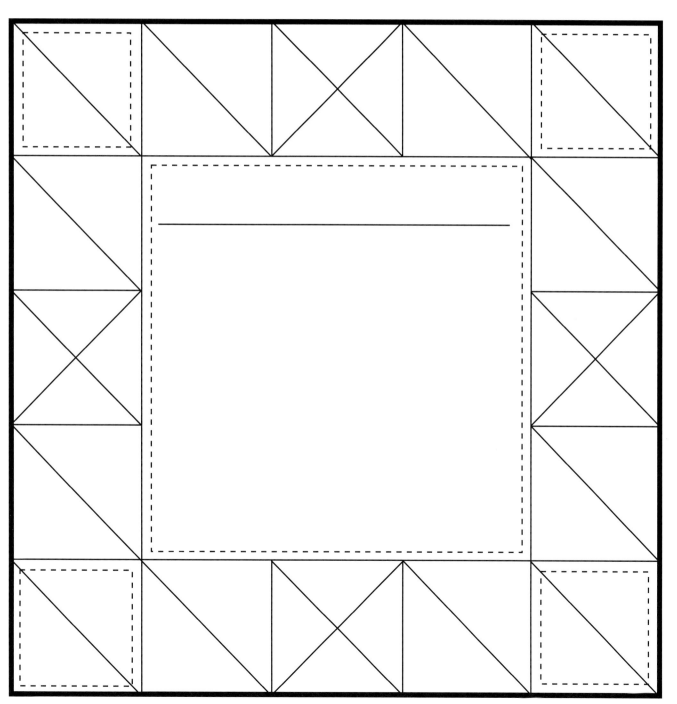

Note to teacher: Use with "Saying Good-Bye" on page 153. Each child will also need an eight-inch square of construction paper.

The Home-School Link
Forming Teacher-Parent Partnerships

Teachers know it, administrators know it, and parents know it too—in order for students to reach their full academic potential, it's vital to develop a cooperative link between home and school. Use these subscriber suggestions to strengthen the link you're forming with your partners in education.

Parent/Teacher Notebook

Believe it or not—it *is* possible to communicate with parents *every* day! Have each child supply a spiral notebook to use only for home-school communications. Before students arrive each morning, write a message on the chalkboard that you'd like students to relay to their parents such as, "Ask me about using a dictionary," or "Our play performance will be Wednesday at 2:00 P.M." When students arrive, their first task of the day is to open their communication notebooks to the next available writing space, write the current date, and copy the message from the chalkboard. Collect the notebooks; then, during the day, quickly check each notebook for a parent message. Sign or initial each notebook as you review it, and write a response, a note of praise (or concern), and/or a reminder as needed. At the end of the day, send the notebooks home with the students. Each student is responsible for sharing his notebook with his parent(s), obtaining a parent's signature and a written message or response (if applicable), and returning the notebook the following school day. Parents will greatly appreciate having an established method of communication, and you will enjoy the ease of implementing such a valuable communication link. As an added bonus, the repetitive routine quickly develops student responsibility.

Elaine Kaplan—Grs. 1–2, Laurel Plains School, New City, NY
Cynthia Pfaff—Gr. 1, Prairie View Elementary, Eden Prairie, MN

Feb. 18, 2002
We experimented with sound today. Ask me about it!
I was amazed by Willy's knowledge of vibration and sound! He is really loving school.
Janice Wilson
EK

Feb. 19, 2002
Our class is having a puppet show on Friday. The principal is coming!

March 14, 2002

Dear Dad,
This week I learned about the solar system. I can tell you the names of all the planets.
Your son,
James

Friday Letter

Keep parents informed about school happenings with weekly letters that are composed and written by their youngsters. Set aside time every Friday for students to review the past week and write friendly letters to their parents. In advance inform parents that you would like them to respond to the letters they receive each Friday. This can be done by writing a letter or comments on the back of the student-written letter. Each Monday, set aside time for students to share the letters and comments their parents have written. Then collect the letters and file them in individual student folders. At the end of the year, bind each child's letter collection between laminated covers. Each resulting booklet is an excellent record of the progress a child has made, as well as a cherished keepsake of his school year.

Paulette Hammond—Gr. 1, Chalkville Elementary School, Birmingham, AL

Outline for Parents

Keep parents informed of what children are learning in your classroom with an attractive, easy-to-read outline. Send an overview of a new theme or project to parents in the form of an outline, and invite them to share information relating to the theme. Parents are eager to share their knowledge and skills when asked, and they enjoy being updated on their children's studies.

Dawn Moore—Gr. 1, Mount View Elementary, Thorndike, ME

Monthly Collaborations

Each month provide an opportunity for students and parents to collaborate on a just-for-fun art project. Consider sending home a seasonal tagboard pattern (like a heart for February or a shamrock for March) for parents and students to collaboratively decorate with tactile objects like seeds, beads, popcorn, cereal, or painted pasta. Include decorating suggestions if desired. Whatever the project, you'll be promoting positive parent-child interactions. Encourage students to bring their made-at-home masterpieces to school so that you can display them for all to see.

Wendy James—Grs. 2–4 Chapter I
Kingsland Elementary School
Kingsland, AR

Designed by: Don and Kim Benz and Katie

Reading Buddies

Date: _____ March 27, 2002

I listened to my child, _____ Winston _____,

read the story titled _____ Gregory Cool

This is what I observed: Winston liked this story a lot. I believe his oral-reading skills are improving. He seems to be reading with more expression. We are still working on observing all punctuation! I am sure we'll read this story several times!

(Please comment on your child's reading improvement and enthusiasm for reading. Also note any trouble areas or concerns such as long pauses or incorrect letter sounds.)

Jenny Wilson
Parent Signature

Reading Buddies

Reading at home can be a rewarding experience for parents and their children. It can also give parents valuable insights into their children's reading capabilities. Strengthen your communication with parents by inviting them to share these insights with you. Each week send home one or more copies of the form on page 160 with each child. Ask that parents listen to their children read student- or parent-selected stories before they complete their forms. If desired, reward those children who return their forms by a designated day of the week. This weekly program encourages students and parents to read together at home, and it relays a message to parents that you value and encourage their input.

Linda P. Lovelace—Gr. 3, Halifax Elementary School, Halifax, VA

Literature-Response Journals

Broaden your students' literature experiences by providing an opportunity for parents and students to respond to literature together. To create a literature-response journal for each student, secure several sheets of notebook paper in a two-pocket folder. Attach a duplicated parent note to the left-hand pocket of the journal. In the note explain that each week students will select different stories to be read at home with their parents. Further explain that when a story has been completed, the parent and child should each write an entry in the journal that describes his or her feelings about the story. Distribute the journals. Have each student personalize the front cover of his journal, then choose a literature selection for the week and place it in a journal pocket.

Have students return their literature-response journals to school each week on a designated day. Review and initial the journal responses—adding brief comments if desired. At the end of the day, have the students carry home their journals along with their new reading selections for the week. This sharing of literature provides wonderful opportunities for extended learning.

Marjorie S. Grutzmacher—Gr. 1, West Side Elementary, Sturgeon Bay, WI

A TALE OF

Parent Survival Guide

Plan for good parent communications by preparing a parent survival guide. Create a booklet that includes your homework policy, discipline plan, and grading guidelines. Also include an outline of skills and topics that will be taught during the school year. Complete the guide by adding techniques and suggestions for ways parents can help their children at home, enrich shared reading, and nurture positive study habits. Present the booklet to parents at the beginning of the school year so that parents are immediately informed—leaving fewer questions as the year progresses.

Debra K. Gustavson—Substitute Teacher, Webster & Siren School Districts, Danbury, WI

Reading Buddies

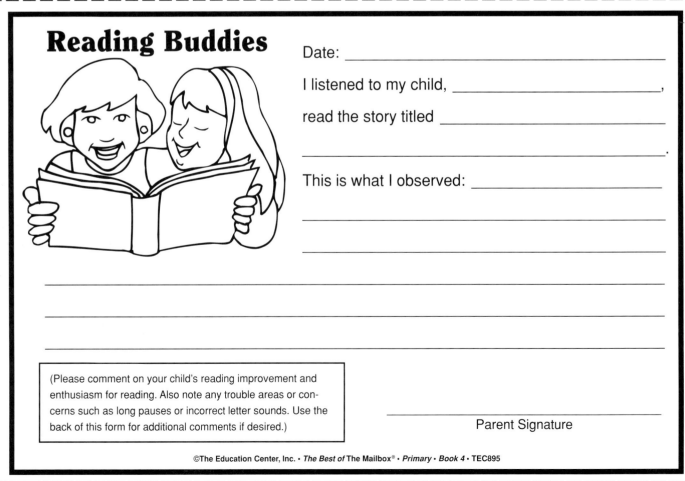

Date: _____

I listened to my child, _____,

read the story titled _____

_____.

This is what I observed: _____

_____

_____

_____

_____

_____

(Please comment on your child's reading improvement and enthusiasm for reading. Also note any trouble areas or concerns such as long pauses or incorrect letter sounds. Use the back of this form for additional comments if desired.)

_____
Parent Signature

Reading Buddies

Date: _____

I listened to my child, _____,

read the story titled _____

_____.

This is what I observed: _____

_____

_____

_____

_____

_____

(Please comment on your child's reading improvement and enthusiasm for reading. Also note any trouble areas or concerns such as long pauses or incorrect letter sounds. Use the back of this form for additional comments if desired.)

_____
Parent Signature

The Sensational Six
Hands-On Activities for the Food Guide Pyramid

March is National Nutrition Month®, so why not enhance your nutrition unit by serving up a hearty helping of these appetizing Food Guide Pyramid activities? They're the perfect recipe to make your youngsters sizzle with nutritional information and beg for seconds!

ideas by Jill Hamilton and Lisa Kelly

Did You Know?

The U.S. Department of Agriculture developed the Food Guide Pyramid to encourage people to improve their diets. It is based on the USDA's research on what foods Americans eat, what nutrients are in these foods, and how to make the best food choices. The Pyramid is an outline of what to eat each day. A range of servings is provided for each major food group. It is not always necessary to eat the maximum servings suggested. The number of servings that a person needs depends on how many calories her body requires. Almost everyone should have at least the lowest number of servings in each range.

Personal Pyramids

Get to the point of the Food Guide Pyramid with the three-dimensional project on page 164. Distribute a white construction-paper copy of the Pyramid pattern to each student. As a class, read each food group and the number of recommended servings; then enlist students' help in naming foods from each group. If desired, have students illustrate one food per group. Explain to students that the foundation of the Pyramid—*bread, cereal, pasta,* and *rice*—should constitute the basis of our diets. Foods at the top of the Pyramid should be eaten proportionately less. When all six groups have been discussed, each student finishes personalizing his Pyramid by completing each sentence and adding his name. Then he cuts out the pattern on the bold lines, folds on the dotted lines, and tapes the tab inside the Pyramid. Encourage students to display their Pyramids on their desks and use them as references during other nutrition activities.

Collecting Servings!

Students will be chomping at the bit to play this self-made center game! To make the game, divide students into six groups and assign each group a different food category. Distribute a stack of discarded magazines, a supply of blank index cards, glue, and scissors to each group. Instruct students to cut out food pictures that represent their assigned categories and glue them on individual index cards. Collect the cards and program the back of each one with the corresponding food group. Laminate the cards for durability; then store them in a decorated lunch bag. Place the bag, crayons, and a class supply of the gameboard (page 165) at a center.

To play the game, each student needs a gameboard. One player removes the food cards, shuffles them, and places them back in the bag. Each player, in turn, draws a card and identifies its food category; then she flips the card to check her answer. If the player is correct, she colors one serving in that category on her gameboard. The student then places the card in a discard pile. If a player gives a correct answer but all the circles for that category are colored, her turn is over. The first player to color all the circles—or servings—on her gameboard wins!

161

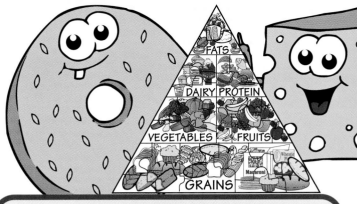

The Fabulous Five

Each of the five major food groups shown on the Pyramid provides nutrients that are needed for maintaining good health. The foods in the sixth group—*fats, oils,* and *sweets*—are needed for a balanced diet, but contain fewer essential nutrients. After sharing the nutrition notes shown with your students, assign a different food group to each of five student teams. Instruct each team to design a colorful poster that promotes the benefits of eating foods from its assigned food group. Provide the teams with white poster board or tagboard, construction paper, markers, and other poster-making supplies. Set aside time for each team to present its poster and talk about the benefits that its food group can provide. Then display the appetizing projects in the school hallway so others can view the benefits of eating a varied diet.

Pyramid Puzzle

Take the puzzle out of the Food Guide Pyramid with this center activity. Cut a large triangle from poster board. Divide the triangle into six sections to resemble the Food Guide Pyramid; then label each section with its corresponding food group. Enlist students' help in cutting food pictures from discarded magazines. Then glue each picture to its corresponding food group on the Pyramid. Laminate the Pyramid for durability before cutting it into puzzle pieces. Store the puzzle in a resealable plastic bag at a center for hands-on exploration. Encourage students who especially enjoy putting together the class puzzle to make their own Food Guide Pyramid puzzles.

Melons are pink.
Berries are blue.
You should eat fruits.
They are good for you!

Jill

Poetry Placemats

Writing poems about the Food Guide Pyramid is twice as much fun when the poems become placemats! Set the mood by reading aloud a few of your favorite food-related poems. (*Food Fight: Poets Join the Fight Against Hunger With Poems to Favorite Foods* edited by Michael J. Rosen [Harcourt Brace & Company, 1996] is a delightfully entertaining collection of food poems.) Then display sample formats like the ones shown below for students to use as they write their poems. To make a placemat, a student glues her written work to a 12" x 18" sheet of colorful construction paper and adds desired decorations. Laminate the projects for durability. Set aside time for each student to share her prose before she takes her placemat home. Time to set the table!

Nutrition Notes

Grains
- provide carbohydrates, a body's main source of fuel
- provide B vitamins that are necessary for normal growth
- provide fiber for good digestion
- provide minerals needed for bone formation

Fruits And Vegetables
- provide vitamin A that is necessary for tissue growth and good vision
- provide vitamin C that is necessary for healing and for healthy bones, teeth, and skin
- provide fiber that helps in the digestion process
- provide vitamin E that helps maintain cell membranes

Dairy Products
- provide proteins needed for cell growth and maintenance
- provide minerals needed for bone formation
- provide vitamins that help in digestion and using energy efficiently
- provide calcium that is needed for bone growth and development, muscles, and blood clotting

Protein Foods
- provide building materials of the body called *amino acids*
- aid tissue growth and the maintenance of cells
- provide energy-producing B vitamins
- provide minerals, like iron, that help the blood provide the tissues with oxygen and prevent anemia

_____ are _____.
_____ are blue.
You should eat _____.
They are good for you!

Try some _____;
Eat some _____.

Taste a _____;
Chomp a _____.

Munch on _____;
Feast on _____.

Gobble _____;
Nibble _____.

Be a smart kid;
Use the Pyramid!

A Ravenous Creature

Set the stage for this nutrition letter-writing activity with an oral reading of "Hungry Mungry" from Shel Silverstein's poetry collection *Where The Sidewalk Ends* (HarperCollins Children's Books, 1974). Hungry Mungry is a child who will eat anything in sight: his extremely large dinner, his parents, the U.S. Army, the universe, and even himself! At the conclusion of this poem, list the *foods* Hungry Mungry ate for dinner on the chalkboard. Ask student volunteers to mark through the unhealthful foods on the list. Then have each student write a letter to Hungry Mungry encouraging him to eat a healthful, balanced diet. Remind students to tell him about the Food Guide Pyramid too. After students complete the letters, mount them on a bulletin board titled "Eat Up This Advice, Hungry Mungry!"

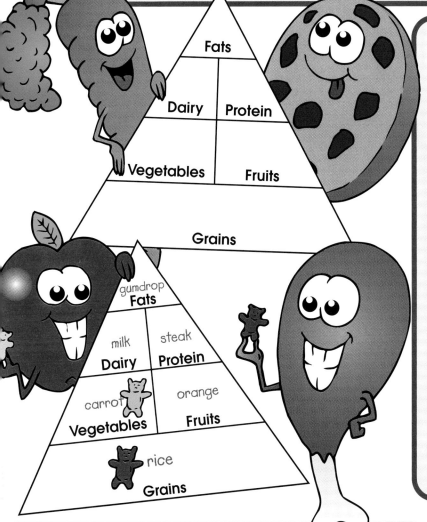

Tasty Lotto

This Food Guide Pyramid game is sure to satisfy your students' appetite for reviewing the food groups. Write a student-generated list of healthful foods on the chalkboard—one food per student. (Be sure foods from each food group are included.) Have each student select a different food from the list, then write its name on one side of an index card and two clues describing it on the other side. Ask that one clue refer to the Food Guide Pyramid. Collect the completed cards and place them in a container. Next give each child a Pyramid-shaped lotto board like the one shown. Instruct him to program each section with a corresponding food from the chalkboard. Also give each student six small, edible snacks to use as markers.

To play the game, draw a food card from the container and read the clues aloud, taking care not to reveal the answer on the back of the card. If a student has this food on his gameboard, he covers it. The first student to cover all his foods announces, "I'm full!" Then he verifies the covered foods by naming them. If time permits have the winning student call the second game. When game time is over, collect the lotto boards for later use and invite students to eat their game markers.

Appetizing Riddles

Add a touch of creative thinking to your Food Guide Pyramid activities with this riddle-writing project. For each student cut a triangle from the front cover of a folded 9" x 12" sheet of white construction paper (see the illustration). To begin, read aloud a food-related riddle book, like *What Am I?: Looking Through Shapes at Apples And Grapes* by N. N. Charles (The Blue Sky Press, 1994), for writing inspiration. Then challenge each student to create a riddle that includes a reference to a food group. Next the child copies his riddle on the front of his construction-paper card. Inside the card he illustrates the answer, making sure that when the card is closed, part of his illustration is seen through the cutout. Allow time for students to share their food riddles with their classmates. If desired, bind the riddles into a class book titled "Food for Thought." Place the book in your classroom library for all to enjoy!

I am sweet.
I have seeds.
I am in the vegetable group.

What am I?

watermelon

Pattern
Use with "Personal Pyramids" on page 161.

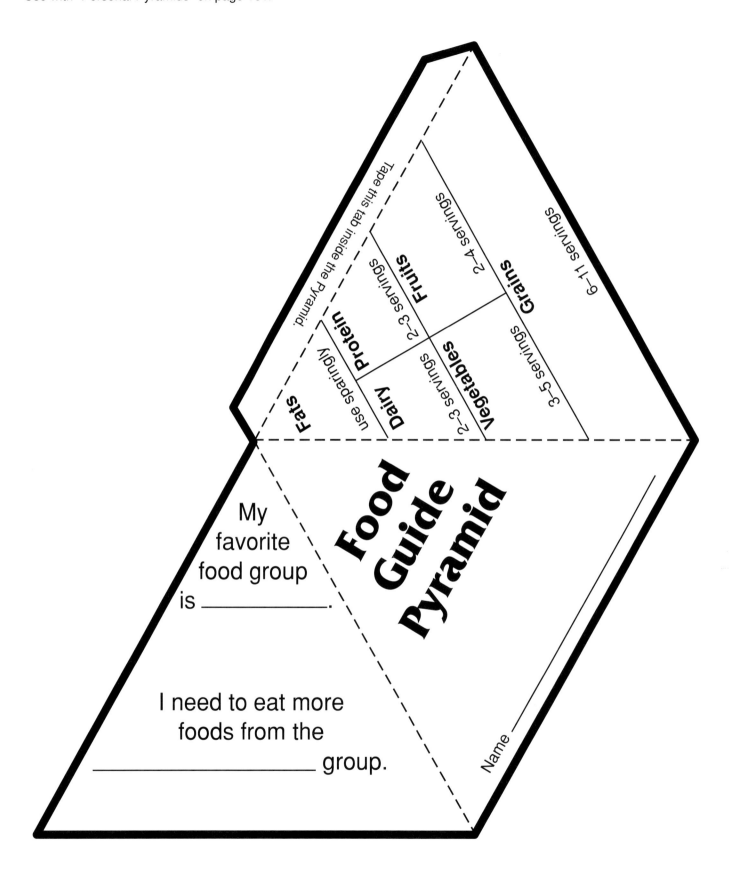

Tape this tab inside the Pyramid.

Grains
6–11 servings

Fruits
2–4 servings

3–5 servings

Vegetables
2–3 servings

Protein
2–3 servings

Dairy

Fats
use sparingly

Food Guide Pyramid

My favorite food group is _____.

I need to eat more foods from the _____ group.

Name _____

Collect All the Servings!

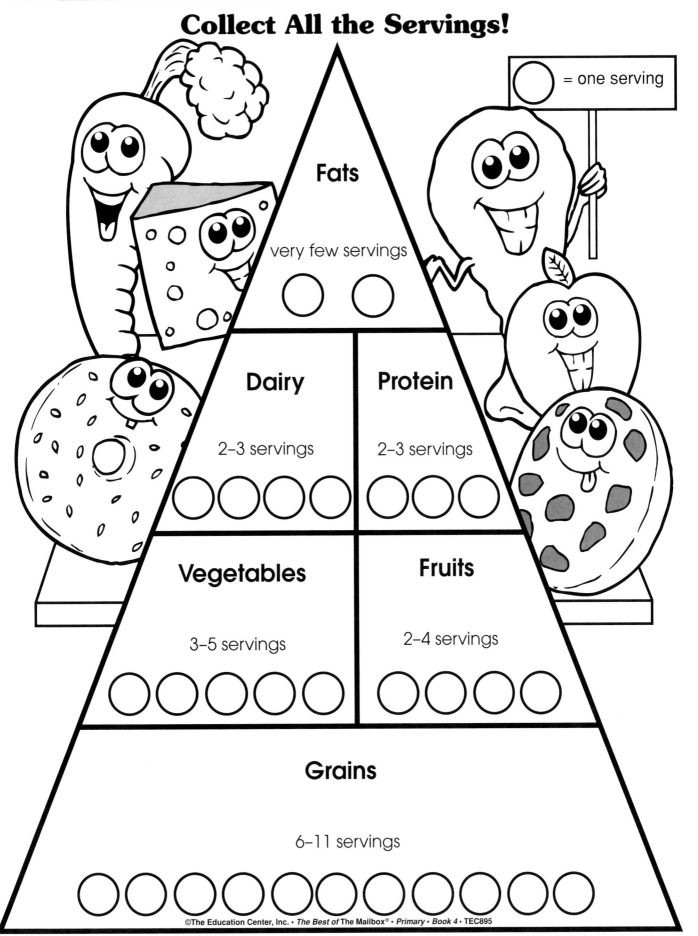

Fats

very few servings

= one serving

Dairy — 2–3 servings

Protein — 2–3 servings

Vegetables — 3–5 servings

Fruits — 2–4 servings

Grains — 6–11 servings

GETTING A JUMP ON PUNCTUATION AND CAPITALIZATION!

If you're constantly looking for ways to improve your students' punctuation and capitalization skills, this collection of teacher-tested ideas will have you jumping for joy!

"BETCHA" CAN'T PUNCTUATE JUST ONE!

Whet your youngsters' appetites for punctuation with this center activity! Gather three disposable bowls and a clean and empty potato chip can. Label the rim of each bowl with a different ending punctuation mark. Then, from yellow construction paper, cut out potato chip shapes that are slightly smaller than the opening of the can. On each chip cutout write a sentence with no ending punctuation; then write the missing punctuation mark on the back of the chip. Laminate the chips for durability and store them in the can. Place the can of chips and the three bowls at a center. A student empties the can of chips and sorts them into the corresponding bowls, checking her work as she goes. Punctuation practice has never been more appetizing!

Lou Murray, Browns Summit, NC

The boy was having a bad day.
When will the dog stop barking?
Look out!

PICTORIAL PUNCTUATION

Here's a picture-perfect way for students to show off their punctuation skills! Mount an interesting photograph or magazine picture near the top of a sheet of chart paper. Draw a vertical line down the left edge of the paper; then, in the resulting column, write an ending punctuation mark on each writing line. Make a second sentence chart in the same manner, making sure that you have one labeled writing line per student. Display the sentence charts in easily accessible locations and place a marker near both of them. Each child takes a turn writing a sentence on one line of a chart. His sentence must relate to the chart's picture and end with the provided punctuation. After all the students have contributed their sentences, post the charts at the front of the room and invite each child to read aloud the sentence that he wrote. Now that's picture-perfect punctuation practice!

MAGNETIC MARKS

This approach to punctuation practice attracts plenty of student interest! Label several individual poster-board rectangles with ending punctuation marks, laminate the rectangles for durability, and attach a self-adhesive magnetic strip to the back of each one. Display the magnetic marks around the border of your chalkboard (or another magnetic writing surface). Write a series of kid-appealing sentences on the chalkboard that do not include ending punctuation. Then have a different student read aloud each sentence and attach the needed magnetic mark. At the end of the lesson, return the magnetic manipulatives to the edge of the writing surface. Plan to repeat the activity periodically, using different sentences each time. In addition, occasionally omit ending punctuation from other chalkboard writing, and let the student who discovers your *error* attach a magnetic mark where it is needed. Who knew punctuation practice could attract so much attention!

Shirley Luetkemeyer—Gr. 1, Null Elementary School, St. Charles, MO

ON THE LOOKOUT

Spark an interest in punctuation and capitalization practice by having students politely point out someone else's mistakes—yours! Have each student program a blank card with the word "Oops!" and store it in her desk. Periodically, as you're writing on the chalkboard or using the overhead projector, omit one or two capital letters and/or punctuation marks. When a student spots a mistake in your writing, she quietly displays her "Oops!" card. Call upon one of your eagle-eyed proofreaders to correct each mistake. Students enjoy and benefit from applying their knowledge of punctuation and capitalization. Plus this approach is a great way to keep students tuned in and motivated!

Sr. Barbara Flynn—Gr. 2
St. Raphael School
Bridgeport, CT

STAYING IN TOUCH

This whole-group activity keeps students in touch with capitalization and punctuation. Give each student a golf ball–sized portion of modeling clay. On the chalkboard write a sentence that is missing a capital letter or a punctuation mark. Challenge each child to identify the missing element, then use his clay to form it. Quickly verify the youngsters' work; then, as the students roll up their clay, erase the sentence and write another one. Repeat the activity as many times as desired. You can bet students will be eager to get their hands on this review activity!

Kristin McLaughlin—Gr. 1
Amity Elementary Center
Douglassville, PA

ZEROING IN

Students zero in on punctuation and capitalization errors with this kid-pleasing activity. Each morning, before the class arrives, write two sentences on the chalkboard that contain punctuation and capitalization errors. As part of your regular morning routine, select a different student to zero in on each sentence. Each child who is chosen uses colorful chalk to draw a large zero around every mistake she sees in the sentence. Then she explains the mistake before she corrects it. This daily grammar review will quickly become a class favorite!

adapted from an idea by Sr. Maribeth Theis—Gr. 2
Mary of Lourdes Elementary
Little Falls, MN

Check It!

✓ Does each sentence begin with a capital letter?

✕ Does each sentence end with a punctuation mark?

M Did you read each word you wrote? Does your writing make sense?

CHECK IT OUT!

Promote a habit of capitalizing and punctuating with a class poster of self-editing guidelines. Custom-design the poster to match your youngsters' writing needs and preface each guideline with a different symbol, letter, or number. Display the poster in a prominent classroom location. Before a student turns in his work, he refers to the poster. After he follows each guideline and makes any needed corrections to his work, he draws the corresponding symbol in the lower left-hand corner of his paper. This clever approach to the editing process teaches students to be responsible for their work.

Mary Anne Pisano—Grs. K–8 Reading Specialist
Lancaster–Lebanon I. U. #13
Manheim, PA

Much Ado About BUGS!

Feeling a little squeamish about exploring the sometimes creepy, sometimes crawly world of bugs? Put your worries aside. This collection of activities is swarming with fascinating facts and enticing activities your students are sure to love. So when you're ready to get the dirt on bugs—dig in!

ideas by Michele Converse Baerns and Jill Hamilton

A Buggy Beginning

Bugs are really amazing animals! To begin your bug unit, enlarge each of the six bug patterns on page 171 onto a 12" x 18" sheet of construction paper. Trim around each shape; then cut each shape into four or five large puzzle pieces. Divide students into six groups and give each group a set of puzzle pieces to assemble. After a group has constructed its puzzle and identified the resulting bug, give the group a book that contains information about its bug and some colorful markers. Challenge the group to label the back of each piece of its puzzle with a different fact about its bug. Set aside time for the groups to share their completed projects. If desired, laminate the completed puzzles and place each puzzle in a large resealable plastic bag. Store the puzzle bags at a center for further hands-on exploration!

What Is an Insect?

Share these ten fascinating facts about insects with your students:

- Insects are small animals with six legs. Insects use their legs to run, walk, jump, dig, and even sing!
- There are approximately five million different kinds of insects in the world.
- Insects wear their skeletons on the outside of their bodies. This *exoskeleton* protects an insect's body like a suit of armor.
- An insect has a heart, a brain, a tummy, air sacs, and nerves. These organs don't look like human organs, but they function in similar ways.
- All insects are cold-blooded. Sometimes big bugs shiver before they fly. What they are really doing is warming up their flight muscles so they'll work!
- Most insects live short lives. Some adult insects only live a few hours!
- Insects do not have noses; they smell with their antennae, or feelers.
- Insects can see, smell, and hear some things that humans cannot.
- Scientists are not sure what insects can feel.
- Insects communicate with each other in a variety of ways. Some insects flash lights, sing, dance, or use smelly chemicals to signal each other.

The Insect Issue

Even though insects—the largest animal group—are often very beneficial to humans, they are not very popular. Take a class poll before you continue your study of insects to find out if your youngsters are in favor of saving or stomping out the insect population. Record the outcome of the class poll; then have students vote again at the completion of the unit. Have students compare the outcomes of the two polls and comment on any changes of opinion.

An Insect's Body

The body of an insect has three sections. The *head*—where eyes, antennae (feelers), and jaws are found; the *thorax*—where legs and wings are attached; and the *abdomen*—where food is digested and eggs are produced. To reinforce the body parts of an insect, have each student make a marshmallow bug. To make the edible bug, use peanut butter to join three large marshmallows—the head, thorax, and abdomen. Poke six pretzel-stick legs into the thorax and two shoestring-licorice feelers into the head. Use peanut butter to attach two mini chocolate-chip eyes to the head and a pair of potato-chip wings (or wing shapes cut from Fruit Roll-Ups®) to the thorax. There you have it, a bug that's good enough to eat!

Parts Are Parts

	People Parts	Insect Parts
head	1	1
chest	1	1
arms	2	0
legs	2	6
antennae	0	2
abdomen	1	1
nose	1	0

Us and Them

Even though humans are very different from insects, they have several similarities. Enlist your students' help in creating a chart like the one shown; then complete the chart under your students' direction. After discussing the similarities and differences that humans and bugs share, use the chart as a springboard for a bug-related math lesson. Pose questions like "If two insects are in a room all alone, how many legs are in the room?" and "If you're counting noses, how many would you count on three people and three insects?" Student interest in math is sure to soar!

Checking Out Bugs

One of the best ways to learn about bugs is to watch them! For this activity each child needs a nine-ounce plastic drink cup, an eight-inch section of nude-colored panty hose that is knotted at one end, and a wooden craft stick. Have each student slide the section of hose onto her cup as shown, then set the craft stick inside the resulting bug observatory.

Take your students outdoors and ask each child to put several blades of grass, a small rock, and a piece of twig in her bug observatory. Then instruct each student to remove her craft stick and search for a bug. (The craft stick can be used to scoop the bug into its temporary home.) Once a student places a bug in her observatory, she slides the panty-hose covering over the top of her cup to prevent the bug's escape. Back in the classroom, distribute copies of page 172 and give each child (or group of children) a hand lens. Ask the students to complete the activity as they observe the bugs they've collected. As soon as everyone has completed the activity, take the students back outdoors so they may return the bugs to their natural habitats. Plan to repeat this activity several times during your study of bugs.

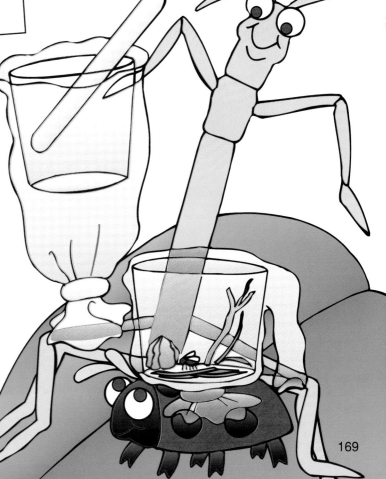

Pam Crane

Figuring With Fireflies

On a summer night, a field of fireflies is a sight to behold! These amazing insects—which are actually beetles, not flies—make a bright greenish light that can be seen at night. *Ten Flashing Fireflies* by Philemon Sturges (North-South Books, 1995) is a fun way to introduce students to these amazing critters. Hidden in the repetitive language of the story are simple addition and subtraction concepts. Plan to read the story more than once. Then during your second or third reading, have volunteers write number sentences on the chalkboard that represent the firefly activity shown in the book's illustrations. Discuss the number patterns that are observed. Later display the book at a center along with a supply of bookmaking materials. No doubt several of your enthusiastic entomologists will be interested in creating variations of this unique bug book.

Ladybug! Ladybug!

Ladybugs have very few enemies. Gardeners love them because they feast on aphids and other insects that attack plants. And the ladybugs' bright colors warn other insects to leave them alone. You see, ladybugs have a very nasty taste! Your students will enjoy creating and eating ladybug cookies as they further investigate these friends of the garden. However, unlike the real thing, these ladybugs are very tasty!

Ladybug Cookies

Ingredients:
1 vanilla wafer
mini chocolate chips
red-, yellow-, or orange-tinted frosting
thin black licorice

Directions:
Spread a layer of frosting on the wafer. Use a length of licorice to visually divide the cookie in half. Position mini chocolate-chip spots and licorice antennae. Yum!

Sarah Ann Lamb—Gr. 3, Lewis Carroll Elementary
Merritt Island, FL

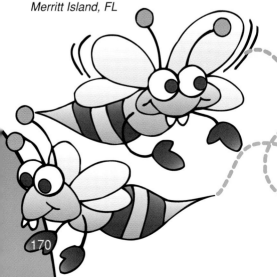

Busy Bees

Bring new meaning to the phrase "busy as bees" with a study of these ever busy insects. Bees—specifically honeybees—are the only insects that produce food eaten by man. Make a list of the different jobs that bees do; then have students compare the chores of these honey-makers to their daily jobs. Wow! Bees really are busy! The next time you have the opportunity to commend your youngsters for being as busy as bees, they'll know exactly what you mean!

Name _____

172

Insects
Bug observation sheet

Bug Watch

Carefully observe your bug. Follow the directions.

1. Write a number in each blank to tell how many parts your bug has:

____ head   ____ thorax
____ abdomen   ____ legs
____ antennae   ____ eyes
____ nose   ____ wings
____ mouth   ____ skeleton

2. Illustrate your bug.

3. Watch your bug carefully. Write what it is doing.

4. Draw a picture of your bug's natural habitat.

©The Education Center, Inc. • *The Best of The Mailbox*® • *Primary* • *Book 4* • TEC895

Note to the teacher: Use this activity with "Checking Out Bugs" on page 169.

Laugh and Learn With Poetry

We've packed a gaggle of giggles and endless learning opportunities into this one-of-a-kind poetry unit! Activities to use with any poem are featured below. One grin-inducing poem and activities to use with it are the focus of the following pages. Could there be any better way to celebrate National Poetry Month in April?

poems and activities by Geoff Mihalenko—Gr. 3
Frank Defino Central School, Marlboro, NJ

Pick Your Poem

Use these "verse-atile" activities with any poem and reinforce the featured language arts skills.

- **Context Clues:** Young detectives must rely on context clues to crack the case of the mystery words! Copy an entire poem, or selected stanzas from it, on chart paper. Use a sticky note to either partially or completely cover one word in each of several lines. Lead students in reading the poem aloud, pausing at each mystery word. Ask youngsters to predict the word by using context clues. Then, with great fanfare, remove the sticky note and reveal the mystery word.

- **Sequencing:** Create a poetic mix-up and reinforce sequencing skills in short order! Select a short poem or choose a stanza from a longer one. Use a wipe-off marker to write each line on a laminated sentence strip. Display the strips in order on a pocket chart. Point to every word as you read aloud each line with the students. Then scramble the strips and have the class direct you in sequencing them correctly.

- **Choral Reading:** Why not make oral-reading practice a group effort? Copy each stanza of a poem on poster-sized paper and then sequentially number the backs of the resulting posters. Divide students into the corresponding number of groups. Give each group a poster and provide time for reading practice. Then collect the posters and stack them in order on an easel, with the first stanza on top. The group who practiced the first stanza reads it aloud. Then move this poster to the back of the stack and continue with the remaining posters in a like manner. For more reading practice, redistribute the posters to different groups and repeat the activity as described.

Easy Answers
(page 175)

In this humorous poem, homework teaches a youngster an unexpected lesson. Use the prereading activity on this page to familiarize students with a variety of timesaving inventions. Then, after several readings of the poem, follow up with the remaining activities.

Prereading Activity
Timesaving Inventions

Since saving time is at the heart of "Easy Answers," a quick investigation of various timesaving machines in use today is in order. Provide a variety of discarded magazines, catalogs, and sales circulars. Have each child cut out a picture of a timesaving invention and glue it near the top of a sheet of writing paper. Below the picture have her write how this invention saves time and how life would be different without it. After each child shares her work with the class, introduce the poem.

Simple-Machine Search

The inventive student in the poem understands that a machine is designed to make life easier. What he hasn't figured out is how to build one! Explain that all machines are based on one or more simple machines. List the six types of simple machines and provide an example of each one. Next give each student a checklist like the one shown. Ask him to find at home or at school at least one example for each type of machine and then list the examples on his paper. To display the students' findings, use yarn to visually divide a bulletin board into six sections. Label one section for each type of simple machine. Give each child six white construction paper squares and have him label and illustrate each square with an example of a different simple machine that he found. Then have him mount his cards in the corresponding bulletin board sections. Now that's a simple-machine reference that really works!

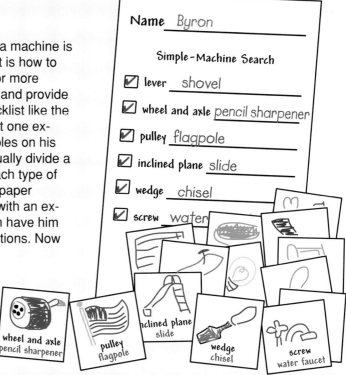

Name Byron

Simple-Machine Search
☑ lever shovel
☑ wheel and axle pencil sharpener
☑ pulley flagpole
☑ inclined plane slide
☑ wedge chisel
☑ screw water

lever
shovel

wheel and axle
pencil sharpener

pulley
flagpole

inclined plane
slide

wedge
chisel

screw
water faucet

Marvelous Motivation Machine

The machine in this poem doesn't help the youngster finish his homework, but this incentive program is sure to motivate your students to complete theirs! Decorate a box and lid to resemble a machine and label it "Homework Machine." Display the box near a poster titled "Homework Points." When a youngster completes her homework, she places it inside the Homework Machine and makes a tally mark on the poster. When you remove the homework from the box, add another tally mark for each paper that is completed neatly and accurately. After the class accumulates a predetermined number of points, award each student with a pass for a homework-free night or plan a special class activity. There's no doubt about it—doing homework pays!

HOMEWORK MACHINE

Easy Answers

I thought homework might be more fun
If I could quickly get it done.
So I made a speedy machine—
The neatest thing you've ever seen.

I built it using copper wire,
Some metal gears, a rubber tire.
It has a bell that rings on top
And flashing lights that never stop.

The next day when I went to school,
I acted very, very cool.
"My machine can do all my work,"
I thought to myself with a smirk.

When I got home, I took the stack
Of homework out of my backpack.
The most homework I'd ever seen—
I put it into my machine.

The lights began to blink and shine.
All systems seemed to work just fine.
The answers magically appeared.
I jumped for joy and then I cheered!

When morning came I wore a grin
As I handed my homework in.
I waited for my teacher's praise.
Instead I saw her eyebrows raise.

My new machine was fast, you see,
But it did not work carefully.
It made some mistakes in its haste,
And everyone knows: haste makes waste.

So thanks to my special device,
I had to do my homework twice.
Now I know it will always pay
To do it the old-fashioned way.

by Geoff Mihalenko

Note to the teacher: Give each student a copy of this page. Read the poem for enjoyment. Then challenge each student to circle the pairs of rhyming words on the page. Next have her draw a star beside each circle that contains a pair of words that end with the same spelling.

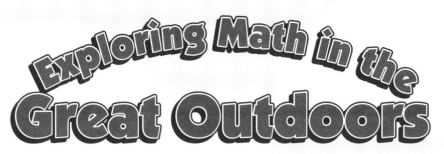

Exploring Math in the Great Outdoors

Give your end-of-the-year math review a creative twist by heading outdoors! A healthy dose of fresh air and sunshine is the perfect way to rejuvenate and reinforce a variety of math skills!

ideas contributed by Monica Cavender

Warming Up to Math

Set the stage for outdoor math adventures by gathering students around an imaginary campfire. Explain that math is all around, even in the great outdoors! Invite youngsters to share examples of math in their everyday environments. Then, if possible, read aloud *Math Curse* by Jon Scieszka (Viking Children's Books, 1995). This experience around the campfire is sure to spark an interest in outdoor math!

Gearing Up

Take a few minutes to gear up your math scouts for outdoor adventure! Explain that in addition to her math expertise, each scout can use a pair of math-spotting binoculars and a scouting journal. Then refer to the following directions to lead students in making their supplies. (*To incorporate math skills, have students measure and cut these items.)

Math-Spotting Binoculars
Supplies to make one pair:
two 9-oz. Dixie® cold cups
clear tape
18" length of yarn*
pencil
access to a hole puncher

Directions:
1. Use the point of the pencil to pierce the bottom of each cup; then carefully tear away the bottom of each cup.
2. Hold the cups side by side. Tape the top rims together.
3. Tape the bottom rims of the cups together; then hole-punch the outside edges of each bottom rim as shown.
4. Securely tie one end of the yarn length in each punched hole.
5. Wear (and use) your math-spotting binoculars during outdoor math adventures!

Scouting Journal
Supplies to make one:
five 6" x 18" sheets of drawing paper*
14" length of raffia (or twine)*
scissors
access to a hole puncher
crayons or markers
glue

Directions:
1. Stack and align the drawing paper; then fold the stack in half.
2. Punch two holes at the top of the stack, near the fold. (Provide assistance as needed.)
3. Thread the raffia through the holes, tie, and fashion a bow from the ends.
4. Color and personalize a cover for your journal.
5. Complete outdoor math activities in your journal as directed by your teacher.

Searching for Sums

Reinforce addition skills with an outdoor sum search! To prepare, list on the chalkboard ten different basic fact sums. Ask each scout to copy the sums near the top of a journal page. Then take the scouts outdoors to search for items that add up to each sum. When a student finds a sum, he writes and solves a number sentence in his journal (see illustration). Then he marks out the sum on his original list. Challenge students to find each listed sum within an allotted amount of time! Now that's "sum" fun!

Kellie Henry—Gr. 3
St. Joseph Grade School
St. Joseph, IL

Outdoor Ordinals

Polish ordinal skills with this outdoor challenge! Label half of a class set of cards with ordinal numbers through "tenth." Label the remaining cards to match. Shuffle each resulting deck. Have an adult helper arrange a line of ten plastic cones in a grassy outdoor area, leaving ample space between them. Have the adult helper take half of the students, a deck of cards, and scorekeeping materials to one end of the cones. Take the remaining students and similar supplies to the opposite end.

To play, each adult simultaneously announces the first ordinal number in her deck. The first player in line jogs to the corresponding cone and touches it. Then he jogs back to the team and asks, "Did I touch the correct cone?" If the team responds "yes," he earns two points and goes to the end of the line. If the team responds "Choose a friend," he selects a teammate and the pair repeats his turn, making sure the correct cone is touched. When the twosome returns, one point is added to the team score. The friend returns to her place in line and the original player goes to the end of the line. The adult then announces the next ordinal number in the deck. Play continues in a like manner until all cards have been played. The team with more points wins. When both teams score equal points, both teams win!

adapted from an idea by Sammie Hardy—Grs. 1–5
Goodrich Elementary
Goodrich, TX

Lively Skip-Counting

This mathematical version of hopscotch hones skip-counting skills! On a paved outdoor surface, use chalk to draw a gameboard like the one shown. Divide students into two groups and have one group line up at each end of the gameboard. Call out a desired multiple and point to Line 1. The first person in Line 1 hops through the gameboard as her classmates skip-count by the number called. When she reaches the end of the gameboard, she proceeds to the end of Line 2 as the first person in Line 2 hops back through the pattern to his classmates' counting. When he reaches the end of the gameboard, the round is over. He walks to the end of Line 1, a different multiple is announced, and another round of hopping and counting begins.

Fractional Finds

A review of fractions is just a step away! If desired, read aloud *Fraction Action* by Loreen Leedy (Holiday House, Inc.; 1996) to review fractional parts of sets. Then head outdoors and arrange your scouts in a horizontal line. Ask each of four scouts to take a giant step forward and then turn to face the class. Lead the remainder of the class in counting the number of classmates in this set. Next, ask individual students to use fractions to describe how many boys (girls) are in the set, how many students in the set are wearing sneakers, and so on. Then have the set of four return to the class line. Repeat the activity a number of times, choosing different students and varying the size of the sets. Continue until each scout has been a part of a set one or more times. When the class is back in the classroom, ask each scout to illustrate and label a favorite fraction from this outdoor experience.

Colors in the Great Outdoors

15
14
13
12
11
10
9
8
7
6
5
4
3
2
1

data collected by ___Nicole___

Colorful Data

Colorful bar graphs result from this outdoor math adventure! To begin, have each child draw lines to divide two journal pages into four sections each. Then have her label the eight resulting sections with the following color words: red, orange, yellow, green, blue, purple, black, and brown. Next, lead your scouts to an outdoor area where they can sit comfortably. Instruct them to quietly observe their surroundings for colors that appear in nature. Then, in their journals, have them list the objects they see by color. Return to the classroom at a predetermined time and give each child a bar graph like the one shown. Ask each child to organize the data she collected on the graph. Set aside time for students to compare the results of their work; then, as a class, discuss why the results of this graphing experience differ.

Bloomin' Calculations

Computation skills are sure to blossom with this thought-provoking activity! If possible, take your scouts outdoors to observe real flowers. Then have each child illustrate in his journal a flower with several individual petals. Next ask him to count the petals on the flower he drew, write this number on the page, and circle it. Finally, challenge each scout to write multiple math equations in his journal that equal the circled number. Encourage students to be creative! After a predetermined amount of time, pair students and have each child check his partner's work. Now that's a creative approach to computation practice!

LIFESAVERS...

LIFESAVERS...
management tips for teachers

Popcorn Payoff

Good behavior pops up everywhere with this positive approach! On your desk display a large, clear plastic container with a lid. Store a supply of popcorn kernels and a one-fourth cup measurer nearby. Each time the class receives a compliment, ask a student volunteer to measure a quarter cup of kernels and pour them into the class container. When it's full, pop the good-behavior kernels in an air popper and serve the tasty snack to the students for a job well done!

Kristin Peluso and Julie Boris—Gr. 1
Clyde C. Cox Elementary
    School
Las Vegas, NV

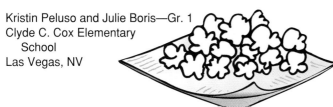

Lesson Plan Lists

Stick with this idea and you'll know at a glance if you have the supplies you need for each day's lessons. As you plan for the upcoming week, label one sticky note per school day. Attach the notes to the corresponding lesson plan page or to an inside cover of your planbook. On each note, list papers to duplicate, supplies to gather, and so on. Cross off the tasks as you finish them. When an entire list is completed, toss it and feel twice the satisfaction—your list is gone and your preparation is complete!

Tiffany L. Gosseen
Hopkins, MO

Record-Keeping Calendars

Tracking students' work habits just got easier! Make a construction paper folder for each child and mount a duplicated calendar page on the front of it. Each day have students store their completed assignments inside their folders. Every afternoon remove the contents of each child's folder. If an assignment is missing, note it in the calendar space for that day. If all work has been completed, stamp the space with a seasonal stamper. At the end of the month, document each child's work habits in your gradebook; then send the folders home. A parent is sure to appreciate this visual record of his or her child's monthly work habits.

Kellie Provost—Gr. 3, Arroyo Mocho Elementary, Livermore, CA

Colorful Reminders

Here's a quick and colorful way to remind yourself about special meetings, appointments, and other important events. For each event for which you want a reminder, write its name and time on a self-adhesive dot. Then peel and stick the preprogrammed dots onto the appropriate spaces in your plan book. Presto! A quick glance at your plan book will remind you of any events scheduled for that school day.

Kristy Osborn—Gr. 3
Abraham Lincoln
    Elementary
Indianapolis, IN

Plans for the week of September 16-20			
MONDAY	8:30-9:00 Language	9:00-9:30 Math	9:40-10:15 Soc. Studies
TUESDAY	8:30-9:00 Language	9:00-9:30 Math	9:40-10:15 Soc. Studies

The Silent Check

Save precious teaching time by keeping class reminders to a minimum. List frequent reminders on the chalkboard, such as "Name on paper," "Desk clear," "Feet on floor," and "Ready to listen." Then begin activities with a silent check. Read aloud the expectations that apply, pausing after each one. If a student has fulfilled it, he makes a large check mark in the air. Students are so eager to "check off" their positive behaviors that they complete each reminder on the spot!

Lu Brunnemer—Gr. 1
Eagle Creek Elementary, Indianapolis, IN

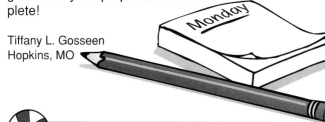

November 1999						
S	M	T	W	T	F	S
	1	2	3	4	5	6
7	8	9	10	11	12	13
14	15	16	17	18	19	20
21	22	23	24	No 25 school!	No 26 school!	27
28	29	30				

Jacob

Leader for the Day

Try this fun alternative to a weekly helper display! Create a fabric or felt chair cover like the one shown (be sure to label both sides). Each day select a classroom leader by slipping the cover over the back of a student's chair. The classroom leader becomes the line leader, paper passer, messenger, and all-around teacher's assistant for the day. At the end of the day, transfer the chair cover to the back of another student's chair. If desired, select the leaders in alphabetical order. Each student will eagerly anticipate her turn as classroom leader, and you'll be boosting self-esteems *and* reinforcing alphabetizing skills!

Margarett Mendenhall—Gr. 1, Mary Feeser Elementary School, Elkhart, IN

This is a neat desk to hide out in during the day.
From the Desk Fairy

Wow, you sure do keep your desk neat and clean!
From the Desk Fairy

I am hiding behind all your neat things.
From the Desk Fairy

I can skate in circles in this neat and clean desk!
From the Desk Fairy

Visits From the Desk Fairy

Promote reading as you motivate students to keep neat-as-a-pin desks! Create a supply of duplicated notes from the Desk Fairy similar to the ones shown. Attach a small sticker or another treat to each one. When the students are out of the room, slip a note from the Desk Fairy into each neatly organized student desk. Once the word gets out, youngsters will eagerly keep tidy desks in anticipation of the Desk Fairy's next visit!

Bonnie Lanterman—Gr. 1, Armstrong Elementary School, Hazelwood, MO

Oops! Notice

How often have you heard the phrase "Oops! I forgot!" when collecting homework assignments? These reminder notices are an effective way to foster responsibility in your students. Duplicate a supply of notices like the one shown. Each time a student forgets to turn in a homework assignment, have him complete and carry home a notice that must be returned with a parent signature the following school day. With this homework plan in place, forgotten homework could soon be obsolete!

Patricia Dent—Gr. 3, Kindle School, Pitman, NJ

Oops! Notice

Dear Mom and Dad ,

Dec. 9, 2001
Date

I forgot to turn in my homework today. My assignment was to put my spelling words in ABC order.

Please sign and date this form. I must return it with my completed homework assignment on Wednesday, Dec. 10, 2001.
day of the week   date

Parent Signature

Date

Love,
Patrick
Student Signature

Spotting Good Behavior

Looking for a colorful way to reinforce positive classroom behavior? This idea really hits the spot! Arrange student desks into groups of four or five. Assign each group of students a different color. Label one manila envelope for each group and display the envelopes on a bulletin board or chalk ledge. Also cut out a supply of round construction-paper circles (spots) in each designated color. Each time you observe a group exhibiting outstanding classroom behavior, slip a colored spot in its envelope. At the end of the week, let each group count the spots it earned. If desired, reward each group that earns a predetermined number of spots for the week with a special privilege or small individual prizes.

Candi Barwinski—Gr. 2
Fleetwood Elementary School
Fleetwood, PA

Blue

Crafty Carryalls

Turn empty Pringles® potato crisps cans into nifty art-supply carryalls! Obtain one Pringles® can (with a snap-on lid) for each student. Cover each container with colorful Con-Tact® paper. Then place inside the container an 8-pack of crayons, a small bottle of glue, a pair of student-size scissors, and other desired art supplies. Have students store their crafty carryalls inside their desks or at another designated location. Now your students' supplies are easily accessible and ready for any project!

Missy Eason and Debra Wingert—Gr. 3
Moulton Branch Elementary
Valdosta, GA

Collecting Class Compliments

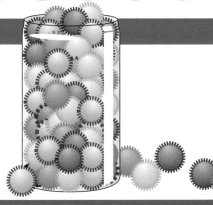

Reinforce positive student behavior with this one-of-a-kind idea. All you need is a clean, empty container and a supply of pom-poms. Each time the class receives a compliment from you or another staff member, drop a pom-pom into the container. When the container is half-full, present each student with a sticker or another small reward; when it's completely filled, plan a class party. You can count on this incentive to keep end-of-the-year behavior in line!

Gina Marinelli—Gr. 2, B. Bernice Young Elementary School, Burlington, NJ

Organizing Back Issues

If you have difficulty remembering which topics are covered in your back issues of *The Mailbox* magazine, try this! Photocopy the table of contents from each back issue and hole-punch the copies for a three-ring binder. Label one divider page for each of the six bimonthly editions. Place the divider pages in the binder and arrange the table-of-contents copies in sequential order behind the dividers. When it's time to plan for the next school year, you'll have an invaluable resource right at your fingertips!

Julie B. Pezzullo, Warwick School Department, Warwick, RI

The Motivation Station

Keep students motivated during the final month of the school year with a motivation station. Cover a large table with an inexpensive tablecloth; then place a variety of items at the table, such as markers, colored pencils, ink pens, writing paper, notepads, stickers, rubber stamps, and stamp pads. Place two or three chairs at the table and label the area "The Motivation Station." Each day before you dismiss the class, announce the names of students who have been thoughtful and responsible throughout the day. Then make arrangements for each mentioned child to spend 15 to 20 minutes of free time at The Motivation Station the following school day. Keep a record of the students who earn visits to the station so that you can personally encourage youngsters who have not yet earned the privilege.

Ann Marie Stephens—Gr. 1, George C. Round Elementary, Manassas, VA

Replenishing Prizes

Here's a nifty way to replenish your supply of inexpensive prizes for next year's class. Invite students to place any unwanted cereal-box toys, giveaways from fast-food restaurants, and other knickknacks in a designated container. Before the start of the new school year, sort through the donations and place the items that are suitable prizes in your classroom prize box.

adapted from an idea by Jill D. Hamilton—Gr. 1 Schoeneck Elementary School, Stevens, PA

Bag It!

This timesaving idea will suit any busy teacher. You need a clear, plastic suit bag labeled for each month (or season) of the school year. When you take down your end-of-the-year classroom decorations, store them in the appropriate suit bag along with any other oversized (or hard-to-store) teaching materials for that time of year. Then sort the classroom decorations and oversized teaching materials that are stored elsewhere in the classroom into the labeled bags. Suspend the bags in a classroom closet. Just think of the time you'll save next year when you have a clear view of each bag's contents!

Denise Baumann—Gr. 2, Rustic Oak Elementary, Pearland, TX

Our Readers Write

Dear Dad,
I need a paper
towel tube by
Tuesday.
Love,
Jerome

Our Readers ▷ Write

First-Class Letters

This year give your student-of-the-week festivities a letter-writing twist! A day or two after the Student Of The Week has shared his special pictures and items with the class, plan a question-and-answer session during which class members may question the spotlighted student about his family, hobbies, and other special interests. At the conclusion of the session, have the Student Of The Week choose a free-time activity while the rest of the class writes letters to him. Compile the completed letters in a decorated folder; then present the folder of fan mail to the honored student at the end of his special week!

Sandy Papendieck—Gr. 3
Levi Leonard Elementary School, Evansville, WI

Handling Classroom Pets

Here's an easy way to monitor the handling of classroom pets. If you prefer that only two students handle classroom pets at any given time, provide two pairs of garden gloves. Explain to students that anyone handling the pets must be wearing a pair of the provided gloves. Not only will you have a management system in place, you will also be promoting a safe and germ-free way for students to handle your classroom creatures.

Caroline Johnson
Upland Unified School District
Rancho, CA

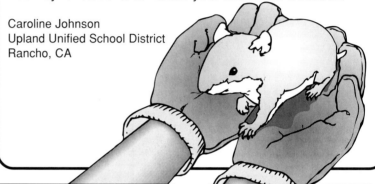

Pass the Photos, Please

Try this picture-perfect approach to class viewing of students' personal photographs. Keep a miniature photo album in your desk. When a student brings photos from home to share with her classmates, insert the photographs into your album; then allow the student to pass the album around the classroom. The pictures will be protected, and individual student viewing will be accomplished in an orderly manner. After the album has been circulated, the student removes her photographs and returns the album to you for safekeeping.

Diane Fortunato—Gr. 2, Carteret School, Bloomfield, NJ

Desktag Tip

Save time and money by laminating back-to-school desktags and using a wipe-off marker to program them. You can have desktags in place when the students arrive, yet you have the flexibility to reprogram them with preferred nicknames. And if a student is a no-show, you can reprogram her desktag for a student who just registered that morning. Then either permanently program the desktags that afternoon or cover the wipe-off programming with lengths of clear book tape (allowing you to later wipe away the programming and reuse the tags).

Luella Brunnemer—Gr. 1
Eagle Creek Elementary
Indianapolis, IN

Hands-On Apron

Your students will enjoy lending a hand with this first-day activity! You will need a plain muslin apron (or jumper), fabric paints, and several small paintbrushes. Lay the apron on a newspaper-covered surface. Using a paintbrush, lightly cover a student's palm with fabric paint; then have her press her handprint on the apron. When the paint is dry, have the student use a permanent marker to write her name near her handprint. Repeat the process until each child has taken a turn. Wear your colorful apron on special days to show your students they are the very best class—hands down!

Colleen Thompson—Gr. 1
Chosen Valley Elementary, Chatfield, MN

Weekly Quotes

Keep parents informed *and* entertained with an easy-to-publish weekly edition of classroom news! Near the end of each day, gather student quotes about the day's events and write them on a dated form like the one shown. On Friday add a note from you and then make a copy for each student. Have each child describe or illustrate her favorite event of the week on the newspaper she's taking home. Extra! Extra! Read all about the week!

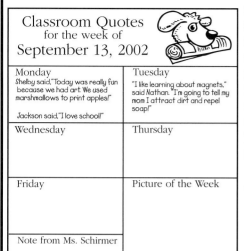

Classroom Quotes
for the week of
September 13, 2002

Monday	Tuesday
Shelby said, "Today was really fun because we had art. We used marshmallows to print apples!" Jackson said, "I love school!"	"I like learning about magnets," said Nathan. "I'm going to tell my mom I attract dirt and repel soap!"
Wednesday	Thursday
Friday	Picture of the Week
Note from Ms. Schirmer	

Christine Schirmer—Gr. 1
Van Zant Elementary School
Marlton, NJ

Off the Wall

Incorporating classroom furnishings and supplies into first-day lessons is a fun way to introduce students to their new surroundings. Have students sort attribute blocks by shapes or Unifix® cubes by colors. Read aloud a fiction and a nonfiction book from the classroom library, and ask students to use the classroom clock to answer time-related questions. Use a globe or map to review the continents and oceans of the world, and refer to the birthday display to create a class graph of student birthdays. This introduction to the classroom is sure to make students feel right at home!

Pamela Reifsneider—Associate Teacher
Newtown Friends School
Newtown, PA

Disposable Smocks

How do you transform a large plastic shopping bag with handles into a disposable paint smock? Cut away the bottom of the bag! To slip on the smock, a child pulls it over his head, poking his head through the main opening and his arms through the handle holes. When the smock comes off, it goes directly in the trash!

Theresa Zule—Teacher Aide K–2
Easton Primary School
Easton, KS

Meet the Class

Instead of sending home the interest inventories that your students complete on the first day of school, collect and publish them in a three-ring notebook. For durability, insert the students' papers into plastic page protectors. Also include a photograph of each student with his interest inventory, if desired. Then arrange for each child to take home the notebook so he can introduce his family to his new classmates. Each time a new student joins your class, update the notebook and then invite him to take it home for the evening so he can quickly get to know his new classmates!

Lynn Lupo-Hudgins
Austin Road Elementary
Stockbridge, GA

Three Class Rules

One, two, three! Take this approach to identifying class rules, and three is all you need! Begin by asking students to brainstorm possible class rules. List their suggestions on an overhead or on the chalkboard. When the list is much too long for anyone to remember, suggest grouping the rules into categories. Three positively stated categories that will include most rules are "Be kind," "Stay safe," and "Follow directions." Lead students to this discovery and then post the class-created rules in a prominent location. Positive results are sure to follow!

Cheryl A. Wade—Gr. 2, Golden Springs Elementary School, Anniston, AL

Year-Round Border

Do you have a year-round display that needs your students' touch? Try this! On the first day of school, review with the class the themes and topics you will teach during the year. Then have each child decorate a scalloped section of bulletin board border with pictures, numbers, and/or words representing the themes and topics in which they are most interested. Keeping the border on display year-round reminds students of what they've learned and what they have to look forward to!

Trisha Owen—Gr. 3, Libbey Elementary School
Wheatland, WY

Framed!

Transform a clear, plastic, picture frame into a versatile teaching tool! Precut a sheet of paper to fit the frame; then program the paper with math problems to answer and slip the paper in the frame. Next attach a library pocket to the back of the frame and tuck an answer key inside. Place the frame, a wipe-off marker, and paper towels at a center. A student solves the problems on the frame, then uses the answer key to check her work. Before she leaves the center, she uses a paper towel to wipe her answers off the frame. Change the frame's programming and answer key as often as desired. Student progress will be crystal clear with this unique learning center!

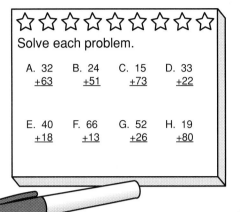

Solve each problem.

A. 32
+63

B. 24
+51

C. 15
+73

D. 33
+22

E. 40
+18

F. 66
+13

G. 52
+26

H. 19
+80

Leslee McWhirter—Gr. 1
Mendel Elementary, Houston, TX

Phone Number Fun

Use phone numbers to "brrring" a real-life context to your math lessons! Ask each student to write his phone number on his paper and use it to complete a math challenge. For example, have each child use the digits in his phone number to create ten, two-digit numerals that are greater than 25. Or ask each student to use the digits to write ten different math facts to solve. Now that's a "phone-omenal" math idea with endless possibilities!

Susan Downs—Gr. 2
Tatum Primary School
Tatum, TX

Daffy Definitions

Promote teamwork with this high-interest vocabulary game! Divide students into small teams. Give each team a dictionary, pencils, and individual blank cards. Secretly assign each team a different vocabulary word. Each team member writes the word on a card; then the team works together to program one member's card with the word's real meaning and each of the remaining cards with an incorrect definition. To play the game, one team presents its vocabulary word and definitions to the rest of the class. Then each remaining team chooses what it believes to be the real definition of the word. When all the guesses are in for that round, award one point for each correct answer. The game is over after each team has presented its vocabulary word. Word for word, this vocabulary-boosting game can't be beat!

Danielle Conforti—Gr. 3
Old Mill School, Sea Girt, NJ

Journal Illustrations

Give daily journal writing a new twist! Start by giving each youngster (and yourself) a journal of blank story-writing paper. Each day write in your journal while students write in theirs. Rather than illustrate your own writing, end each writing session by selecting one child to add illustrations to your entry. It's a great opportunity for students to showcase their comprehension skills and artistic talents. And as an added bonus, they get to know their teacher better too. There's little doubt that your journal will quickly become the most-read and best-illustrated volume in the classroom!

Last night I went to see my dad. I told him about our accident yesterday with the math manipulatives. He laughed so hard he almost fell out of his wheelchair!

Linda Stec—Gr. 3
Deford Elementary School
Deford, MI

Glue Solution

Put a lid on sticky situations! When students are completing art projects at their desks, give each student a plastic milk-jug lid that contains an individual portion of glue. After a child finishes his project, he places his milk-jug lid in a designated area. When the extra glue hardens (in a day or two), simply bend the lid and pop out the hardened glue. The milk-jug lids are ready to use again, and there's no gluey mess!

Del Bull—Gr. 1
Jesse Boyd Elementary
Spartanburg, SC

Special Guests

Ensuring that every student has a special guest for a class performance can be tricky with so many parents working outside of the home. This tip will help. If a youngster's adult family member is unable to attend, make arrangements for him to invite a sibling or another friend from within your school. Each of your students will be pleased to have a familiar face in the audience, and your students' special guests will feel honored too!

Eleanor Beson—Special Education Grs. K–6
Ballard School, South Glens Falls, NY

Word Wheel

Put a new spin on sight words with a recycled Rolodex® card file. Type each word from the Dolch list of the 250 most commonly used words (or another desired list) on a self-sticking label. Remove the alphabetized dividers from the card file and then stick each prepared label on an individual card. There you have it. A word wheel with plenty of appeal!

Marni Krams—Special Education, Royal Palm Elementary
Lauderhill, FL

Weekly Reflections

This end-of-the-week writing activity is a winner! Every Friday have each student write and date a personal evaluation of his past school week in a "Weekly Reflections" journal. Then, either collect the journals and pen a positive response to each child's entry, or send them home so parents can read and respond to their youngster's writing. The weekly evaluations motivate students to do their best throughout the week, and the adult-written replies are wonderful self-esteem boosters for students!

Judy Wetzel—Gr. 2, Woodburn School
Falls Church, VA

Kindness Counts

Promote **r**andom **a**cts of **k**indness with a R.A.K. cube. Cut the top from an empty tissue cube. Have students brainstorm different ways to be kind to others and list their ideas on chart paper. Then copy these ideas onto individual paper strips and deposit them in the prepared cube. Periodically remove a paper strip from the cube, read aloud the act of kindness that's listed, and encourage students to put it into action. A few days later, invite the class to talk about the benefits of sharing this act of kindness with others. No doubt students will agree, R.A.K.s are A-OK!

Janet Finley Landry—Gr. 3
Wren Hollow Elementary, Ballwin, MO

Individual Paint Palettes

Take the pain out of class painting projects with individual paint palettes! Give each child a five-inch square of leftover laminating film. To disperse paint, squeeze dollops of desired tempera paints directly on the palettes. When it's time for cleanup, allow the paint on the palettes to dry before removing it (it crumbles easily). Presto! The palettes are ready to be reused!

Charlotte Cross—A.R.T.S.
Fletcher Elementary, Fletcher, OK

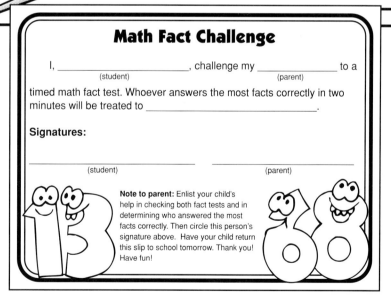

Math Fact Challenge

I, _____, challenge my _____ to a
　　　　　(student)　　　　　　　　　　　　　　　(parent)
timed math fact test. Whoever answers the most facts correctly in two minutes will be treated to _____.

Signatures:

_____　　　_____
　　　　(student)　　　　　　　　　　　　　　(parent)

Note to parent: Enlist your child's help in checking both fact tests and in determining who answered the most facts correctly. Then circle this person's signature above. Have your child return this slip to school tomorrow. Thank you! Have fun!

Durable Bookmarks

These easy-to-make bookmarks are clear winners with kids! Use a paper cutter to cut laminating film leftovers into slightly oversized bookmark shapes. Trim each shape with paper edgers to create a decorative edge, and then press a colorful sticker at the top of the shape. The bookmark is ready to use!

Pat Kourt—LMS
Thomas-Fay-Custer Unified Schools
Thomas, OK

Math Fact Showdown

Here's a homework assignment students request time and again! Send each child home with two identical copies of a timed fact test and a Math Fact Challenge like the one shown. A child and parent fill out the challenge, take the test, and then determine who answered the most math facts correctly. Ask each student to return the completed challenge sheet the following school day. Learning math facts quickly becomes a top priority!

Maria Smith, Bess Race Elementary, Crowly, TX

Cocoa Changes

Students observe changes in matter with this tasty science activity! Give each student a paper napkin, a small candy cane, several minimarshmallows, and a Styrofoam® cup that contains premeasured powdered cocoa mix. Carefully pour hot water into each child's cup. Direct the students to use their candy canes to stir the cocoa into the water. Then have the students add the marshmallows and stir a bit longer. While the cocoa is cooling, discuss the changes that take place in the cocoa, the candy canes, and the marshmallows. Now that's a science activity that really melts in your mouth!

Nancy Osborn—Grs. 1–2
Monica Leary Elementary School
Rush, NY

Dictionary Sleuths

Whet your youngsters' appetites for dictionary practice with this step-by-step approach. Choose a mystery word; then write the first letter of the word on the chalkboard. Ask each student to crack open his dictionary to this letter. Then add to the suspense by revealing only one letter of the mystery word at a time. For example, if the mystery word is *reindeer,* write *r* on the board. Then add the *e* and have students turn to the *re-* words. Continue adding one letter at a time until the word is guessed by a student, each child has located it in his dictionary, and the definition has been read aloud. Don't be surprised if your supersleuths get good at guessing and locating mystery words before all the letters are given!

Candy Whelan—Gr. 3
Garlough Elementary
West St. Paul, MN

Winter Warm-Up

Energize your class on a cold, wintry day with this marvelous movement activity. Post the song, and sing it several times as a class. Each time through, insert the name of a different student. When a student is selected, she immediately performs a jump. The rest of the youngsters copy the jump as they sing the final two lines of the song. Your students will jump for joy when it's time for winter warm-up!

My Jump
(sung to the tune of "Frère Jacques")
This is [name]; this is [name].
Watch [his/her] jump; watch [his/her] jump.
Now you try it; now you try it.
Jump, jump, jump.
Jump, jump, jump.

Susan T. Brown—Grs. K–2, Palmyra Elementary, Palmyra, VA

Flannelboard Substitute

Need an instant flannelboard or just an extra one? Cut a large rectangle from felt and attach a piece of magnetic tape to each corner. Simply display the felt on a magnetic surface or chalkboard. When you're finished, fold the felt in half with the magnets to the inside to create a handy storage space for pieces.

Janelle Yelton—Gr. 3, Remington Elementary, Wolcott, IN

Find That State

Pique your students' interest in United States geography with this fact-filled map activity. Display a U.S. map on a bulletin board. Label each of 50 index cards with the name of a different state and an interesting fact about it. Place the cards in a container near the map. Each day ask a student to draw a card from the container, read it to the class, and find the corresponding state on the map. Then help the student pin the card on the bulletin board and use a length of yarn to connect the card and its corresponding state. In 50 days youngsters will be acquainted with all 50 states!

Corrien Mateo—Gr. 3 ESL
  Resource
Oakwood Elementary
Lemont, IL

Utah
Utah's Great Salt Lake is North America's largest salt lake. It is only about 15 feet deep.

Fly's-Eye View

Bring a bird's-eye view into focus with this literature-related mapping activity. Read aloud Jim Aylesworth's *Old Black Fly* (Henry Holt and Company, 1995), which gives a rollicking account of a family in hot pursuit of a fly. Then have students imagine that a distant relative of the old black fly has landed on the classroom ceiling. Ask each child to draw the classroom from the fly's perspective. Invite that old black fly back into your classroom as needed for further mapping fun.

Brigid Lund
Plymouth, MN

Dear Dad,
I need a paper towel tube by Tuesday.
Love,
Jerome

It's in the Bag!

The next time a child needs to replenish a school supply or you're requesting that students contribute to a class project, try this! Have each child write a short note to his parent(s) on the outside of a folded paper sack that, when unfolded, can be used to carry the needed supply to school! These unique requests really deliver!

Janice Keer—Grs. 1–2
Irvin Pertzsch School
Onalaska, WI

Soaking Up Knowledge

Get students absorbed in learning with this clever idea! Show the class a dry, natural sponge. Then place the sponge in a shallow container of water and have students observe it soaking up the water. Tell them that just as the sponge soaks up water, their brains can soak up knowledge. Showcase the sponge and container for a constant reminder of this analogy. Then conclude each day by inviting students to share the knowledge they've soaked up!

Jo Fryer—Gr. 1
Kildeer Countryside School
Long Grove, IL

SLURP!

Ketchup Day

What in the world is Ketchup Day? A day to catch up, of course! Keep a plastic bottle of unopened ketchup in your closet. Periodically display the container and proclaim a designated amount of time for catching up on incomplete work. Students who are all caught up may participate in quiet free-time activities. Isn't it amazing how a bit of ketchup can increase the appeal of just about anything?

Jo Fryer—Gr. 1

BILL'S Squeeze Ketchup

Helping Verbs

Need a hand teaching some of the most common helping verbs? This song, sung to the tune of the "Mickey Mouse Club March," is sure to help!

Helping Verbs
Have, has, had,
Is, am, are,
Be, being, and been.

Helping verbs, helping verbs.
Helping verbs, helping verbs.
Forever, ever keep them in our
Minds, minds, minds.

Come along and join our verbs and
Sing our language song.
Have, has, had,
Is, am, are,
Be, being, and been.

Debra Kain—Gr. 2
Sewell School
Sewell, NJ

Hubba Hubba!

Believe it or not, you can give flash card review a facelift by simply inserting four or more seasonal cards into the deck! To make the cards, attach stickers to precut cards, and then label the cards with a desired response (see provided list for suggestions). Student interest in flash cards immediately increases!

Month	Picture	Response
Sept.	owl	hoot, hoot
Oct.	scarecrow	caw, caw
Nov.	turkey	gobble, gobble
Dec.	Santa	ho, ho, ho
Jan.	Snowflake	Let it snow, snow, snow!
Feb.	heart	hubba, hubba
March	pig	oink, oink
April	raindrop	drip, drop
May	bee	buzz, buzz
June	cow	moo, moo

Laura J. Williams—Gr. 3
Flint Hills Christian School
Manhattan, KS

Hubba
Hubba

Fact Finder

For a fun review of math facts, try this unique flash-card game. Have each child arrange an equal number of fact cards on her desk so that only the fact problems can be seen. To begin play, choose a fact answer and say, "Fact finders, search for the sum of 12." Each student who has a fact card that equals 12 raises her hand. When a student is called upon, she reads aloud her math fact and answer. If it is a correct match, she places the card in a discard pile on her desk. Continue play in this manner, citing a different fact answer each time. The first child to discard all of her cards wins the game.

Judy Chunn—Grs. 2–3
Westminster School
Nashville, TN

Save Those Trays

The plastic trays that hold frozen microwave dinners have a multitude of classroom uses. Keep glitter, sequins, and other art supplies tidy in individual trays. Or use the trays to store and distribute small manipulatives like macaroni pieces, buttons, and dried beans. Since the trays are not easily tipped over, they are also perfect for holding different colors of tempera paint. Start your collection of trays today!

Lee Anne Tragle—Substitute Teacher
Centreville, VA

Hard at Work

Keep your youngsters wrapped up in learning with this unique door decoration! Purchase a roll of yellow caution tape from a hardware store; then randomly wrap the tape around your classroom door. If desired, wrap a length of the tape around each child's desk or chair. Post the title "Hard at Work" and a learning permit that has been authorized by the school principal on or near the door. Whether you're fighting off spring fever or your students are taking achievement tests, you can count on your new decor to build learning enthusiasm.

Chantelle M. Gist—Grs. K–4
Title I Reading/Writing
Reid Elementary School
Springfield, OH

Hard at Work

Learning Permit

Earth Day Math

Head outdoors on Earth Day (April 22) to reinforce measurement skills and promote environmental awareness. Each child needs a paper grocery bag, a ruler, disposable plastic gloves, and a marker. Instruct students to collect trash from the school grounds. Before each item of trash is bagged, a student measures its length in inches and records the measurement on the outside of his bag. After a set amount of time, have each student transfer his trash collection into a trash receptacle, then tally the measurements on his bag to determine how many inches of trash he collected. The message is clear—trash really adds up. As a follow-up, have students suggest ways to take better care of our Earth.

Sheila Asbury—Gr. 2, Hidden Valley Elementary School, Charlotte, NC

Magic Carpets

Use this high-flying idea to introduce lessons that involve faraway places. Give each child a small rug or carpet sample that's large enough to sit on. (Inquire at carpet stores for outdated or unwanted samples.) Then, using fabric paints or markers, have each child personalize her magic carpet. Invite students to sit on their magic carpets each time you plan to explore a faraway place. What a wonderful way to travel!

Donna Henry
Portsmouth Catholic
  School
Portsmouth, VA

Plant Discovery

Cultivate interest in an upcoming plant unit with this unique introduction. Display a collection of items that have plant-related origins, such as a cotton T-shirt, chewing gum, vanilla extract, paper, an eraser, chocolate, and burlap. Post the question "What do these items have in common?" Also place a container labeled "Predictions" and a supply of scrap paper at the display. Ask students to study the objects and submit their predictions. A few days later, list the predictions on the chalkboard. Review the list; then reveal the correct answer. Even if a correct prediction was not made, you'll have sprouted plenty of interest in plants!

Mary Howard Cook—Gr. 2
McAlpine Elementary School
Charlotte, NC

I think they all came from Mrs. Cook's house.

Summer Letter Writing

Inspire students to maintain their writing skills during summer break by giving each child a small gift and a promise. To prepare each gift, place three decorated sheets of stationery and a stamped, self-addressed envelope in a decorated bag. Distribute the bags on the last day of school. Invite each child to write a friendly letter to you this summer. Suggest that students describe special summer happenings in their letters. Promise to reply to each letter that you receive. It may be as much of a treat for you to read about your students' summer adventures as it will be for them to get letters from you!

Debbie Tofflemire—Gr. 1
West Indianola School
Topeka, KS

Something New

This summer add to your collection of classroom displays! Before you head home for summer vacation, photocopy your favorite bulletin-board ideas from past issues of *The* Primary *Mailbox*®. Gather the supplies you'll need to prepare the lettering and any other teacher-created elements. Then—during the summer—trace, cut out, and color the bulletin-board components. Store the cutouts for each bulletin board, along with your photocopy of the display, in a gallon-size resealable plastic bag. Next school year, when you have oodles of time-consuming things to do in addition to your bulletin boards, you can reach for your bulletin-board bags and change a display in no time!

Betsy Ruggiano—Gr. 3
Featherbed Lane School
Clark, NJ

Book Bonanza

If you have several unused book-club bonus points, this end-of-the-year behavior incentive plan is for you! Use your points to purchase one children's book per student. During the last few weeks of school, end each school day with a drawing. Invite those students who have exhibited positive behaviors throughout the day to enter. Before dismissal draw two names and allow each winning student to choose a book from your collection. If you draw the name of a child who has already won a book, reward the student with a smaller treat such as a pencil or a piece of sugarless gum; then draw another name. This plan not only encourages positive behavior—it encourages summer reading, too!

Colleen Proffitt—Gr. 2
Doe Elementary
Mountain City, TN

Games Galore

Here's a game plan for the final week of school! Designate the next-to-last day of school as Game Day. Explain that each student who has completed all of her outstanding work may bring her favorite game to school on that day. On Game Day, divide the participants into small groups and have each group member take a turn teaching her group how to play her favorite game. Students will definitely be motivated to complete their work and a fun time will be had by all!

Judy Johnson—Grs. 1–2, St. Mary's Academy, Englewood, CO

Photographic Memories

Viewing photographs is a great way for students to reminisce about their school year. When composing your end-of-the-year parent correspondence, include snapshots from field trips, classroom activities, and other school events. A personal message from you, along with a photo or two, will be treasured by your students and their parents. The results of this effort will be long lasting and appreciated.

Pauline R. Lawson—Gr. 1
Fuquay-Varina Elementary
Fuquay-Varina, NC

Answer Keys

Page 97

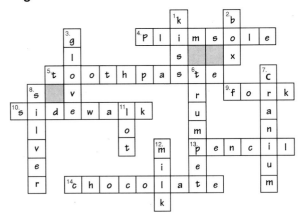

Page 151

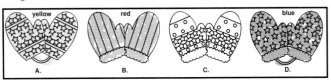